Internationa

Books in the Politics Study Guides series

International Politics

An Introductory Guide

Alasdair Blair and Steven Curtis

Edinburgh University Press

For Abbie, Jakob and William

© Alasdair Blair and Steven Curtis, 2009

Edinburgh University Press Ltd
22 George Square, Edinburgh
www.euppublishing.com

Typeset in 11/13pt Monotype Baskerville by
Servis Filmsetting Ltd, Stockport, Cheshire, and
printed and bound in Great Britain by
CPI Antony Rowe, Chippenham and Eastbourne

A CIP record for this book is available from the British Library

ISBN 978 0 7486 2415 7 (paperback)

The right of Alasdair Blair and Steven Curtis to be identified
as authors of this work has been asserted in accordance with the
Copyright, Designs and Patents Act 1988.

Published with the support of the Edinburgh University
Scholarly Publishing Initiatives Fund

Contents

Boxes

Tables

Figures

Abbreviations

ABM	anti-ballistic missile
AIDS	acquired immune deficiency syndrome
ANZUS	Australian, New Zealand and US Alliance
APEC	Asia-Pacific Economic Cooperation
ASEAN	Association of South East Asian Nations
AU	African Union
BMA	British Medical Association
CAP	Common Agricultural Policy
CCTV	close circuit television
CEE	Central and Eastern Europe
CFSP	Common Foreign and Security Policy
CIA	Central Intelligence Agency
CIS	Commonwealth of Independent States
CMEA	Council for Mutual Economic Assistance (USSR)
CPSU	Communist Party of the Soviet Union
CSCE	Conference on Security and Cooperation in Europe
ECB	European Central Bank
ECOSOC	Economic and Social Council of the United Nations
ECSC	European Coal and Steel Community
EDC	European Defence Community
EEC	European Economic Community
EMS	European Monetary System
EMU	Economic and monetary union
EPC	European Political Cooperation
EU	European Union
Euratom	European Atomic Energy Community
FDR	Federal Republic of Germany (West Germany)
GATT	General Agreement on Tariffs and Trade
GDP	gross domestic product
GDR	German Democratic Republic (East Germany)
GNP	gross national product
IAEA	International Atomic Energy Agency
IBRD	International Bank for Reconstruction and Development

ICBM	intercontinental ballistic missile
IGBP	International Geosphere-Biosphere Programme
IGO	intergovernmental organisation
ILO	International Labour Organisation
IMF	International Monetary Fund
INF	intermediate nuclear forces
INGO	international non-governmental organisation
IPCC	Intergovernmental Panel on Climate Change
IPE	international political economy
IR	International Relations
JHA	justice and home affairs
LDC	less developed country
MAD	mutual assured destruction
MNC	multinational corporation
NAFTA	North American Free Trade Agreement
NAM	Non-Aligned Movement
NATO	North Atlantic Treaty Organisation
NGO	non-governmental organisation
NPT	Nuclear Non-Proliferation Treaty
OAU	Organisation of African Unity
OEEC	Organisation for European Economic Cooperation
OPEC	Organisation of Petroleum Exporting Countries
PLO	Palestinian Liberation Organisation
PMCs	private military companies
RPF	Rwandan Patriotic Front
PRC	People's Republic of China
QMV	qualified majority voting
SALT	Strategic Arms Limitation Talks
SDI	Strategic Defence Initiative
SEA	Single European Act
SLBM	submarine-launched ballistic missiles
START	Strategic Arms Reduction Talks
UN	United Nations
UNEP	United Nations Environment Programme
UNICEF	United Nations International Children's Emergency Fund
UNSCOM	United Nations Special Commission
USSR	Union of Soviet Socialist Republics

WHO	World Health Organisation
WILPF	Women's International League for Peace and Freedom
WMD	weapons of mass destruction
WMO	World Meteorological Organisation
WTO	World Trade Organisation

Preface

This introductory textbook has been influenced by our experience of researching and teaching the subject of International Relations (IR) for over fifteen years each. We have structured the book into chapters that provide a general introduction to the subject-matter. This includes devoting a significant proportion of the book to providing historical context for the subject-matter to ensure that the reader has a solid grasp of recent events. In writing this textbook we have been conscious that it is geared toward the needs of both college and university students. While we have endeavoured to make the subject as accessible as possible, we have also sought to impress that this is a challenging subject that requires wider reading. This is a task that has been aided by lengthy conversations with colleagues and students over the years at the different universities in which we have worked. We are particularly grateful to the kind support that Brian Hocking provided in the early stages of our careers, and to the advice and comments that Sean McGough gave us when we were initially planning this book. Elsewhere, the staff at Edinburgh University Press, in particular our editor Nicola Ramsey, have offered important and invaluable advice, while Duncan Watts provided the encouragement that was essential for us to complete this book. Finally, we would like to express our love and thanks to our families. It is to our children that this book is dedicated.

Leicester and London
February 2009

Introduction

Contents

Overview

This introductory chapter provides an overview of the key issues which relate to the study of international politics. This is a subject which covers a wide range of topics, from climate change to nuclear proliferation. The formal study of international politics is a relatively recent phenomenon, commencing in the early years of the twentieth century. At that time much of the focus was attached to the role of nation-states, with relatively little attention being given to the influence of non-state actors. As the twentieth century progressed, these non-state actors became increasingly prominent. This reflected the growing interconnectedness of international politics. Non-state actors vary in size and form, ranging from intergovernmental organisations such as the World Trade Organisation (WTO) to multinational corporations (MNCs) such as Microsoft. For many individuals this shift away from nation-states has been tied up with the process of globalisation. This chapter is concerned with outlining the main topics that are relevant to the study of international politics and in so doing provides a foundation for the chapters that follow.

Key issues to be covered in this chapter

- An introduction to international politics as an academic subject area
- An outline of the role that state and non-state actors play in international politics
- An awareness of the ways in which the study of international politics can be approached from a theoretical angle

Why study international politics?

The study of international politics can appear unrelated to everyday life. It is common to find individuals commenting that what happens on the other side of the world is of little relevance to their own lives. Sitting in the relative comfort of a developed country, some might conclude that the economic and political crisis of a **Third World** state is of no concern to them. This is an extremely simplistic view. Apart from the moral issues surrounding the need for the advantaged to assist the disadvantaged, the fact of the matter is that we live in an interconnected world. To illustrate this point we will use the two case studies of **climate change** and the 2001 invasion of Afghanistan.

Our first case study of climate change is the most pressing issue that the world faces according to the latest UN Development Report.[1] Climate change refers to the process of **global warming** whereby the earth's atmosphere is heating up because of an increase in carbon emissions from industrial growth that is typified by pollution from vehicles, aircraft, houses and power stations. Much of the responsibility for global warming rests with the developed countries, and, as we show in Figure 1.1, nearly half of all global fossil fuel emissions have occurred since the 1970s.

The rapid industrialisation of **developing countries**, such as Brazil, India and China, means that there is the very real threat of even greater carbon emissions. These emissions are particularly influenced by the burning of **fossil fuels** which are often the easiest and cheapest means of energy, but which have the worst impact

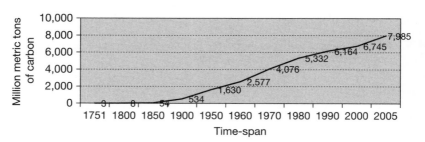

Source: Carbon Dioxide Information Analysis Centre, at: http://cdiac.ornl.gov/ftp/ndp030/CSV-FILES/global.1751_2005.csv.

Figure 1.1 Global carbon emissions, 1751–2005

in terms of accelerating global warming. As the majority of the countries in the world can be regarded as developing countries, it is evident that the potential for climate change as a result of economic growth is significant. To put this state of affairs into context, it has been estimated that if everyone in the world generated greenhouse gases at the same rate as the developed countries then we would need nine planets to sustain life. Something clearly has to be done to remedy this situation.

The problem that the world faces is that it is hard to imagine how everyone in the developing world could have a standard of living comparable to that enjoyed in the developed world without a dramatic increase in global pollution. This is a particularly complex problem as developing countries tend to have a greater reliance on carbon-based sources of energy, such as coal, which are often the cheapest and most readily available. Moreover, as we will see in Chapter 9, the decisions taken by consumers and policy-makers tend to be shaped by the economic factors, such as price, rather than environmental concerns. In a nutshell, policy-makers in the develop-ing world stress that efforts to lessen environmental impact would lower their economic growth rates. This state of affairs creates many problematic questions. How can developed countries ask developing countries to reduce their greenhouse gas emissions when they are closely tied to their economic growth? Is it right for citizens in the developed world to enjoy the benefits of clean water, public housing and consumer products, such as televisions and washing machines, while citizens in the developing world go without because of the threat of global warming?

The answers to these questions are complicated, given that both developed and developing countries have expressed reservations about meeting the carbon emission reductions that were set out in the 1997 **Kyoto Protocol**. For instance, the United States under President George W. Bush (2001–9) refused to accept the cuts in carbon emissions set out in the protocol, with this decision limiting the opportunity for tackling climate change given the fact that the United States is presently responsible for the most carbon emissions in the world (Figures 1.2 and 1.3). Policy-makers in Washington argue that reductions in carbon emissions would reduce US com-petitiveness vis-à-vis other countries. This particularly applies to

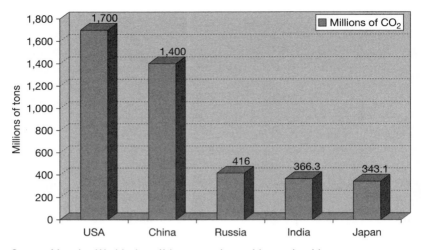

Source: Mapping Worlds, http://show.mappingworlds.com/world.

Figure 1.2 Top five producers of CO_2 emissions

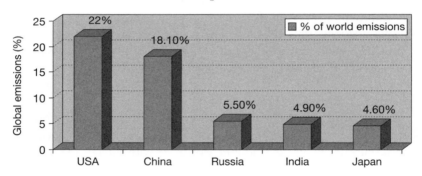

Source: Mapping Worlds, http://show.mappingworlds.com/world.

Figure 1.3 Top five producers of CO_2 emissions as world percentage

developing countries such as China, which is itself the second largest source of carbon emissions. However, while this may lead to the conclusion that reducing carbon emissions by developing countries is unlikely when leading developed countries are unwilling to do the same, the UK Treasury Department, Stern Review Report (2006) emphasised that it was actually in the economic interests of countries to tackle the effects of climate change today rather than having to deal with the impact in the future. This is because the Review estimates that if the developed world fails to take action now, then the overall costs and risks of climate change would be equivalent to losing 5 per cent of global GDP each year from now into perpetuity, with the possibility that this could rise to 20 per cent of GDP. By contrast, if action is taken in the form of reducing greenhouse gas emissions then it is possible that the costs can be limited to around 1 per cent of GDP each year.[2]

In seeking to find a solution to these problems, one answer is for those countries which agree on the need to reduce carbon emissions to undertake such a course of action. As European Union (EU) member states played a significant role in drawing up the 1997 Kyoto agreement, in 1998 the then fifteen member states agreed to reduce their carbon emissions to 8 per cent below 1990 levels by the year 2012. Concern in the United Kingdom over the impact of climate change resulted in the government establishing in September 2006 the Office of Climate Change to specifically tackle the subject. Another answer is for organisations such as the United Nations (UN) to highlight the threat posed by global warming through such activities as the UN Environment Programme (UNEP).[3] The UNEP has also collaborated with the World Meteorological Organisation (WMO) to establish the Intergovernmental Panel on Climate Change (IPCC) in 1988 to highlight the problems of climate change, and the significance of this work was reflected in the award of a Nobel Prize in 2007.[4] Individuals can also demonstrate to governments the importance of responding to the challenge of global warming, and this has resulted in many commentators pointing to the role that **civil society** plays in international politics. Finally, **non-governmental organisations** (NGOs), such as Friends of the Earth and Greenpeace,[5] have been active in highlighting environmental concerns, while the International Geosphere-Biosphere Programme (IGBP) is a research programme which was specifically created to study the impact of global climate change.[6] All this work is reflected in the Earth Charter, which provides a statement on a global consensus for a sustainable Earth.[7]

However, while the Stern Review makes the economic argument for taking action now, the problem is how to get countries and individuals to take action when there are costs involved. This is essentially an economics conundrum of trying to achieve a balance of maintaining economic growth and preventing climate change which centres on comparing the costs incurred against the future benefits. To achieve change there has to be an approach which combines a mixture of incentives and penalties that will help to reduce carbon emissions. Basic incentives could come in the form of providing grants to insulate houses and installing alternative energy systems, such as solar panels, to reduce energy consumption. By contrast, penalties could come in the form of a carbon tax that would aim to encourage individuals to switch from carbon-based energy to renewable energy.

In analysing the case study of climate change it is apparent that this is an issue which affects all countries and draws in opinions from a range of actors including governments, **intergovernmental organisations (IGOs)**, such as the UN and EU, NGOs, such as Greenpeace, as well as wider civil society. But while climate change affects all countries, and although there is a need for both developed and developing countries to address issues of carbon emissions, it has none the less been predicted that the impact of climate change is likely to hit the developing world harder than the developed world. In part, this is because people living in the developed world are more likely to be protected from rising sea levels through flood defences – not every capital city that is close to the sea can have the luxury of London's Thames Barrier. The IPCC has predicted that 'the effects of climate change are expected to be greatest in developing countries in terms of loss of life, and relative effects on investment and economy'.[8] It is a point that was made clear by the United Kingdom relief and development charity, Tearfund, which published a report in 2006 that estimated that there were already an estimated twenty-five million environmental refugees as a result of climate change which had brought about floods, storms and rising tides.[9] Thus, set aside from the economic debates that endlessly engulf discussions on climate change, it is evident that this story is in essence a story of human survival that is highlighted by the fact that half of the world's population are within 100 km of the sea and a tenth are within 10 km. Such is the fear of rising sea levels in low-lying countries that, in 2008, the President of Maldives took the decision to divert a share of the country's tourist revenues to create an insurance fund to buy a new homeland given that most parts of the Maldives are only 1.5 m above sea level and UN forecasts indicate that sea levels are likely to rise by 59 cm by 2100.[10]

Our second case study relates to the American-led invasion of Afghanistan in October 2001. This invasion was in response to the 11 September 2001 attacks on the United States when hijackers affiliated with the terrorist organisation **al-Qaeda** crashed commercial aircraft into the twin towers of the World Trade Center, resulting in the collapse of both towers. A further aircraft crashed into the Pentagon and a fourth crashed into a field in Pennsylvania. The purpose of the invasion of Afghanistan was to destroy al-Qaeda and capture its leader, Osama bin Laden, as well as to remove the Taliban regime that had provided al-Qaeda with a safe haven. The origins of al-Qaeda can be traced back to the 1979 Soviet invasion of Afghanistan, which pitted Afghan **mujahideen** fighters against Soviet troops and Afghan Marxists. At a time of **Cold War** tension, the United States viewed this conflict in ideological terms and provided financial support to the mujahideen so that they could fight the Soviet Union troops.

Afghanistan became a proxy battleground for the Cold War between the United States and the Soviet Union. After ten years of fighting, the Soviet Union withdrew its troops in 1989 and this led to an initial conclusion that Afghanistan and the United States were victorious. The same year marked the end of Soviet domination of Eastern Europe, and by the end of 1991 the Soviet Union had disintegrated and the Cold War was over.[11] The emergence of a post-Cold War order resulted in an early assessment that the world would be a safer place in the absence of **superpower** confrontation. This did not prove so for Afghanistan, which disintegrated into civil war and led to the rise of the Taliban which from the mid-1990s provided a safe haven for Osama bin Laden (who had previously been based in Sudan).

In the post-Cold War world **rogue states** and stateless terrorist organisations, such as al-Qaeda, provided new threats to states. This was evidenced by bombs exploding in hotels containing American soldiers in Aden and the Yemen in 1992, the attack on the World Trade Center in 1993, bombing campaigns against American Embassies in Tanzania and Kenya in 1998 and the bombing of the USS *Cole* in 2000. The culmination of these attacks was the events of 11 September 2001. This resulted in the American-led **war on terror** that involved the invasion of Afghanistan in 2001 and, more controversially, Iraq in 2003.

Although the invasions raised questions about the legitimacy of the action, because the UN Security Council resolutions Nos. 1368[12] and 1373[13] that dealt with Afghanistan did not expressly authorise the use of force – a point that we will explore in more detail in Chapter 10 – it is telling that recent assessments suggest that the world is not necessarily safer as a result of the invasions of Afghanistan and Iraq. At the time of writing (Sping 2009) Osama bin Laden has not been caught and it has been argued that the threat from terrorism has increased because of a new generation of radicalised Islamists. This is a point that has been made by the British Foreign Secretary, David Miliband, who noted in January 2009 that the United States' war on terror was 'misleading and mistaken', and has acted as a gel to unite extremists against the West.[14] Although he was not a member of Cabinet at the time it is, however, interesting to note that Miliband did not object to the decision taken by the then Prime Minister, Tony Blair, to support the war on terror and as such his announcement in January 2009 marks a significant change from previous government policy.

Afghanistan itself has not become a more peaceful or stable country. In 2008 the Brookings Institution, a Washington-based think-tank, recognised Afghanistan as being the world's second weakest state and one of only three failed states (the others are Somalia and the Democratic Republic of the Congo).[15] As we note in Chapters 7 and 10, failed states and, more generally, weak states pose particular problems to global security because they are ungovernable and, therefore, enable terrorist organisations to flourish. Weak states also export other problems, such as the migration of people. In the case of Afghanistan, it is also noticeable that some eight years after the invasion and the deployment of thousands of foreign troops to the country, it is none the less still regarded as one of the world's largest opium producers and, as such, is a direct source of the instability caused by heroin use throughout the world.

From our analysis of the American-led invasion of Afghanistan it can be seen that the world has not automatically become a safer place as the terrorist threat has not rescinded. The broader war on terror has also had a profound effect on the countries that waged the war. Afghanistan and Iraq remain largely ungovernable countries, while the United States has been criticised for the tactics that it has used in the war on terror. The events of September 2001 also fundamentally changed the way in which we live our lives, with a dramatic expansion in intelligence gathering by the state through the interception of communications which has eroded individual privacy, while airport security has been significantly increased. So the next time you have to take your shoes off to be scanned before you board an aeroplane, consider the sequence of events that led to this reality of modern life.

An overview of international politics

From the above examples it should be evident that the study of international politics is concerned with understanding the interconnected relationships affecting the world in which we live. It is often variously referred to as the study of world politics, global politics or international politics, but all of these descriptions fit within the academic subject of International Relations (IR).

As an academic discipline, IR seeks to examine topics such as war, peace, poverty, economic development, the relationships between states and the role of **non-state actors**. It is a subject which requires an understanding of international history, economics, law, sociology, political science and, in some instances, the subject-matter of IR is taught within these academic disciplines. It does, however, need to be emphasised that IR is a separate academic discipline, albeit a modern one that was heavily influenced by the horrors of the First World War which resulted in the death of some nine million people. This led directly to the creation of the first professorship in IR at Aberystwyth University in 1919, which formally marked the birth of the discipline. This book seeks to provide an introduction to this subject.

The formal study of IR is a relatively recent concern with its origins being rooted in the necessity of trying to understand the factors which led to the First World War and, more crucially, ways in which the potential for conflict between states could be regulated. The first institutional attempt to regulate conflict was the establishment of the League of Nations on 24 April 1919. It sought to promote the notion of **collective security** by binding its members to respect the territorial integrity of other states and thereby reduce the potential for aggression. As we will examine in more detail in Chapter 2, the League of Nations failed because some member states did not respect these objectives and the lessons from this experience informed the establishment of the UN in 1945. The UN has, however, not been without criticism as it has regularly suffered from an inability to establish a collective identity. One of the reasons for this has been the desire of nation-states to protect their own interests, and this in turn provides further evidence of why it has often been so difficult to uphold **international law**, a point that we explore in Chapter 10.

One of the most defining features of the twentieth century was the Cold War conflict between the two superpowers of the United States and the Soviet Union. This was a conflict that was shaped by the ideological confrontation between **capitalism** and **communism**. Although military power was very much at the foreground of the superpower confrontation, we show in Chapter 3 that the conflicts which took place during the Cold War did not involve the superpowers directly engaging in military conflict with each other. Rather, they were often what came to be known as proxy wars. A focus on military power continued into the early years of the post-Cold War period when the collapse of communism in Central and Eastern Europe and the break-up of the Warsaw Pact produced as much discussion about post-Cold War security structures as it did about the economic challenges and opportunities that emerged from this change.

With the end of the Cold War, academics in the early 1990s began to highlight the importance of the notion of 'soft power',[16] which, as we show in Box 1.1 below, was considerably different to traditional concepts of 'hard power' that centred on military and economic strength. In its basic form, soft power referred to the ability of a state to indirectly gain influence abroad through such means as culture and ideology. Thus, after the end of the Cold War the Soviet Union's main successor, Russia, has had little soft power because of its lack of attractiveness to other states. The United States, by contrast, has traditionally enjoyed a lot of soft power that has centred on the English language, democratic ideals and the global reach of its media industry, in particular Hollywood. In a similar vein, much has been

Box 1.1 Comparing hard and soft power

	Hard power	Soft power
Focus	Achieving direct outcomes through military and economic might.	Achieving indirect outcomes through culture and ideology.
Method	Using inducements and threats to get a desirable outcome. In other words, using the so-called 'carrot and stick' approach.	Using the attractiveness of your culture and national values to shape the preferences of others. In other words, attempting to co-opt rather than coerce other countries into positions that you would prefer.
Examples	Military force and economic sanctions.	Public diplomacy, media and culture.
Actors	Main focus is on the role of nation-states.	Nation-states are important, but NGOs and MNCs also have soft power.
Utility	Hard power is generally portrayed as a type of power that political leaders can directly control. However, this does not mean that they always have full control over the outcomes. For instance, the United States ultimately failed to achieve its outcome	Soft power is a more difficult and less predictable type of power for political leaders to control. This is in part because many of the resources that are relevant to soft power, such as culture and media, are outside government control. Moreover, whereas

Hard power	Soft power
in the Vietnam War, there is debate over the success of the hard power approach of the American-led 'war on terror', while economic sanctions do not always produce their desired outcomes. For instance, sanctions often result in an increase in the popularity of the leadership of the targeted country as the domestic population unites against the external threat.	'success' in hard power can be measured in military and economic terms and outcomes, soft power 'success' is dependent on the degree to which it is viewed as being attractive by the targeted audience. As such, the outcomes are often more difficult to predict and can take longer to take hold than hard power.

written about the soft power influence of the EU in contradistinction to the relative weakness of its military influence.[17]

Just as there has been a change in terms of the increased attention to soft power, there has also been a shift in the approach to economic power. The second half of the twentieth century witnessed the rise of big business, particularly the spread and influence of **multinational corporations (MNCs)** that, as we show in Chapter 8, have in many cases wealth and influence equal to the power of some nation-states. This emphasis on power beyond the nation-state was emphasised by the existence of organisations such as the EU and the ability of transnational pressure groups to advance arguments and opinions that transcend state boundaries. In an ever more globalised world, developments such as these have challenged state authority. Yet the global credit crunch of the first decade of the twenty-first century has highlighted that far from withering away, the nation-state continues to be the primary actor in IR. It is a point that we demonstrate in Chapters

7 and 9. The uncertain economic conditions which wiped billions of pounds off the balance sheets of companies in the first decade of the twenty-first century has redressed the balance of influence at a global level, with the state being the only institution having the capacity to respond to such global economic challenges.

These developments have further highlighted the interconnectedness of the world in which we live, and some of the most dramatic events of recent years have been the changes that have taken place in formerly closed societies and one-party states, many of which have become democracies. In fact, democratic government has become the predominant form of political organisation. Such changes have in turn meant that the focus of IR has shifted away from the Cold War bipolar East–West division, as we no longer refer to a capitalist–communist division of the globe. This was, of course, a rather crude delineation, as during the Cold War there were a significant number of countries, such as India, which tried not to align themselves to either of the superpowers.

Today the predominant division in IR is between rich and poor countries, and this largely conforms to a North–South division. One of the more significant features of this gap is the fact that for many countries the division in wealth between rich and poor countries has actually increased over recent years. Many academics rightly ask the question whether there are particular factors that have influenced this division. For some, the poverty endured by many nations is a result of corrupt leadership. For others, it is the product of the structural conditions of the global economy. Think about the fact that the main global organisations and institutions are for the most part controlled or shaped by rich countries. The work of the International Monetary Fund (IMF) and the World Bank is greatly influenced by the interests of rich and powerful countries, while the UN is governed by a Security Council that has at its core five permanent members comprising Britain, France, the United States, Russia and China (otherwise known as the P5). Also, while these countries are also the five recognised nuclear powers, it is telling that the permanent membership does not include any representation from South America or Africa. Britain and France have populations of roughly sixty million each and are permanent members and yet India, with a population over one billion, is not.

Looking to answer these points is not an easy task and to a large extent there is not one correct answer. This is both the beauty and beast of the subject of IR which does not conform to a set of pre-scribed laws or facts as might be the case were you studying a science. Instead, this is a subject where you will find many different arguments relating to the same point of analysis. Many of these arguments are rooted in theories, which, as we stress in Chapter 6, have a significant role in structuring information into more manageable forms of inter-pretation. Some of this information can be particularly challenging to both our intellect and our emotions. IR is a subject that is laced with the tragedy of death, repression and poverty. One of the most chilling points to note is the ability of humans to impart pain on each other. The Nazi regime murdered six million Jews in the holocaust, more Soviet citizens died as a result of Stalin's internal repression than were killed during the Second World War and, as recently as 1994, the world stood by and watched some 800,000 people being killed in Rwanda in a matter of months.

From the foregoing discussion it should be evident that IR is concerned with studying a wide range of topics that go beyond just focusing on peace, conflict and the role of the state. The economic discrepancies between rich and poor nations and the ways in which these inequalities can be reduced are equally important areas of analysis. This focus on economic and social issues extends to the influence of such non-state actors as NGOs, IGOs and MNCs. As much of this activity takes place within the international arena, IR is not for the most part concerned with the study of the domestic poli-tics of nation-states. Yet that is not to say that domestic politics do not impact on the international level, as changes in national governments can result in states pursuing different preferences in their negotiations with other states. Mikhail Gorbachev's 1985 appointment as General Secretary of the Soviet Communist Party had a dramatic impact in accelerating the process of domestic economic and political reform as well as creating a climate in which disarmament negotiations could take place with the United States.

Sub-disciplines

The range of topics covered by IR means that the subject-matter has tended to be grouped into specific sub-disciplines. To take an example, security studies is concerned with matters relating to peace and security. During the Cold War this was a particularly prominent area of study, with scholars examining why the superpowers did not enter into direct conflict with each other. The end of the Cold War and the emergence of other security challenges broadened this subject area to take account of new threats, such as **terrorism**, environmental degradation and social and political instability due to large migration flows. Many of these topics overlap with concerns from other academic disciplines. Whereas scholars of international politics might focus on security concerns relating to the movement of people, an economist might focus on the impact that migration has on national wage rates.

This interconnection between economics and politics is reflected in the presence of the sub-discipline of international political economy (IPE). It is a field of study that pays attention to the trading and financial relations between nations, with scholars looking at such topics as the way in which nation-states enter into co-operative arrangements in order to facilitate trade and the implications that economic globalisation presents to the **sovereignty** of nation-states. But beyond these issues there are other fundamental concerns which affect the **international system**. One of the most pressing is the growing economic inequality between nations. Inequalities are often presented in the format of the division between the rich **North** and the poor **South**, and the way in which aid and debt impact on these relationships. A student of IPE might, therefore, be asked to find out why there has been a widening in the gap between rich and poor nations. Moreover, this focus on the relationships between countries is increasingly set within the context of globalisation, with some commentators starting to question the extent to which it is possible to separate the roles of state and non-state actors or to clearly distinguish domestic from international realms.

The relevance of theory

In trying to understand these issues, IR scholars make use of theories to enable them to obtain a clearer understanding. Why is it then the case that students of international politics regularly question the relevancy of theory to their studies? One answer to this question is that many students often approach the subject from the angle of recounting events. This means that the analysis of international politics can appear similar to the approach taken by an international historian. This is a crucial mistake. International politics is more than just the narrating of events, dates and people. Our understanding of the Cold War cannot be reduced to a chronological account of what happened.

We need to go beyond merely describing events and instead offer an analysis of why they happened. Why have African states been troubled by so much conflict in the post-1945 era? How would you explain the prominence of non-state actors in international politics? What factors explain the reasoning behind the 2003 Iraq war? In answering these questions we need to go beyond listing the events that have taken place. Moreover, in many cases the volume of information with which a student is faced means that it is impossible to cover all the relevant points. We, therefore, need to know which information to use and which to leave out. This is a decision that is made easier through the use of theory.

Theories are of considerable help because they provide a structure that allows us to make decisions about the relevance of the information that we use. Thus, whereas students often consider theories to be complex and hard to understand, the fact of the matter is that theories exist to simplify our study of international politics. In this sense, they help to bring order to our studies and there are many different theories which seek to provide alternative explanations of the events that have taken place as well as to offer predictions for the future pattern of events.

Theories are subject to considerable debate because they offer differing interpretations of the same events. In line with all social science subjects, the objective of each theory is to offer the most compelling argument, although that is not to say that one specific theory can be used to understand all events. To this end, we are often faced with a theoretical toolbox whereby one theory will offer a better explanation of an event than another. It is also true that just as the nature of international politics changes, so too do the theories which seek to explain what is happening. This means that some theories that appeared relevant fifty years ago might appear less relevant today.

In providing an introduction to the utility of theory we are going to concentrate on four main theories which offer differing perspectives of

Table 1.1 Summary of the main theories of international politics

	Realism	Liberalism	Marxism	Constructivism
Main actors	States	States, IGOs, MNCs and NGOs	Social classes: capitalists and workers.	Individuals, states and domestic and international societies.
Focus	Stresses the anarchical nature of world politics and argues that states are preoccupied with guaranteeing their own security.	Emphasises opportunities for co-operation between states and highlights the importance of the international economy.	Criticises the capitalist accumulation of resources and the exploitation of workers.	Explores how states and world politics are socially constructed and how they change through time.

the study of international politics. They are **Realism, Liberalism, Marxism** and **Constructivism**, and as Table 1.1 highlights they are individually quite different from each other. A fuller discussion of these issues is provided in Chapter 6.

Realism

The first of these four main theories is Realism. The Realist approach emphasises that there is no overarching world government or accepted authority. As we note in Box 1.2, Realists view international politics as an anarchic environment because the absence of a higher political authority creates a competitive environment in which states seek to preserve their sovereignty. Realists stress that nation-states are the most important actors in international politics, and, because they seek to protect their own interests, this means that they are less likely to co-operate with other states. It is a view which attaches importance to the power of the state, while such matters as economic growth or the development of the state are seen as being

---

Box 1.2 Realism

- Focus on the military conflict between states.
- Considers that the world is anarchic with states competing for power and security.
- Has been a dominant theoretical base for understanding world politics, although in recent years its position has been challenged by developments such as globalisation.

---

of lesser importance. In this sense, Realists would argue that powerful countries use organisations such as the UN as a means of extending and maintaining their influence rather than as part of a collective approach to security.

Such a take on events can be traced back to the fifth century BC when the Greek historian Thucydides (460–404 BC) noted that the underlying cause of the Peloponnesian war (431–404 BC) between Athens and Sparta was the way in which the growth of the power of Athens resulted in Sparta becoming fearful for its own security.[18] Thus, faced with an imbalance of power, Sparta felt it necessary to go to war rather than wait to be attacked by Athens. This Realist approach would later be emphasised in the writings of Niccolò Machiavelli (1469–1537) in the sixteenth century, who in his book, *The Prince*, stressed the importance of military strength over such issues as the economic wealth of the nation.[19] In the twentieth century the Realist approach was initially influenced by the British historian, E. H. Carr (1892–1982), who analysed the breakdown in international relations during the 1930s.[20] After the Second World War the US diplomat, George Kennan (1904–2005), and the University of Chicago political scientist, Hans Morgenthau (1904–80), were key figures in the development of Realist thinking. Having escaped from Nazi Germany, Morgenthau argued in *Politics Among Nations* (1948) that international politics is a struggle for power.[21] But while there are considerable strengths to this view, a key criticism of Realism has been the way in which it views economics and politics as well as domestic and international politics as being different areas of activity. At the same time, the emphasis attached to the state as the key actor means that Realism does not take into consideration the influence of non-state actors such as **interest groups**.

Liberalism

The Realist anarchic view is not shared by Liberal theorists, who question the dominance of nation-states and instead emphasise the extent to which it is possible to achieve peace and compromise in international politics.[22] Liberalism stresses that it is possible for states to enter into co-operation with each other, and that the **national interest** goes beyond the military need to defend territory which is at the core of Realist thinking (see Box 1.3). This basically means that whereas Realists emphasise the sovereign integrity of nation-states, Liberalism notes that while nation-states may be sovereign they, none the less, exist in a broader pattern of interconnecting relationships which fundamentally means that the state cannot just do as it chooses. In this sense Liberal theorists would emphasise the importance of IGOs, while Realist scholars would stress that IGOs are of little consequence to international politics.

The Liberal view of international politics achieved prominence after the First World War when there was a concerted effort to achieve international co-operation through the League of Nations. Realists subsequently labelled these Liberal plans for the peaceful ordering of international politics as **idealism**. The potential for states to enter into co-operation with each other was further emphasised after the Second World War when the UN was created and during the late 1960s and 1970s, a time of growing economic **interdependence** between nations. Yet repeatedly the ascendancy

---

Box 1.3 Liberalism

- Focuses on the growing economic interdependence between states.
- Emphasises the importance of non-state actors.
- Examines attempts to deal with global issues such as global warming (the Kyoto Protocol) and human rights (the International Criminal Court).

of Liberal views was short-lived, as the competing interests of nation-states were highlighted by the Second World War and the periods of high tension during the Cold War. Although the end of the Cold War brought Liberal thinking back to the fore of international politics, the period since September 2001 has once again seen a shift to concerns with conflict and state security as a result of the war on terror.

Marxism

The Marxist theory is based on the writings of Karl Marx (1818–83) and his collaborator, Friedrich Engels (1820–95). This theory is considerably different from Realist and Liberal interpretations, because it stresses the way in which the capitalist economy dominates international politics. This means that Marxist thinkers emphasise the structure of international politics as being primarily an economic, in which the elites which dominate many states and non-state actors represent the capitalist economic class. As we explore in Box 1.4, the Marxist view notes that inequalities between and within nations are the result of this capitalist economic system, which ensures that the working class gains little and as such introduces students to the relevance of structure and agency in politics and IR debates. Put simply, structure and agency is a concept that is used to highlight the way in which the structures of society shape the choices that can be taken by individuals through their own agency.

It is a theoretical approach which continues to be relevant despite the collapse of Communist rule in the former Soviet Union. This is because

Box 1.4 Marxism

- Focuses on the economic exploitation of poorer states by the most developed states.
- Highlights the exploitation of Third World states prior to them gaining independence.
- Stresses the reality of neo-colonialism after independence: the IMF, World Bank and MNCs (and possibly NGOs) constrain poorer states' ability to develop.
- Emphasises the growing disparity in wealth between North and South.

its critique of capitalism can be used to highlight the gaps between the rich North and the poor South, and the way in which some regions such as Africa remain relatively impoverished. Thus, Marxists would argue that the trading relationships between a large MNC and a poor country would more than likely favour the interests of the MNC, which in turn further strengthens its position in the global economy. This situation is often linked to the concept of **neo-colonialism**, which refers to the way in which powerful countries and modern capitalist businesses have been able to exert influence on former colonies, even though the latter have gained formal independence. For Marxists, these inequalities can be overcome only by structural and collective reform.

Constructivism

Whereas the Realist, Liberal and Marxist views emphasise the way in which international politics is conducted at a level above the individual, Constructivists argue that individuals are able to exercise considerable influence in shaping events. This is a view of international politics which stresses that the international system is socially constructed. Influenced by the writings of Alexander Wendt (1958–), the Constructivist approach counters the Realist argument that there is an inherent level of **anarchy** in the international system.[23] Constructivists, therefore, argue that state interests and identities are shaped by the ideas that exist within the system (Box 1.5). To this end,

---

Box 1.5 Constructivism

- Seeks to demonstrate how key aspects of international politics have been socially constructed whereby they are the result of social interaction.
- Challenges many of the key assumptions of Realism, which stresses that the dynamics of international relations are shaped by the structure of the international system. Constructivists stress that these structures are themselves determined by social practice.
- Changing social practices can lead to fundamental change of international structures.

Constructivists emphasise that their approach to the study of international politics provides an opportunity to foresee change within the international system in a way that other theories cannot. Thus, whereas Realism, Liberalism and Marxism do not provide adequate theoretical explanations to explain such events as the collapse of the Soviet Union and the fall of the Berlin Wall, Constructivists would argue that their theory can explain these events.

Summary

In this chapter we have provided an overview of the nature of international politics and you should be aware of the broad range of subjects with which it is concerned. This ranges from military force to environmental concerns. You should also be aware of the fact that there are considerable differences in the wealth and influence of nation-states, while at the same time there has been a dramatic increase in the number of non-state actors. Our introduction to the topic of globalisation shows that while there is a considerable degree of interconnectedness between nations, it is nevertheless the case that some areas, such as central Asia and sub-Saharan Africa, have been less affected by these changes. This is a point confirmed by Andrew Hurrell and Ngaire Woods, who note that what has been 'neglected in liberal and other writings about globalisation is one particularly important feature of world politics: inequality'.[24]

The basic picture that is emerging from this introduction is that we live in an unequal world. The 2007 UN Human Development Report notes that some 2.6 billion people live on less than US$2 a day.[25] This equates to 40 per cent of the world's population. The disparity between rich and poor countries is growing. Nearly one billion people entered the twenty-first century unable to read a book or sign their name, of which two-thirds were women.[26]

As students of IR it is important that such statistical evidence is not just recounted as part of an historical narrative. We need to ask why and how such situations exist. Why is it the case that the gap between rich and poor countries has widened over the course of the twentieth century? Why do India and Pakistan possess nuclear weapons and yet are unable to provide clean drinking water to all of their populations? The answers to these questions are never as simple as they may seem at first sight. The chapters which follow seek to unravel these and other questions and provide a comprehensive introduction to the subject of international politics. In Chapters 2 to 5 we explore the development of the international system since 1900. Due to the nature of this introductory guide, we will focus on globally significant trends and events, but this is not to deny the importance of regional political and security dynamics which have been expertly addressed elsewhere.[27] In Chapters 6 to 12 we take a more theoretical, conceptual and thematic approach to examining the key issues of international politics.

· ·

✔ What you should have learnt from reading this chapter

- International politics affects everyone and encompasses a vast range of topics.

- Sovereignty is a key concept in IR.

- Nation-states vary considerably in terms of their size and influence. There is also a broad level of distinction between the rich North and the poor South.

- There has been an explosion in the number of non-state actors, such as IGOs, NGOs and MNCs. These non-state actors can exert considerable influence on international politics.

- Theoretical explanations are important because they help to structure our analysis of international politics.

❓ Likely examination questions

What is meant by sovereignty?

To what extent do we live in an anarchical world?

To what extent do non-state actors challenge the ability of states to manage international affairs?

Has globalisation exacerbated the problem of economic inequality between North and South?

Why do non-governmental organisations seek to influence the decisions that nation-states take?

Under what conditions are states most likely to use force in world politics?

Why has it been so difficult to negotiate a solution to the problem of global warming?

Was the United States correct to oppose the Kyoto protocol?

Why are theories relevant to the study of international relations?

To what extent has economic power eclipsed military power?

 ## Helpful websites

General reference

BBC at: www.bbc.co.uk

Keesings at: www.keesings.com

Intute at: www.intute.ac.uk/socialsciences

Spartacus Educational at: www.spartacus.schoolnet.co.uk

Internet Modern History Sourcebook at: www.fordham.edu/halsall/mod/modsbook.html

The Avalon Project at: avalon.law.yale.edu/default.asp

Project Gutenberg at: www.gutenberg.org/wiki/Main_Page

Reference maps

Mapping Worlds at: www.mappingworlds.com

UK National Archives Maps in Time at: www.nationalarchives.gov.uk/cabinetpapers/themes/maps-interactive/maps-in-time.htm?&1918

International organisations

United Nations at: www.un.org

European Union at: http://europa.eu

World Bank at: www.worldbank.org

North Atlantic Treaty Organisation at: www.nato.int

Climate change

UK Met Office at: www.metoffice.gov.uk/climatechange

UK Climate Impacts Programme at: www.ukcip.org.uk

UK Office of Climate Change at: www.occ.gov.uk/index.htm

Intergovernmental Panel on Climate Change at: www.ipcc.ch

UN Framework Convention on Climate Change at: http://unfccc.int/2860.php

CGD's Climate Change Research at: www.cgd.ucar.edu/ccr

Stern Review on Economics of Climate Change at: www.hm-treasury.gov.
uk/sternreview_index.htm

Archives

UK National Archives at: www.learningcurve.gov.uk/default.htm

Newspapers

The Guardian at: www.guardian.co.uk

The Times at: www.timesonline.co.uk

Research

Chatham House at: www.chathamhouse.org.uk

Royal United Services Institute at: www.rusi.org

Brookings Institution at: www.brookings.edu

Woodrow Wilson International Center for Scholars at: www.wilsoncenter.
org/index.cfm

Royal Institute for International Relations at: www.egmontinstitute.be

Netherlands Institute of International Relations at: www.clingendael.nl

Pugwash Conferences on Science and World Affairs at: www.pugwash.org

Rand Corporation at: www.rand.org

Stockholm International Peace Research Institute (SIPRI) at: www.sipri.org

British American Security Information Council (BASIC) at: www.basicint.org

Verification Research, Training and Information Centre (VERTIC) at: www.
vertic.org

Professional associations

Political Studies Association at: www.psa.ac.uk

British International Studies Association at: www.bisa.ac.uk

University Association for Contemporary European Studies at: www.
uaces.org

American Political Science Association at: www.apsa.net.org

 ## Suggestions for further reading

Introductory texts

M. Nicholson, *International Relations: A Concise Introduction*, 2nd edn
(Palgrave, 2002).

K. L. Shimko, *International Relations: Perspectives and Controversies* (Houghton Miffin, 2005).

P. Sutch and J. Elias, *International Relations: The Basics* (Routledge, 2007).

P. Wilkinson, *International Relations: A Very Short Introduction* (Oxford University Press, 2007).

Comprehensive textbooks

J. Baylis, S. Smith and P. Owens (eds), *The Globalization of World Politics*, 4th edn (Oxford University Press, 2008).

C. Brown and K. Ainley, *Understanding International Relations*, 3rd edn (Palgrave, 2005).

J. Edkins and M. Zehfuss (eds), *Global Politics: A New Introduction* (Routledge, 2009).

J. Goldstein, *International Relations*, 5th edn (Longman, 2003).

R. Little and M. Smith (eds), *Perspectives on World Politics*, 3rd edn (Routledge, 2006).

T. Salmon and M. Imber (eds), *Issues in International Relations*, 2nd edn (Routledge, 2008).

B. White, R. Little and M. Smith (eds), *Issues in World Politics* (Palgrave, 2005).

N. Woods (ed.), *Explaining International Relations Since 1945* (Oxford University Press, 1996).

Great Powers to Superpowers

Contents

Overview

Having provided a general overview of the main issues that relate to the study of IR in Chapter 1, we are now going to go look at the historical origins of the subject-matter. In this chapter our primary focus is on the period from 1900 to 1945, although we also look at key developments in the nineteenth century. The reason that we are chiefly concerned with developments from 1900 onwards is that the discipline of IR is, for the most part, concerned with recent developments. As we noted in Chapter 1, this is a subject that was principally conceived in the aftermath of the First World War, with the first professorship of IR being established in 1919. In looking at this recent history, it is evident that the last one hundred years have witnessed key changes in the structure and organisation of international politics, with the period from 1900 to 1945 witnessing the onslaught of two world wars, a global economic crisis and the rise of superpower conflict. In examining these issues the chapter pays attention to the rise of the superpower conflict that dominated the second half of the twentieth century.

Key issues to be covered in this chapter

- The changing nature of power and influence in international politics
- The origins of the First World War and the implications of the Versailles peace treaty
- The factors which led to the Second World War and the post-war settlement
- The demise of the European colonial powers and the emergence of superpower rivalry

The onset of total war

Whereas the twentieth century was dominated by two world wars and a **Cold War** conflict, many individuals lived in relative peace throughout the nineteenth century. This was despite the fact that the early years of the nineteenth century were dominated by France's quest to control the European continent under the influence of Napoleon, who had crowned himself Emperor in 1804.[1] The ensuing conflicts with the other **Great Powers** resulted in the ascendancy of Austria, Britain, Prussia and Russia over France, with the conduct of international politics being formalised at the Congress of Vienna of 1814–15.

The Congress, which lasted from 1 November 1814 to 8 June 1815, was a conference of ambassadors of the major European powers which sought to settle the map of Europe after the defeat of Napoleon. This included depriving France of the territory conquered by Napoleon. The major achievement of the Congress was the re-establishment of a **balance of power** among the Great Powers of Europe, which in turn created an environment within which peace could flourish. That peace was broken by the Crimean War of 1853–6, and there were also notable conflicts over the unification of Germany and Italy between 1859 and 1871. After 1871 peace returned to Europe and this relative harmony continued until the First World War of 1914–18. What then were the factors that broke the peace?

There are many arguments over the reasons for the outbreak of the First World War. One of the most common themes concerns the competition for power among European nations. This particularly applied to Germany, which, after becoming a unified state in 1871, sought to match the influence of Britain, France and Russia.[2] Germany challenged the *Pax Britannica* at the turn of the century by building up its navy and seeking out territory that it could colonise and markets that it could trade with. There were few options for Germany to obtain new markets and territory because by 1900 much of the international system had been conquered: the majority of Africa, Asia and the Middle East were dominated by Britain and France; Russia along with Japan and Britain exercised influence in China; and the United States exercised influence in Latin America.

Somewhat inevitably Germany argued that this was to its disadvantage. Its search for new territories was as much about its desire to increase its world status as it was about its need to obtain new markets that would assist with its economic expansion. It should, therefore, be evident that while peace existed in Europe after 1871, this was an increasingly uneasy peace as tension and rivalry between the dominant countries came to the fore.

Germany's ambitions challenged the positions of Britain, France and Russia, who in turn concluded agreements with each other to protect their interests. Known as the 'Entente powers', this meant that by the early 1900s there were in effect two power blocs in Europe. The first was a rather loose alliance between Britain, France and Russia. The second was Germany's alliance with the Austro-Hungarian Empire.

The First World War

Despite these tensions, the opening shots of the First World War were not fired by France, Britain, Germany or Russia. Instead, they were fired by a Serb nationalist at Archduke Franz Ferdinand who was heir to the Austro-Hungarian Empire. Students of history need to ask why this incident resulted in a war that lasted for four years between 1914–18? As Paul Kennedy has written, 'the June 1914 assassination is one of the best-known examples in history of a particular event triggering a general crisis, and then a world war'.[3] The answer to the question that we posed is that the Austro-Hungarian empire decided to retaliate against Serbia in the wake of the assassination. Yet by that stage the Austro-Hungarian Empire was a ghost of its former influence, and Germany's alliance with it resulted in the German government offering the empire its unconditional support on 5–6 July 1914. At first glance some might argue that the First World War was an accidental war which came about through the coincidence of the assassination. Another view is that Germany was on a war footing in the early years of the twentieth century and wanted war so that it could break up the power blocs of continental Europe.

The First World War had a dramatic impact on all countries. It was the world's first 'total war' where the full weight of industrial

Table 2.1 War expenditure and deaths, 1914–18[4]		
	Expenditure ($bn)	**Dead**
Britain	43.8	723,000
British empire	5.8	198,000
France	28.2	1,398,000
Russia	16.3	1,811,000
Italy	14.7	578,000
United States	36.2	114,000
Other	2.0	599,000
Total Entente/Allied	147.0	5,421,000
Germany	47.0	2,037,000
Austria-Hungary	13.4	1,100,000
Bulgaria-Turkey	1.1	892,000
Total Central Powers	61.5	4,029,000
Total	**208.5**	**9,450,000**

production had been used to fight the war. As we show in Table 2.1, vast economic resources were used to support the war effort; a war which was also about mass death as millions of soldiers were killed – over 400,000 troops were killed at the battle of Verdun in 1916 alone. Despite this carnage, the war was primarily fought in open country-side and did not result in the vast infrastructure damage wrought on the cities of Europe in the Second World War. Although outwardly the battlefields quickly returned to their former agricultural use, the war brought about wider change in terms of the geographical map of Europe. The Austro-Hungarian and Ottoman empires collapsed and tsarist rule in Russia was overthrown by the 1917 Bolshevik revo-lution. Susan Carruthers is, therefore, quite right to ask the question: 'Had anyone really won the war?'[5]

Although all the countries that participated in the war were cer-tainly affected by it, the devastation was more keenly felt in those countries where the land conflict had taken place, particularly

France. At the end of the war there was a desire by France to obtain economic and financial resources from Germany to assist with its own reconstruction – known as **reparations**. These issues were discussed in six months of negotiations at the Paris Peace Conference, which took place after the signing of the Allied armistice with Germany on 11 November 1918 and officially marked the end of the war. The outcome of these discussions was the Treaty of Versailles of 28 June 1919, which was heavily influenced by the views of American President Woodrow Wilson (1856–1924) who advanced a set of principles that became known as his 'Fourteen Points' (see Box 2.1). For President Wilson, at the core of these points was the principle of national **self-determination** that was laid down in the fourteenth point: 'A general association of nations must be formed under specific covenants for the purposes of affording mutual guarantees of political independence and territorial integrity to great and small states alike.' Wilson's argument centred on the belief that stability and peace could be achieved only by moving away from the old practice of balance of power to instead having a system based on democratic states. Indeed, President Wilson argued that the American entry into the First World War in 1917 had been shaped by a desire to 'make the world safe for democracy'. Thus, after the collapse of the Ottoman, Russian and Austro-Hungarian empires, there emerged a number of new nation-states as we show in Figure 2.1: Bulgaria, Hungary, Poland, Czechoslovakia, Yugoslavia, Finland, Romania, Estonia, Latvia and Lithuania.

This process of self-determination was not without its problems as territorial boundaries were contentious matters that rarely satisfied all parties. Determined that the new state of Poland should have a sea outlet, the peace-makers annexed part of Germany into the new Poland, thereby resulting in German nationals being located in the new country. The peace settlement also resulted in France regaining the industrial area of Alsace–Lorraine which had been annexed by Germany after the war of 1870–1, while France was also awarded occupation of the Saar for fifteen years. A further condition of the peace settlement was that Germany lost its empire and underwent a process of demilitarisation. Such changes angered many Germans who witnessed the reduction in the size, population and strength of their country. Moreover, when combined with France's insistence on

Source: www.nationalarchives.gov.uk/pathways/firstworldwar/index.htm.

Figure 2.1 The borders of European states in 1919

reparations, it meant that far from providing a platform for stability the peace settlement in fact sowed the seeds for further turmoil and conflict.

This potential for future conflict went beyond the European continent. During the First World War Britain waged a campaign in Sinai and Palestine against forces from Germany and the Ottoman empire. Following its collapse at the end of the First World War the Ottoman empire was partitioned by the 1920 Treaty of Sèvres, although Britain and France had already concluded the secret Sykes–Picot pact in May 1916 carving up the Ottoman empire. The outcome was that after the First World War Turkish controlled territory in the Middle East was divided up into various British and

Box 2.1 The Versailles Settlement and President Wilson's Fourteen Points

The Versailles Settlement was influenced by the 'Fourteen Points' of American President Woodrow Wilson. It created new states in the Balkans and Central and Eastern Europe after the collapse of the Ottoman and Austro-Hungarian empires and established a League of Nations to deter future conflict. Germany was punished for starting the war and lost approximately 13 per cent of its land and population. This included losing Alsace and Lorraine to France and the so-called 'Polish corridor' to Poland, which meant that East Prussia was cut off from the rest of Germany. Additionally, Germany was disarmed, made to pay reparations to the victorious powers and it was agreed that an allied occupation army was to be based in the Rhineland for fifteen years. Somewhat inevitably many Germans resented the terms of the Versailles Settlement which many analysts regarded as being too hard on Germany. It was, therefore, not surprising that subsequent German governments challenged the Versailles settlement.

President Wilson's Fourteen Points

  I. Open covenants of peace, openly arrived at.
 II. Absolute freedom of navigation upon the seas, outside territorial waters, alike in peace and war.
III. The removal, so far as possible, of all economic barriers and the establishment of an equality of trade conditions among all the nations consenting to the peace.
 IV. National armaments to be reduced to the lowest point consistent with public safety.
  V. Impartial adjustment of all colonial claims.
 VI. The evacuation of all Russian territory.
VII. Belgium must be evacuated and restored, without any attempt to delimit sovereignty which she enjoys in common with all free nations.
VIII. All French territory should be freed and the invaded provinces restored, and the wrong done to France by Prussia in 1871 in the matter of Alsace–Lorraine should be righted.
 IX. A readjustment of the frontiers of Italy should be effected along clearly recognisable lines of nationality.
  X. The peoples of Austria-Hungary should be accorded the freest opportunity for autonomous development.

XI.   Romania, Serbia and Montenegro should be evacuated; occu-
      pied territories restored; Serbia accorded free and secure
      access to the sea.

XII. The Turkish portions of the present Ottoman empire should be
      assured a secure sovereignty, but the other nationalities which
      are now under Turkish rule should be assured an undoubted
      security of life and absolutely unmolested opportunity of auton-
      omous development.

XIII. An independent Polish state should be erected which should
      include the territories inhabited by indisputably Polish popula-
      tions, which should be assured a free and secure access to the
      seas.

XIV. A general association of nations must be formed under specific
      covenants for the purposes of affording mutual guarantees of
      political independence and territorial integrity to great and small
      states alike.

Source: M. Howard, *The First World War: A Very Short Introduction* (Oxford
University Press 2001), pp. 120–1. Also electronically available at World War I
DocumentArchive:http://wwi.lib.byu.edu/index.php/President_Wilson%27s_
Fourteen_Points.

French administered areas, with Britain getting control of Palestine
and France getting control of Lebanon. The upshot of these events
was to create a complicated state of affairs over the future administration of the Middle East. It was a situation that had been reinforced by the then British Foreign Secretary, Arthur James Balfour,
putting forward a declaration in 1917 that favoured the creation of
a Jewish homeland in Palestine. Known thereafter as the Balfour
Declaration, it became an important focal point in campaigns for a
Jewish state and for many it sowed the seeds of future discord in the
Middle East.

Despite this potential for future conflict, in the wake of the First
World War there emerged the first major attempt to regulate differences between states through the creation of the League of Nations
on 24 April 1919. The League sought to provide a framework that
would deter future wars. Central to this was the commitment in
Article 10 that its members were to preserve each other's territorial

integrity, with members able to take collective action against aggressor states. Fundamentally, however, the League did not prove strong enough to regulate the aggression that would emerge in the inter-war period and this consequently led to its downfall.[6] The League's demise also marked a move away from an **Idealist** view of collective security and the emergence of **Realism** as the main theoretical approach (see Chapter 6).[7]

The Second World War

American influence on the post-war settlement reflected the changing nature of world power. Whereas the nineteenth century had been dominated by Britain, the dawn of the twentieth century saw the rise of the United States. But while the United States quickly availed itself in having a major share of world trade, its rise took place in tandem with a greater interconnection of the world economy.

The stark reality of this changed economic climate was evidenced by the 1929 economic crisis that was marked by the Wall Street crash. The Wall Street crash set off a chain of events resulting in the **Great Depression**, which by the early 1930s had affected much of the world's industrialised economies. Germany was badly affected by the adverse economic conditions, and by 1932 some six million Germans were registered unemployed. The severity of this situation was compounded by a decline in German industrial production because of the overall reduction in world trade. At a time of economic instability the popularity of the Nazi Party increased as its anti-semitic message became a galvanising theme for many Germans. Hitler's message that the Jews were to blame for Germany's economic catastrophe, combined with his use of propaganda, resulted in him being appointed Chancellor of Germany in January 1933.[8] Hitler's ascent to power was followed by the immediate rearmament of Germany which was achieved through a dramatic rise in public expenditure. This rearmament reversed Germany's economic malaise and increased the country's economic output to such an extent that in a short space of time it was no longer affected by the Great Depression. To this end the post-war settlement did not result in the peace for which the signatories of the Treaty of Versailles had hoped. As Henry Kissinger has commented, 'the framers of the Versailles settlement achieved the precise opposite of what they had set out to do'.[9] It was consequently the case that the 1920s and 1930s were marked by resentment and economic and political crises.

Although Hitler managed to cure the problem of unemployment and increase Germany's economic output, he had wider foreign policy ambitions that centred on strengthening Germany's political and military influence.[10] In 1936 Germany reoccupied the Rhineland and in 1938 it annexed Austria. Other European leaders did not have the stomach to directly confront these territorial advances and acknowledged Germany's expansion through a policy of **appeasement**. The apotheosis of appeasement was the **Munich Agreement** of 30 September 1938 in which France and Britain agreed to Germany's annexation of the Sudetenland in Czechoslovakia, which was an area that had a majority German population. For many European countries this annexation was a price worth paying to avoid war, and upon returning from Munich the British Prime Minister, Neville Chamberlain, spoke of the agreement as 'peace in our time'. Yet the agreement did not stop Germany's ambitions and one year later in 1939 it occupied the rest of Czechoslovakia.

Concerned about Germany's onward march, Britain gave a security guarantee to Poland, and when Germany invaded Poland on 1 September 1939 the British Cabinet concluded on 2 September that 'there should be no negotiation with Germany unless she was first prepared to give an understanding to withdraw her troops from Poland and Danzig' and 'that it was undesirable to allow Germany longer than until midnight, 2nd/3rd September to make up her mind on these points'.[11] When Germany did not adhere to this ultimatum the Second World War began in Europe on 3 September 1939 (see Box 2.2). The origins of the Second World War can be directly traced to the outcome of the First World War.[12] As John Keegan has commented, 'The Second World War, when it came in 1939, was unquestionably the outcome of the First, and in large measure its continuation. Its circumstances – the dissatisfaction of the German-speaking peoples with their standing among other nations – were the same, and so were its immediate causes, a dispute between a German-speaking ruler and a Slav neighbour.'[13]

Tension and conflict in the inter-war period was also to be found in Asia where Japan sought new markets and raw materials to feed its

Box 2.2 Historical background to the Second World War

- 1919   Treaty of Versailles.
- 1924   Dawes Plan scales down reparations.
- 1925   Locarno Treaty.
- 1926   Germany enters the League of Nations.
- 1929   Wall Street crash.
- 1930   Allied troops leave the Rhineland five years ahead of planned withdrawal.
- 1933   Adolf Hitler becomes Chancellor of Germany and Germany leaves the League of Nations.
- 1934   Hitler introduces conscription.
- 1935   Italy invades Abyssinia.
- 1936   Remilitarisation of the Rhineland (March).
- 1938   Anschluss between Germany and Austria (March); Munich conference which cedes the Sudetenland to Germany (September).
- 1939   Germany invades Czechoslovakia (March); Pact of Steel between Hitler and Mussolini (May); Nazi–Soviet Pact (23 August); Germany invades Poland (1 September); Britain and France declare war on Germany (3 September).
- 1940   Italy enters war as an ally of Germany (June).
- 1941   Germany invades the Soviet Union (June); Japan attacks the United States at Pearl Harbor (December).

growing economy. This resulted in the expansion of its influence into China and, by 1933, it controlled Manchuria through the establishment of the puppet state of 'Manchuguo'. The League of Nations did nothing in response to this blatant act of aggression and this situation 'can be regarded as the beginning of the violence that developed into the Second World War'.[14] In 1939 the United States withdrew from the 1911 Treaty of Commerce and imposed an embargo on exports of oil and scrap iron to Japan. Although American oil exports to Japan were not significant, it served to increase the tension between the two countries.

This tension resulted in all-out war after Japan's surprise attack on the American fleet at Pearl Harbor on 7 December 1941. Winston Churchill regarded the United States entry into the war to be a deciding factor, and would later note that 'Hitler's fate was sealed. Mussolini's fate was sealed. As for the Japanese, they would be ground to powder. All the rest was merely the proper application of overwhelming force.' [15] A Grand Alliance was then formed between the United States, the Soviet Union and Britain to fight the Axis powers of Germany, Italy and Japan. The conflict culminated in an Allied victory in Europe on 8 May 1945 with the surrender of Germany. The war finally came to a conclusion with the surrender of Japan on 2 September 1945. The Japanese surrender came as a direct result of the American use of atomic bombs on the cities of Hiroshima and Nagasaki. To date, this remains the only ever use of nuclear weapons.

The use of advanced weapons meant that the costs of the Second World War were far greater than those the First World War. Apart from the vast economic costs incurred in fighting and the destruction wrought by the war, it is estimated that over sixty million people, both civilian and military, were killed. The surrender of Germany also brought to an end the persecution and genocide which had been a dominant feature of Nazi Germany. Over a twelve-year period the Nazi regime persecuted the Jewish population, which eventually led to a holocaust that murdered some 5.8 million Jews.[16] This sickening attempt to create a racially pure Germany also resulted in the regime persecuting other groups, such as the disabled, the Roma and those who were perceived to be ideologically at odds with the Nazi Party. By 1945 nearly two out of three European Jews had been killed as part of Hitler's final solution, and, as Table 2.2 shows, this resulted in over 80 per cent of the Jewish population being killed in many European countries.

Post-war settlement

The Second World War claimed over sixty million lives, two-thirds of which were civilians, and in many countries the population losses were particularly stark. Between 10 and 20 per cent of the populations of Poland, Yugoslavia and the Soviet Union were killed. At the end of the war the great European cities of Cologne, Berlin and Vienna resembled a wasteland of rubble. Britain – which was not subject to the atrocities of the land campaign – suffered

Table 2.2 The Nazi genocide of the Jews[17]				
Country	Jewish population	Estimated number of Jews killed		
		Lowest	Highest	% of Jewish population
Poland	3,300,000	2,350,000	2,900,000	88
Soviet Union	2,100,000	700,000	1,000,000	48
Romania	500,000	200,000	420,000	49
Czechoslovakia	360,000	233,000	300,000	83
Germany	240,000	160,000	200,000	83
Hungary	403,000	180,000	200,000	50
Lithuania	155,000		135,000	87
France	300,000	60,000	130,000	43
Holland	150,000	104,000	120,000	80
Latvia	95,000		85,000	89
Yugoslavia	75,000	55,000	65,000	87
Greece	75,000	57,000	60,000	80
Austria	60,000		40,000	67
Belgium	100,000	25,000	40,000	48
Italy	75,000	8,500	15,000	26
Bulgaria	50,000		7,000	14
Denmark		Below 100		
Luxembourg		3,000		
Norway		1,000		
Total	8,388,000	4,194,200	5,721,000	68

extensive damage through air bombardment, while its economic might had been shattered through having spent some 25 per cent of its total wealth fighting the war. Thus, at the end of the war there was a significant lack of basic infrastructure in many of the countries that had been involved in the conflict. There was, therefore, a desire by many states to establish structures that would end the problem of conflict between states through the creation of new organisations. The drive to construct a new international system had in fact commenced before the end of the Second World War. This was evidenced by the development of the United Nations system and the economic organisations that emerged out of the **Bretton Woods** negotiations of 1944–6 that were attended by some forty-four countries.[18] The latter included the General Agreement on Tariffs and Trade (GATT), the International Bank for Reconstruction and Development (IBRD) and the International Monetary Fund (IMF).

Set against a background of the 1930s depression and the experience of the Second World War, governments were motivated to engage in new forms of international co-operation to ensure that the post-war period would not be marked by financial disaster whereby nation-states returned to the **protectionism** of the 1930s. As one commentator has noted, 'the war years provided the furnace within which some of the most important post-war organisations were fashioned'.[19] The emergence of new bodies of international co-operation went hand-in-hand with an increase in the number of participating states, with this development being heavily influenced by the process of **decolonisation** which was a dominant feature of the twentieth century. Whereas there were 192 members of the UN in 2009, there were only fifty-one original members in 1945 (see Figures 2.2 and 2.3).

Such changes meant that there was a dramatic re-ordering of influence in world politics. This was most starkly evidenced by the emergence of the Soviet Union and the United States as the dominant powers in the post-war world. They were the only countries who were able to marshal the necessary economic, military or political resources that were necessary to exercise global influence. Although the Soviet Union had been significantly affected by the war effort, it had sizeable resources upon which it could draw. For the United States, the war stimulated an economy which had grown considerably since 1939. Its trade surplus had grown fat through exporting products, and by 1945 it was estimated that some 45 per cent of all global manufactures took place in the United States which as a result proved to be the main source of credit for the world economy after the war.

In an effort to establish the parameters of the post-war world a number of **summits** took place from early 1945 onwards, of which the most important were held at Yalta in the Crimea in February 1945 and just outside Berlin at Potsdam in July–August 1945. The meetings were attended by the United States, the Soviet Union and Britain, collectively known as the gathering of the 'Big Three'. Britain's participation was influenced by its wartime role and because its empire still stretched around the world. Despite being exhausted by the war and having suffered from problems of imperial over-stretch since the turn of the century, British foreign policy-makers none the less continued to think in global terms. As we show in Figure 2.4 this was most clearly summed up by Churchill's vision of Britain being at the centre of three interlocking circles: the Atlantic relationship with the United States and Canada; the British Empire and Commonwealth; and Western Europe.

The future of Europe, especially the position of Germany, were key items of discussion at the meetings in Yalta and Potsdam. At Yalta it was agreed that Germany would be divided into four occu-pation zones that would be governed by the United States, the Soviet Union, Britain and France. Such a decision essentially divided Europe into **spheres of influence**. While a further agreement also included a 'Declaration on Liberated Europe' committing the coun-tries to recognising the right to hold free elections in the liberated countries, the United States and Britain conceded at Yalta that the Soviet Union should have 'friendly' neighbours in Eastern Europe.

By the time of the Potsdam conference the United States was becoming more suspicious of Soviet motives. At Potsdam the United States was represented by Harry Truman who had become president after Franklin Roosevelt's death on 12 April 1945.[20] Truman was sceptical of Soviet motives, and some have argued that his decision to drop atomic bombs on Japan four days after the end of the Potsdam conference was as much influenced by his desire to expedite the end of the war in the East as it was to impress on the Soviet Union the power and influence of the United States. The atomic bomb provided the United States with an unrivalled ability not only to win wars but also to prevent them taking place. As Williamson and

Source: www.un.org/Depts/Cartographic/map/profile/world45.pdf.

Figure 2.2 Map of the world in 1945

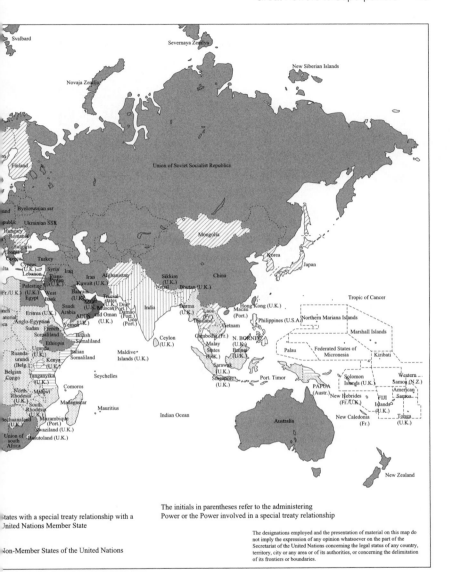

The initials in parentheses refer to the administering
Power or the Power involved in a special treaty relationship

States with a special treaty relationship with a
United Nations Member State

Non-Member States of the United Nations

The designations employed and the presentation of material on this map do
not imply the expression of any opinion whatsoever on the part of the
Secretariat of the United Nations concerning the legal status of any country,
territory, city or any area or of its authorities, or concerning the delimitation
of its frontiers or boundaries.

Source: www.un.org/Depts/Cartographic/map/profile/world00.pdf.

Figure 2.3 Map of the world in 2006

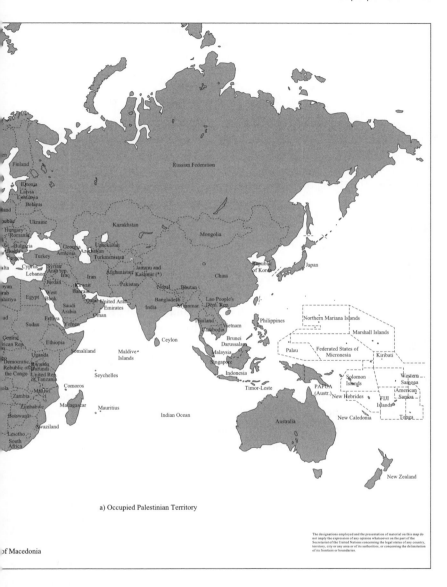

a) Occupied Palestinian Territory

of Macedonia

The designations employed and the presentation of material on this map do
not imply the expression of any opinion whatsoever on the part of the
Secretariat of the United Nations concerning the legal status of any country,
territory, city or any area or of its authorities, or concerning the delimitation
of its frontiers or boundaries.

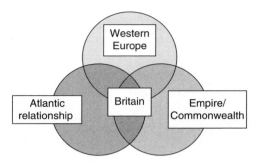

Figure 2.4 The three interlocking circles of British foreign policy in 1945

Rearden have commented, 'Truman quickly realized that what he had in his hands was not only a devastating means of waging war but an asset of unrivalled potential for preserving peace as well.' [21]

Truman's suspicions of the Soviet Union's post-war motives were compounded by its announcement at the conference that it had reached agreement on the boundaries of Poland with the Communist government in Warsaw. The effect of this was the surrendering of East Prussia to Poland. This fait accompli shored up American suspicions that the Soviet Union wanted to establish a network of client states, a view further compounded by Moscow's refusal to co-operate with France, Britain and the United States in the reconstruction of Germany. The Soviet attitude was basically to extract as many resources as it could from its occupation zone of Germany in order to accelerate the reconstruction of the Soviet economy. In contrast, Britain, France and the United States wanted to build up the German economy allowing it to become economically self-sufficient and, thus, not place a burden on their own economies. It was a view that would lead to the merging of the British and American occupation zones in January 1947 to establish what became known as 'Bizonia'. France also merged its zone in the spring of 1947 to create what in due course would become the Federal Republic of Germany (FDR or West Germany). The net effect of this state of affairs was to divide Germany and Berlin between Western and Soviet spheres of influence.

From the foregoing information it is should be apparent that the post-war world was to be be shaped principally by the United States and the Soviet Union. Yet, in contrast to the First World War, no peace treaty was signed after the Second World War. The interests of the American-led **Western bloc** and the Soviet-led **Eastern bloc** dominated many of the organisations that emerged in the post-war period. While an additional division also emerged between the interests of states located in the **North** and the **South** following decolonisation, the key factor that shaped IR in the post-1945 period was the **bipolar** division between the Soviet Union and the United States. In reflecting upon these events it could be asked whether more could have been done to prevent Stalin from dominating Eastern Europe after the end of the Second World War.

Summary

In this chapter we have provided a broad introduction to the major developments of the nineteenth century and set out the most important changes that took place in the first half of the twentieth century. This was a period which saw a shift in the global balance of power away from the European imperial powers to the United States and the Soviet Union. The ensuing superpower rivalry can be traced back to the Bolshevik revolution in Russia in 1917 which pitted an ideological clash between communism and capitalism. Thus, the Grand Alliance which brought the United States and the Soviet Union together during the Second World War was in every sense a marriage of convenience that masked the mistrust and suspicion which existed between both countries. The Soviet Union, which accounted for some twenty-five million of the sixty million casualties during the Second World War, considered that the Western allies had been content to allow it to take the brunt of the fighting with Nazi Germany. It is a view supported by the delay until 1944 of the Western allies invasion of Europe.

As the war in Europe came to an end, a key issue was gaining control of Germany's technological expertise. This specifically applied to Germany's expertise in rocket-propelled weapons, and especially the knowledge of Wernher von Braun who was the central figure in Germany's rocket development programme. Along with other skilled German scientists, von Braun was extracted to America by US military intelligence officers and the knowledge and skills that they brought proved to be crucial to the development of the

US space programme. The United States was also suspicious about the political motives of the Soviet Union as its armed forces began to move towards Germany in the later years of the war. A question which no doubt dogged the minds of Western leaders was whether Soviet troops would return home at the end of the war or whether they would seek to establish a buffer zone for the protection for the Soviet motherland.

....

✔ What you should have learnt from reading this chapter

- The origins of the First World War can be traced to a number of imperial, nationalist and economic tensions.

- A combination of the Great Depression and the reparations imposed on Germany at the end of the First World War influenced the outbreak of the Second World War.

- The League of Nations was not strong enough to regulate the aggression that took place in the years after 1919.

- The economic devastation, political instability and human loss brought about by the Second World War meant that there was an impetus to establish new structures that would hopefully bring an end to conflict between states.

- The Second World War brought about a re-ordering of influence in world politics that was signified by the emergence of the United States and the Soviet Union as world superpowers, as well as the creation of newly independent states as a result of decolonisation.

- The Cold War developed from the superpowers' different approaches to the nature of the post-war world.

? Likely examination questions

What were the factors that influenced the outbreak of the First World War?

To what extent did the Treaty of Versailles contribute to the instability of the inter-war period?

What were the consequences of the First World War?

What was the significance of Woodrow Wilson's Fourteen Points?

Why did the League of Nations fail?

Was appeasement the correct policy to pursue against Hitler?

In what ways can the Second World War be attributed to the policies pursued by Hitler?

What caused the Second World War?

To what extent was the Cold War inevitable in the wake of the defeat of Germany in 1945?

Why was Europe divided into spheres of influence after 1945?

 ## Helpful websites

General information

History World at: www.historyworld.net

First World War

First World War http://www.firstworldwar.com/

World War I Document Archive at: http://wwi.lib.byu.edu/index.php/Main_Page

Covenant of the League of Nations at: http://avalon.law.yale.edu/20th_century/leagcov.asp

UK National Archives at: www.nationalarchives.gov.uk/pathways/firstworldwar/index.htm

UK Cabinet Papers on the League of Nations at: www.nationalarchives.gov.uk/cabinetpapers/themes/league-of-nations.htm

Inter-war period

Treaties, pacts and axes at: www.nationalarchives.gov.uk/cabinetpapers/themes/treaties-pacts-axes.htm

Inter-war treaties and pacts at: www.nationalarchives.gov.uk/cabinetpapers/themes/interwar-treaties-pacts.htm

German threat and rearmament at: www.nationalarchives.gov.uk/cabinetpapers/themes/german-threat-rearmament.htm

Descent into war at: www.nationalarchives.gov.uk/cabinetpapers/themes/descent-into-war.htm

Appeasement and war at: www.nationalarchives.gov.uk/cabinetpapers/themes/appeasement-and-war.htm

Second World War

Second World War at: www.secondworldwar.co.uk

BBC website at: www.bbc.co.uk/history/worldwars/wwtwo

History learning site at: www.historylearningsite.co.uk/WORLD%20 WAR%20TWO.htm

UK National Archives at: www.learningcurve.gov.uk/coldwar/G2/default. htm

Imperial War Museum at: http://london.iwm.org

US Holocaust Memorial Museum at: www.ushmm.org

Nazi genocide at: www.bbc.co.uk/history/worldwars/genocide

World at War at: http://worldatwar.net

 ## Suggestions for further reading

Historical surveys

P. Calvocoressi, *World Politics Since 1945*, 9th edn (Longman, 2008).

E. Hobsbawm, *Age of Extremes: The Short Twentieth Century 1914–91* (Michael Joseph, 1999).

P. Kennedy, *The Rise and Fall of the Great Powers: Economic Change and Military Conflict from 1500 to 2000* (Fontana Press, 1988).

W. C. McWilliams and H. Piotrowski, *The World Since 1945: A History of International Relations*, 6th edn (Lynne Rienner, 2005).

J. W. Young and J. Kent, *International Relations Since 1945: A Global History* (Oxford University Press, 2003).

First and Second World Wars

A. P. Adamthwaite, *Making of the Second World War* (George Allen and Unwin, 1979).

E. H. Carr, *The Twenty Years' Crisis: 1919–1939* (Palgrave, 2001).

S. L. Carruthers, 'International history, 1900–1945', in J. Baylis and S. Smith (eds), *The Globalization of World Politics*, 3rd edn (Oxford University Press, 2005), pp. 63–91.

M. L. Dockrill and J. D. Gould, *Peace without Promise: Britain and the Peace Conferences 1919–1923* (Batsford, 1981).

N. Ferguson, *The War of the World: History's Age of Hatred* (Allen Lane, 2006).

E. Goldstein, *The First World War Peace Settlements, 1919–1925* (Longman, 2002).

M. Howard, *The First World War: A Very Short Introduction* (Oxford University Press, 2002).

S. Marks, *The Illusion of Peace: International Relations in Europe 1918–1933* (Macmillan, 1976).

C. Nicolson, *The Longman Companion to the First World War* (Longman, 2001).

R. J. Overy, *The Origins of the Second World War*, 2nd edn (Longman, 1999).

R. A. C. Parker, *Chamberlain and Appeasement: British Policy and the Coming of the Second World War* (Macmillan, 1993).

S. Steiner, *The Lights that Failed: European International History 1919–1933* (Oxford University Press, 2005).

CHAPTER 3

The Cold War

Contents

Overview

The Second World War alliance that was formed between the Soviet Union and the United States to defeat Hitler was in every sense an alliance of necessity. In this chapter we examine how this alliance dissolved into a Cold War conflict. This chapter explores the ideological division that sat at the centre of the Cold War conflict and the nature of the bipolar division of international politics. Attention is focused on the way in which the struggle for power between the superpowers led to various conflicts which did not result in direct war. This was because in the wake of the Cuban missile crisis the superpowers became more aware of the potential for conflicts to escalate into a nuclear war. Such wariness over possible devastation that could emerge from a Cold War conflict between the superpowers in turn resulted in a warming in relations between the United States and the Soviet Union which became known as the era of détente.

Key issues to be covered in this chapter

- The ideological basis of the Cold War
- The reasons why the Cold War conflict spread to Third World countries
- The advent of nuclear weapons, their impact on the security structure and the nature of war in the post-1945 system
- The potential for compromise in the Cold War era

Early Cold War

Whereas the Western allies viewed the division of Europe to be a temporary state of affairs, it rapidly became apparent that the Soviet Union regarded it as a permanent fixture and ensured that governments favourable to its interests were installed in those countries that fell within its sphere of influence. This prompted Winston Churchill to observe in his March 1946 speech at Fulton, Missouri that:

> From Stettin in the Baltic to Trieste in the Adriatic, an iron curtain has descended across the Continent. Behind that line lie all the capitals of the ancient states of Central and Eastern Europe. Warsaw, Berlin, Prague, Vienna, Budapest, Belgrade, Bucharest and Sofia, all these famous cities and the populations around them lie in what I must call the Soviet sphere, and all are subject in one form or another, not only to Soviet influence but to a very high and, in many cases, increasing measure of control from Moscow.

Despite the fact that he was no longer prime minister, Churchill's reference to the emergence of an **iron curtain** meant the speech proved to be one of the most significant of the **Cold War**. The speech emphasised the need for the United States to adopt a stronger anti-Soviet policy. Such a change of tack had been signalled a month earlier when the US diplomat George Kennan argued in his famous 'long telegram' of 22 February 1946 that the United States should develop a policy of **containment** which referred to the need for it to challenge the march of Soviet power, as outlined in Box 3.1.

This change of tactic was triggered by the realisation that there existed a power vacuum among the countries of Western Europe. Britain was unable to maintain a global role at a time of rationing basic products at home. It was a situation that was further compounded by the winter of 1947, the worst that Britain had experienced since 1881, which resulted in a decline in manufacturing output and a conclusion by policy-makers in London that Britain would have to reduce its overseas commitments. Britain was incapable of continuing to provide support to Greece at a time when the government in Athens was seriously threatened by the attempts

Box 3.1 US policy of containment

- Influenced by the context of Britain's withdrawal from Greece and Turkey.
- George Kennan's 'long telegram' provided a basis for US foreign policy in the post-1945 era.
- The United States sought to strengthen alliances with non-communist governments to deter the possibility of Soviet-backed coups.
- The United States aimed to tackle the weak economic conditions that fostered poverty and thereby provided what many regarded to be a breeding ground for communism.
- CIA funds were used to support the defeat of communism.

of Communist guerrillas to take power. Yet if this had been allowed to happen, it certainly would have weakened the influence of the Western allies in this area.

The immediate response to the security vacuum was to be found in the United States. President Harry Truman pledged American support in March 1947 for 'free peoples who are resisting subjugation by armed minorities or by outside pressures'.[1] Former US Secretary of State, Henry Kissinger, considered that this meant that the United States was taking on 'the historical responsibility for preserving the balance of power'.[2] The **Truman Doctrine** marked the start of a more active American foreign policy of which Western Europe was the most immediate beneficiary. A few months later in June 1947, US Secretary of State, General George Marshall, outlined a plan to offer economic assistance to aid the recovery of all European states. The **Marshall Plan** stated that:

> Europe's requirements for the next three or four years of foreign food and other essential products – principally from America – are so much greater than her present ability to pay that she must have substantial additional help or face economic, social, and political deterioration of a very grave character.

This policy extended to the Soviet Union, although Moscow rejected Washington's offer, which in any case had a number of strings attached. The US administration was a keen advocate of the removal of trade barriers in order to strengthen the economies of Western Europe which would in turn offer a ready market for the United States to trade with.

Barely two years after the end of the Second World War there was a bipolar division of Europe based on Soviet and American spheres of influence. While Box 3.2 highlights that the origins of the tension between the two countries can be traced to before the Second World War, it was nevertheless the case that the first conflict of the Cold War took place in June 1948 over Berlin. The German capital lay in the heart of the Soviet zone of occupation and Soviet leader, Joseph Stalin, took the decision to sever rail and road communication to Berlin to force it to succumb to Soviet domination. The West responsed to the Berlin blockade with a massive airlift which provided the necessary fuel and food supplies for the citizens of West Berlin and prompted the Soviet Union to end its blockade in May 1949. This test of Western resolve to the Soviet challenge was formalised through the creation of the North Atlantic Treaty Organisation (NATO) in April 1949.

Despite this initial focus on Europe, the Cold War impacted on countries at a global level. The first sign of this occurred in China in 1949 when the communists under the leadership of Mao Zedong emerged victorious at the end of a thirty-year **civil war**. American concern about the impact of the communist victory was heightened when communist North Korea attacked South Korea in June 1950. The United States was caught off guard by this invasion even though there had been a number of border incidents between North and South Korea. To outside observers the North Korean attack was interpreted as being part of a general communist offensive strategy, with the Soviet Union backing the North Korean Stalinist regime of Kim ll Sung. The invasion was viewed by many as a test of the willingness of the United States to confront this aggressive strategy, with policy-makers in Washington painting a picture of the spread of communism in South Korea as part of a broader **domino theory**. The argument here was that 'if Stalin were not stopped in Korea he would advance and states would fall in succession to communism until it dominated Europe and Asia or started a Third World War'.[3] A fear of looking weak meant that as the North

Korean forces moved south the United States called on the UN to name North Korea as an aggressor.

The upshot was a conflict that involved many countries fighting under UN command, including the United States and the United Kingdom. The conflict lasted three years and claimed in excess of three million lives. The significance of the Korean War was fivefold. First, it massively increased the Cold War tension, whereby a civil war had resulted in the participation of foreign countries on both sides. Secondly, it shifted the focus of the Cold War to other corners of the world, and meant that it now suddenly had a regional focus on Asia. Thirdly, policy-makers became aware of the potential danger posed by regional conflicts which could in due course lead to a global war. Fourthly, it was the first test of the UN. Fifthly, it fuelled anti-communist rhetoric in the United States that was typified by the rabid views of Senator Joe McCarthy.

In reviewing the early years of the Cold War it is evident that 1947 was a key turning point beyond which there was little chance of retreat for either **superpower**. This year was marked by a crisis in Greece and, as Box 3.2 notes, the start of the institutionalisation of the Cold War through the Truman Doctrine and Marshall Plan. This period saw the gradual suppression of any resistance to Soviet takeover in Eastern Europe and culminated in the communist coup in Czechoslovakia in 1948. The subsequent Berlin blockade of 1948, the creation of NATO and the formation of the Federal Republic of Germany (FDR) in 1949 signified the formalisation and consolidation of emerging power blocs in Europe. The Soviet Union's successful test of its first nuclear weapon in 1949 formally ended the US atomic monopoly, while the Korean War highlighted the **globalisation** of the Cold War and influenced the build up of US military forces because it increased the sense of insecurity in Washington.

IR scholars are often divided over the factors that resulted in the wartime alliance of the United States and the Soviet Union moving into a post-war confrontation. The traditional or 'orthodox' view has attached emphasis to the expansionist and aggressive policies of the Soviet Union, which are set within the class struggle advocated in **Marxism**–Leninism. According to the orthodox view, the expansionist policies pursued by the Soviet Union resulted in the United

Box 3.2 Origins of the Cold War

- 1917   The source of conflict can be traced back to the Russian revolution and the resulting ideological conflict between Marxism and capitalism.
- 1939–45   The wartime alliance was a marriage of convenience – there were successive strains between the countries over such issues as the development of a second front. The Soviet Union bore the brunt of the land conflict until the 1944 Normandy landings.
- 1945   Yalta Conference. The United States used the atomic bomb on 6 August.
- 1946   Winston Churchill's 'iron curtain' speech.
- 1947   Crisis in Greece, Truman Doctrine and Marshall Plan.
- 1948   Communist takeover in Czechoslovakia and start of Berlin blockade.
- 1949   Creation of NATO, establishment FDR (West Germany) (i.e., formalisation of the division of Germany) and Chinese revolution.

States responding through the development of alliances which would challenge Soviet policy. Thus, orthodox historians stress that the Soviet Union sought to undermine non-communist powers, being reinforced by the views set out in Kennan's 'long telegram' and Churchill's 'iron curtain' speech.

This view is rejected by 'revisionist' writers, who argue that the Soviet Union should not be held responsible for the outbreak of the Cold War. Such an argument rests on the fact that the Soviet Union only just avoided defeat during the Second World War and the huge human and economic losses that it incurred meant that it was a devastated nation by 1945. The United States was by contrast a prosperous country in search of markets in which to expand its capitalist trade, which would in turn increase its economic and political influence. Revisionist writers, therefore, argue that in the face of this threat of US domination, Soviet leaders justly protected their own security interests through a sphere of influence in Eastern Europe as well as through supporting revolutionary movements throughout the world. Moreover, just as it could be argued that Churchill's speech was influential in the development of US policy in the post-war period, it could also be argued that this speech threatened the Soviet Union and, therefore, influenced Stalin's decision to take a controlling interest in Eastern Europe.

Decolonisation

Just as the post-1945 period was marked by **superpower** tension, a further defining feature of the period was the process of decolonisation. This is despite the fact that decolonisation dates back to the late eighteenth and early nineteenth centuries when Latin American countries and the United States fought wars of national liberation against the British, Portuguese and Spanish empires. Moreover, rather than this being a sign of a retreat from **colonialism** it was the case that in the late nineteenth and early twentieth centuries a number of countries were engaged in an active policy of **imperialism**.[4] Among others, Belgium, Britain, France, Italy, the Netherlands and Portugal acquired new colonial territories in Africa and Asia. Indeed, by the end of the Second World War most of Africa and Asia was under colonial rule (see Figure 2.2). This was further highlighted at the establishment of the UN on 26 June 1945, when only twelve of the forty-nine founding members were from Africa and Asia. This figure is even worse when you take into account that of these twelve states, Egypt, India, Lebanon, Iraq and Syria were not fully independent. This meant that the only independent African and Asian states who were founder members of the UN were South Africa, Ethiopia, Liberia, the Philippines, Saudi Arabia, Iran and Turkey, of which the last three were never colonised themselves.

Towards the end of the Second World War some imperial powers recognised the need for constitutional change in the colonies so as to provide greater local control. In Britain's case this desire to grant independence could be traced back to the 1931 Statute of Westminster which granted independence to Australia, New Zealand, Canada and South Africa. In 1944 France held a conference in Brazzaville, where agreement was reached on the end to forced labour and the expansion of African involvement in local politics. In 1946 Britain established African majorities in legislative councils in Nigeria and the Gold Coast (Ghana). However, the colonial powers initially viewed these changes as a means of appeasing the local population in an overall context of still maintaining colonial rule rather than as setting out a route map for independence. Indeed, after the Second World War the colonial powers sought to develop their African possessions so as to enhance their prosperity. Crucially this desire to retain influence and control went against the fact that the encouragement of development led to political, social and economic unrest which was an important factor influencing the shift towards decolonisation.

When Britain granted independence to India and Pakistan in 1947 this signalled the start of a process of decolonisation which principally affected Africa, the Caribbean and parts of Asia. In 1945 the continent of Africa was still largely controlled by the European imperial powers, with only Egypt, Liberia and Ethiopia being independent countries. Yet, as Table 3.1 highlights, by 1965 most of the continent was independent of direct colonial rule, with the momentum towards independence having partly been triggered by Indian self-rule.

One of the most pressing issues after the Second World War was the desire to establish a Jewish homeland as set out in the 1917 Balfour Declaration. To this end the UN General Assembly agreed in Resolution 181 of 29 November 1947 on a plan to partition Palestine into Jewish and Arab states, with Jerusalem to act as an international city (Figure 3.1).[5] However, while the plan was agreed to by Jewish leaders, it was rejected by Palestinians and the Arab states who considered it to be an unjust division imposed by outside powers given that at the time the Arabs of Palestine outnumbered the Jews by two to one. As a result the plan was never implemented and the Palestinians went on to assemble forces to oppose the partition. This has principally taken the form of the Palestinian Liberation Organisation (PLO), although a plethora of other organisations, such as Hamas, also exist which seek to fight the Palestinian cause. The years since 1947 have seen a succession of wars in 1948, 1956, 1967, 1973, 1982, 2006 and most recently the conflict in Gaza in 2009. The first conflict erupted in 1948 when Britain withdrew from the region, resulting in a declaration by the Jews on the creation of the state of Israel and the establishment of the West Bank and the Gaza Strip as specific areas for the Palestinians (Figures 3.1 and 3.2). At the root of these conflicts has been the desire for a Palestinian

Table 3.1 Decolonisation

Country	Colonial power	Year of independence
India	Britain	1947
Pakistan	Britain	1947
Sri Lanka	Britain	1948
Indonesia	Netherlands	1949
Libya	Italy	1951
Sudan	Britain	1956
Tunisia	France	1956
Morocco	France	1956
Ghana	Britain	1957
Malaya	Britain	1957
Guinea	Britain	1958
Benin	France	1960
Togo	France	1960
Somalia	Italy/Britain	1960
Cameroon	France	1960
Central African Republic	France	1960
Chad	France	1960
Congo	Belgium	1960
Gabon	France	1960
Ivory Coast	France	1960
Madagascar	France	1960
Mali	France	1960
Mauritania	France	1960
Niger	France	1960
Senegal	France	1960
Upper Volta	France	1960
Zaire	Britain	1961
Nigeria	Britain	1961

Table 3.1 (*cont.*)

Country	Colonial power	Year of independence
Sierra Leone	Britain	1961
Tanganyika	Britain	1961
Uganda	Britain	1962
Burundi	Belgium	1962
Rwanda	Belgium	1962
Algeria	Britain	1962
Zanzibar	Britain	1963
Kenya	Britain	1963
Malawi	Britain	1964
Zambia	Britain	1964
Gambia	Britain	1965
Botswana	Britain	1966
Lesotho	Britain	1966
Equatorial Guinea	Spain	1968
Mauritius	Britain	1968
Swaziland	Britain	1968
Guinea Bissau	Portugal	1974
Mozambique	Portugal	1975
Cape Verde	Portugal	1975
Comoros	France	1975
São Tomé and Principe	Portugal	1975
Angola	Portugal	1975
Western Sahara	Spain	1976
Seychelles	Britain	1975
Djibouti	France	1977
Zimbabwe	Britain	1980
Namibia	South Africa	1990

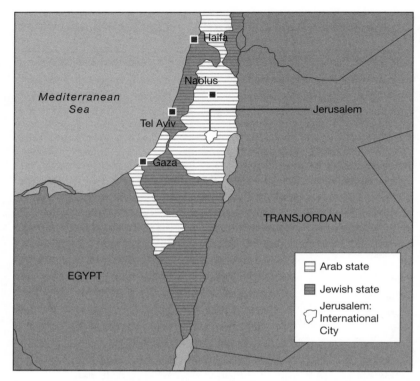

Source: http://news.bbc.co.uk/1/shared/spl/hi/middle_east/03/v3_israel_palestin-ians/maps/html/israel_founded.stm

Figure 3.1 UN plan to partition Palestine, 1947

homeland which has resulted in the Middle East being one of the most unstable regions in the world.

Decolonisation often resulted in the swift transfer of power as the colonial authorities were faced with pressures for independence that they could not resist. In many instances the euphoria granted by independence quickly changed as the new states became embroiled in a cycle of corruption, factionalism, coups and **civil war** (see Box 3.3). Why was this the case? The answer to this question is basically a combination of factors that include the legacy of colonial rule, problems of patronage, an underdeveloped state apparatus, the presence of tribalism and climate and resource problems.

Source: http://news.bbc.co.uk/1/shared/spl/hi/middle_east/03/v3_israel_palestin-ians/maps/html/israel_founded.stm.

Figure 3.2 Establishment of the West Bank and Gaza Strip, 1949

Of these factors the legacy of colonial rule is one of the most regularly cited reasons for the economic and political malaise that has dominated newly independent states in the post-colonial period. It was certainly the case that the colonies were staggeringly underprepared for independence in terms of having an educated population who were capable of running the country. And as this situation could not be resolved quickly it created frustration as the local population had thought that independence would lead to greater social provision.

A further problem was that the colonial powers had operated a system of patronage and indirect rule. It has to be remembered that many of the countries that the colonial powers controlled were many times greater in size than their own country: for example, the small state of Belgium controlled the Congo which was larger than

---

Box 3.3 Legacy of colonial rule

- Newly independent states were often ill-prepared to act as democracies.
- The boundaries of many of the states were drawn up by colonial rulers and did not always reflect the reality of where population groups were based.
- Leaders now had access to state funds and contracts, and were able to ensure the loyalty of groups through patronage.
- Many of the new states had an underdeveloped infrastructure, including a poorly educated population.
- Investment often took place in urban areas with rural areas seeing little state activity.
- Many independent states, particularly in Africa, suffered from problems of a difficult climate, poor soil quality and a dependence on a limited number of crops, which meant that their economies were vulnerable to many factors that were beyond the control of the state.

Western Europe. Yet the leaders of the newly created countries now had access to state funds and were able to offer contracts for work which ensured the loyalty of groups through patronage. Many leaders also sought to enrich themselves and, in some instances, this resulted in the emergence of a 'clientelism state' because the state became the supreme patron. Corruption accordingly became a normal part of political activity because the independent countries lacked democratic traditions. In some states, such as Zaire (now the Congo), the looting of the state's resources was so massive that the regimes were termed 'kleptocracies'.

This situation was compounded by the presence of tribalism. During the colonial era tribal chiefs had the ability to raise taxes and administer law, and this meant that the colonial masters did not have to spend resources on developing an administrative network. However, tribal chiefs who had benefited from indirect rule did not want to give up their privileges, while tribal chiefs had often set themselves up as alternative centres of power to the government. This has meant that tribal groupings have presented a huge challenge to African states whereby in some countries, such as Uganda and Nigeria, the presence of large tribes competing for power has resulted in a lack of political stability.

Related to this point is the fact that many of the states that were created did not conform to natural borders. In essence, they were just a series of lines drawn on the map by the colonial powers, with the presence of colonial forces and administrative bureaucracy being the gel keeping the countries together. Thus, when the colonial powers left the structures which had provided stability were eroded, and this meant that the newly created states were left open to ethnic and tribal conflict which has resulted in many of the states becoming regarded as being weak and in some instances as failed states (see Chapters 7 and 10). A final point to note is that many states have suffered from climate and resource problems that have included disease, drought, famine and a dependence on a limited number of products that have exposed the country to fluctuations in the world economy.

In examining the movement towards independence it is apparent that it provided further evidence of the declining influence of European powers. This was particularly evidenced by the 1956 Suez crisis in which Britain, France and Israel conspired to invade Egypt in response to the Egyptian leader's, Colonel Nasser, seizure of the Suez canal. The sight of British paratroopers invading Egypt brought with it worldwide condemnation, with the British government being specifically criticised by US President Eisenhower and in the face of severe American economic pressure British troops retreated from Egypt. If the British government had not been aware of it before, the Suez adventure once and for all put rest to its claim to be a global power. As Geir Lundestad has noted, American intervention had different long-term effects for policy-makers in London and Paris: 'London repair relations by once again emphasizing the importance of the "special relationship" with the United States; in Paris the humiliation strengthened determination to pursue European integration, in part to make Europe stronger but also vis-à-vis the US'.[6]

For the superpowers the creation of newly independent states offered a key opportunity to extend their influence. As there were often competing power groups within the countries the superpowers tended to back groups that they considered would further their own aims. In the majority of instances such decisions did not reflect the overall needs of the countries concerned. The United States advo-cated a policy of intervention in its own 'backyard' of Latin America to keep out other powers. This was a region with poor levels of eco-nomic development where the ownership of land tended to rest in a few hands and where exporting products such as coffee were at the mercy of global markets.

Guatemala was typical of this picture where in the early 1950s 75 per cent of the country's wealth rested in the hands of 2 per cent of the population. In 1950 Jacobo Arbenz was elected President with a view to changing this situation through the re-appropriation of land, which was a policy that went against the interests of the capitalist landowners. In the early Cold War the United States viewed what was in essence a domestic economic struggle as an ideological conflict between **capitalism** and **communism** and responded with the US Central Intelligence Agency (CIA) backing a coup in 1954 that resulted in the overthrow of the democratically elected government.

Non-Aligned Movement
Many countries rightly rejected the superpower pressure to choose sides. At the Bandung conference of 18–24 April 1955 twenty-nine African and Asia states took a decision to stay out of the Cold War conflict. Within this group of countries, the influence of such leaders as Nehru (India), Nasser (Egypt), Sukarno (Indonesia), Castro (Cuba) and Tito (Yugoslavia) resulted in the creation of the **Non-Aligned Movement (NAM)** in 1961 (see Box 3.4). In practical terms, the NAM followed a policy of 'active neutrality' whereby it advocated engagement with both superpowers during the Cold War and, at the same time, sought to develop the social and economic wellbeing of its members. In the post-Cold War world the NAM's focus has shifted away from a concern about the global balance of power to instead paying attention to key concerns of debt relief, trade and investment, the impact of globalisation and health issues such as AIDS.

Cold War confrontation and compromise

The tension of the early Cold War years put both superpowers on a war footing and saw the conflict move out of its European origins. The successful Soviet nuclear test of 29 August 1949 provoked the

Box 3.4 The Non-Aligned Movement

- As of 2008 the NAM comprised 118 developing countries.
- One of the criteria for membership is that members cannot be involved in alliances or defence pacts with the main world powers.
- The NAM does not have a constitution or permanent secretariat. The key decision-making body is the Conference of Heads of State and Government which meets every three years.
- The NAM's large and diverse membership means that it is often difficult for it to reach a consensus.

United States into assessing the significance of this development for American security. On 15 April 1950 the US National Security Council published a report entitled 'United States Objectives and Programs for National Security', referred to as NSC-68, which called for a significant expansion in American military capacity. The report specifically noted that what was necessary was 'a build-up of military strength by the United States and its allies to a point at which the combined strength will be superior . . . to the forces that can be brought to bear by the Soviet Union and its satellites'.[7]

A significant amount of the build up of forces took place in the European theatre, with the security of Western European countries being guaranteed by the presence of American troops and the stationing of conventional and nuclear weapons. NATO provided an added security blanket as Article 5 of the North Atlantic Treaty stressed that an attack on one country was an attack on all countries, thereby embedding the nature of collective defence. The Soviet Union was just as busy building up its force levels and established the **Warsaw Pact** in May 1955, which was itself a direct response to the re-militarisation of West Germany in 1954. By the early 1950s an institutionalisation of the Cold War had occurred with both superpowers seeking to establish spheres of influence that would maximise their reach and influence on global politics (see Box 3.5).

Stalin's death in 1953 brought with it a reappraisal of Soviet strategy as his successor, Nikita Khrushchev, aimed to normalise relations

Box 3.5 Expansion of the Cold War

- 1950   Start of the Korean War.
- 1953   Death of Joseph Stalin and end of the Korean War.
- 1954   Soviet Union starts establishing relations with the Third World.
- 1954   Partition of Vietnam.
- 1955   Germany joins NATO and creation of the Warsaw Pact.
- 1956   Hungarian uprising.

with the outside world. This did not mean that the Soviet Union sought to roll-back its troops from the various countries in which they were stationed. Rather, Khrushchev wanted to maintain a socialist bloc of states in Eastern Europe and to develop relations with non-European states, notably in the Third World where many groups opposed the capitalist **West**. However, while Khrushchev sought to modernise Soviet society, his efforts led to wider unrest with protests taking place in Poland and Hungary. The Soviet response was to suppress the riots and in so doing left some 25,000 people dead in Hungary in 1956.

Under Khrushchev's leadership mixed messages emerged from the Soviet Union, where his efforts to seek some form of co-existence with Western countries went hand-in-hand with continued Soviet support for wars of national liberation. Such support antagonised the United States, and tension between the two superpowers increased with the Soviet Union being the first country to launch a satellite in 1957. Known as Sputnik, this event shocked the United States because it meant that the Soviet Union had developed intercontinental ballistic missiles (ICBM). A direct consequence of this was to increase the perception in the United States that it was behind the Soviet Union in the nuclear **arms race**, and this proved to be a key subject in the run up to the 1960 US Presidential elections; John F. Kennedy argued that the missile gap suggested American weakness.

This perception of American weakness in the Cold War conflict was emphasised by the Soviet and East German decision in August 1961 to start the process of erecting a barricade around East Berlin to stop East Germans escaping via West Berlin. Although the erection of the Berlin Wall did not impact on the status of West Berlin, it none the less demonstrated the extent to which Western powers were powerless to stop Soviet policy.

Cuban missile crisis

Superpower tension increased when the Soviet Union shot down an American U-2 spy plane on 1 May 1960 – a significant propaganda coup for the Soviets. The tension between the superpowers was brought to a head on 14 October 1962 when an American U-2 spy plane flying over Cuba took photos of Soviet soldiers erecting intermediate- and medium-ranged nuclear missiles. Such action contradicted pledges given by the Soviet premier Khrushchev not to send offensive weapons to Cuba and US President Kennedy regarded this as an extremely serious issue which nearly brought the world to the brink of nuclear war. In reflecting why the Soviet Union took the decision to build nuclear missile bases in Cuba, John Young stressed that a contributing factor might have been President Kennedy's inaction over the erection of the Berlin Wall.[8]

Cuba presented the United States with a different situation to that in Berlin. In 1961 President Kennedy sanctioned a CIA invasion plan to overthrow the Cuban leader, Fidel Castro. The invasion, which took place at the Bay of Pigs on 17 April 1961, was a spectacular failure as the invaders never got off the beach and thereby did not create the popular uprising against Castro that the United States had hope for. In many respects, the American invasion tilted Castro further towards the Soviet Union, and when the Soviet Union took the decision to base nuclear weapons on Cuba it meant that Cuba was placed at the centre of the Cold War conflict. Policy-makers in Washington responded by establishing a quarantine around Cuba to prevent more missiles arriving and at the same time demanded the removal of the missiles already there. After a number of difficult diplomatic discussions a compromise solution was achieved, whereby Khrushchev agreed to remove the missiles from Cuba as long as the United States pledged not to invade the island. Yet, the potential for nuclear conflict had been real as both countries had stood 'eyeball to eyeball'.

Box 3.6 Intensification of the Cold War

- 1957   Launch of Sputnik demonstrates Soviet ICBM capability.
- 1959   Cuban revolution results in Castro assuming office.
- 1960   Sino-Soviet split.
- 1960   U-2 American spy plane shot down.
- 1961   Kennedy becomes US President. Failed American Bay of Pigs invasion of Cuba. Berlin Wall is built. Soviet Union detonates the biggest nuclear explosion and launches the first man into orbit.
- 1962   Cuban missile crisis.

The commonly held view that a nuclear catastrophe had narrowly been avoided meant that there was a need to ensure that the Cold War could not turn into a **hot war**. For Robert McMahon this meant that 'having peered into the nuclear abyss, US and Soviet leaders recognised the need to avoid future Cuba-type confrontation and began to take some significant steps in that direction'.[9] For the United States, this meant that it had to reappraise its foreign policy so that it no longer aimed to remove the Soviet Union. What this meant in practice was that the United States had to live in a world in which it could not exercise **hegemony** and in which it had to exist with the Soviet Union. As we see in Box 3.7, this brought about the need for better communication between both countries and as a result a telephone 'hot line' was set up between the Kremlin and the White House.

The shock of the Cuban missile crisis forced the superpowers to reappraise their need for dialogue and this in turn brought about the start of a process of limiting and controlling nuclear weapons. Such an approach was amplified by the spread of states which possessed nuclear weapons. Britain (1952), France (1960) and China (1964) all became nuclear powers. This concern led to the 1963 Test Ban Treaty which prohibited nuclear weapon tests or any other nuclear explosion in the atmosphere, outer space and under water. Although though the Treaty did not stop underground tests, the setting of such limitations highlighted a common acknowledgement of the need to stop contamination via radioactive substances.

Box 3.7 Consequences of the Cuban missile crisis

- Need to ensure that the Cold War could not turn into a hot war.
- The United States had to live in a world in which it had to exist with the Soviet Union.
- The aim of peaceful co-existence emphasised by the creation of the 'hot line' between the Kremlin and the White House.
- Start of a process of limiting and controlling nuclear weapons.
- The crisis also demonstrated to the United States the importance of nuclear superiority.

Five years later the 1968 Nuclear Non-Proliferation Treaty (NPT) sought to limit the further spread of nuclear weapons. Under the NPT, non-nuclear weapon states were prohibited from, *inter alia*, possessing, manufacturing or acquiring nuclear weapons or other nuclear explosive devices. All signatories, including nuclear weapon states, were also committed to the goal of total nuclear disarmament. Yet, despite these goals, several states went on to acquire a nuclear capability, notably India and Pakistan. Israel is also recognised by many to posses nuclear weapons, although the government of Israel itself has never acknowledged that it has acquired a nuclear weapon capability.

Vietnam War

The process of **decolonisation** was also evident in Asia, with Britain granting independence to Burma and Ceylon in 1948. Elsewhere in Asia the Netherlands and France were less willing to grant independence and wanted to maintain control of the East Indies and Indo-China. As a consequence, conflict emerged in these countries between the colonial powers and national forces wanting independence. Having advocated a policy of **self-determination**, the United States contradicted itself by supporting the colonial powers and highlighted the fact that 'the attitude of the United States on decolonisation issues was never clear-cut'.[10] Whereas the United States had been a strong supporter of decolonisation in the post-1945 era and had been critical of what it regarded as French and British **colonialism** during the Suez crisis of 1956, the spread of the Cold War to Asia in the 1950s meant that policy-makers in Washington were prepared to defend empires. This inevitably caused further resentment towards the West by Sukarno and Ho Chi Minh, who were the respective nationalist leaders of Indonesia and Vietnam. The Soviet Union and China responded opportunistically to this situation by seizing the chance to develop relations in south-east Asia; in early 1950 both countries formally recognised Ho Chi Minh's Democratic Republic of Vietnam.

The end of Korean War and the advent of the hot line between the superpowers did not create a climate of Cold War stability. In 1954 – just one year after the end of the Korean War – a conflict emerged between North and South Vietnam. Between 1946 and 1954 Vietnam struggled to gain independence from France, and in the end the country was divided into North and South Vietnam. The North came under communist control and the South was controlled by those who had collaborated with France. Although this conflict raised the spectre of the spread of communism in Asia, it did not provoke an immediate response from external powers such as the United States to get directly involved. That is not to say that there was not an American presence in Vietnam in the immediate years after 1954 when French forces had been defeated at Dien Bien Phu. Nicholas White informs us that by 1954 the United States was actually shouldering 75 per cent of the cost of France's war against the Vietminh.[11] By the time of President Kennedy's assassination in November 1963 there were some 17,000 American 'advisers' in South Vietnam and military aid was provided to the South Vietnamese government. Five years later the American commitment to South Vietnam had increased to over 500,000 troops being engaged in a conflict with North Vietnamese forces that were being supported by Moscow and Beijing.

For the student of IR, the interesting question about the Vietnam War was that it took place at a time of supposedly reduced Cold War tension in the wake of the Cuban missile crisis. What, then, were the factors that contributed to the Vietnam War? The answer to this question is that while there was a thaw in American–Soviet relations after the Cuban missile crisis, at the same time there was an increase in tension in American–Chinese relations. The United States was particularly concerned about what it regarded as China's expansionist policies in southeast Asia, with Presidents Kennedy and Johnson being determined to contain China and stop what they perceived to be the spread of communism in the region. As Mitchell Hall argues, the United States 'believed the loss of South Vietnam would threaten other states in the region and endanger America's standing in the world'.[12] This was referred to as the domino theory. At the same time the war provided an opportunity for the United States to demonstrate its ability and willingness to respond to communist threats through a policy of containment that had served as the bedrock of American policy in the post-1945 era.

The Vietnam War proved to be deeply unpopular and claimed the lives of more than 58,000 American troops, while three to four million Vietnamese were killed on both sides. In the end the United States failed to achieve its goal of stopping the collapse of South Vietnam and in 1975 Vietnam became unified under communist control. Yet contrary to American predictions, the communist victory in Vietnam did not result in the spread of communism to other countries in the region. The domino theory did not hold true; the United States had wrongly regarded the civil war nature of the conflict in Vietnam as being part of a broader Cold War struggle against international communism.

Emergence and decline of détente

One of the paradoxes of the late 1960s was that just as the United States was becoming ever more involved in what it regarded as a key Cold War conflict in Vietnam, there emerged a set of conditions that led to the warming of relations between the two superpowers (see Box 3.8). This became known as the era of **détente**, which basically meant a lessening of tension in international politics. But while initial signs of détente had been evident in the wake of the Cuban missile crisis through the establishment of the 'hot line' agreement and the 1963 Partial Test Ban Treaty, it was nevertheless the case that an undercurrent of tension remained between the superpowers as each wanted to maintain its own influence. In 1968 the Soviet Union asserted its authority by invading Czechoslovakia to suppress

Box 3.8 Stability of the Cold War

- 1963 Hot line agreement between the United States and the Soviet Union. Signing of the Test Ban Treaty. US President Kennedy assassinated and Lyndon Johnson appointed his successor.
- 1964 Khrushchev falls from power and is replaced by Leonid Brezhnev.
- 1968 Nuclear Non-Proliferation Treaty is signed. Soviet forces invade Czechoslovakia (Prague Spring).
- 1968 Start of détente and the SALT process.
- 1969 Advancement of the Brezhnev Doctrine of limited sovereignty for communist states. Richard Nixon becomes US President. US spacecraft Apollo 11 lands on the moon.

the reforms that had been put in place by politicians in Prague. This emphasis on Soviet influence would be further highlighted in 1969 by the announcement of the **Brezhnev Doctrine**, which advanced the concept of limited **sovereignty** for the communist pro-Moscow states.

Despite this tension, however, there was a genuine concern that the relations between the superpowers should be improved. The pressure for détente came from many different angles. Within Western Europe the origins of détente lay in the policies of the West German Chancellor, Willy Brandt, who advocated negotiating with the Eastern bloc. Known as the policy of **Ostpolitik**, it produced a number of agreements that recognised the status of East Germany and Berlin, and also brought about the abandonment of the previous **Hallstein Doctrine** which had stressed that West Germany was the sole representative of the German state.

A common theme underlying détente was the superpowers' mutual fear of nuclear war. The dawn of **Mutual Assured Destruction (MAD)** and the development of an arms race with the advent of ICBMs and submarine-launched ballistic missiles (SLBMs) meant that by the end of the 1960s both superpowers were faced with a basic choice of either accelerating or slowing down the arms race. The decision to pursue a policy of détente owed much to Richard Nixon assuming the American presidency in 1969 with him stressing the development of an 'era of negotiations' in his inaugural speech. Along with his adviser, Henry Kissinger, he was keen to reduce Cold War tension, end the Vietnam War and accept the broad notion of nuclear parity with the Soviet Union. Such a strategy was based on Nixon's concern that throughout the 1960s America's 'tendency to become preoccupied with only one or two problems at a time had led to a deterioration of policy on all fronts'.[13] This included the development of a policy of rapprochement with China whereby the United States sought to expose the deteriorating relations between the Soviet Union and China. For the United States, the benefit of opening up a dialogue with Beijing was that policy-makers in Washington hoped that it would result in a more fluid **international system** that was less grounded in the rigidity of the American–Soviet relationship. At the same time, it was also a way of moving on from the Vietnam War by demonstrating that the United States had policies that championed the development of peaceful relations.

One of the most significant developments during the détente period was the Helsinki Final Act that was signed in 1975 by thirty-five nations including the Soviet Union and the United States. This agreement was the final act of the **Conference on Security and Cooperation in Europe (CSCE)** and was seen as a significant step in reducing Cold War tensions. This was because the agreement recognised national boundaries, thereby consolidating Soviet influence in Central and Eastern Europe. For the Soviet Union this was a particularly important development because, in the absence of a peace treaty after the Second World War, it wanted formal recognition of Soviet influence in Central and Eastern Europe. As Michael Alexander has commented, 'Soviet governments needed to see the *post bellum* realities formalized'.[14] And while many commentators regarded this as an agreement to sell out the interests of Central and Eastern Europe to the Soviet Union, the West viewed this as a necessary concession to improve **East–West** relations. Moreover, as the agreement included a declaration on **human rights**, it provided an opportunity for the West to criticise Soviet policy in subsequent years. The emphasis by the United States on human rights issues was, however, very much a policy of double standards. While it sought to highlight human rights abuses in the Soviet bloc, at the same time it continued to support administrations that were known for their human rights violations. This included supporting President Mobuto of Zaire and the Shah of Iran.

Arms limitations

The United States considered that détente had to be based on real outcomes rather than just a change in diplomatic atmosphere. This particularly applied to halting **nuclear proliferation**, of which the January 1972 Strategic Arms Limitation Talks (SALT) agreement placed limitations on the weaponry that each superpower could have (see Box 3.9). The SALT agreement proved to be a highpoint for President Nixon, because just two weeks later individuals who were working for his re-election campaign were arrested for braking into the headquarters of the Democratic Party. Because this took place at the Watergate hotel and office complex in Washington DC, the events which ultimately led to President Nixon's resignation (and his replacement by Vice President Gerald Ford) are commonly known as the 'Watergate scandal'.

Nixon's departure coincided with increased American doubts about the value of détente as there was a belief that the Soviet Union was gaining military superiority and that the SALT process had favoured Moscow (see Box 3.10). There was also a concern about Soviet support for the spread of communism abroad as highlighted by its support of revolutionary forces in Ethiopia in 1975 and Angola in 1978. Yet the United States equally offered its support to friendly countries and movements that shared its aims, especially in South

---

Box 3.9 SALT agreement

- 'Interim Agreement on Offensive Missiles'.
- ICBMs: 1,054 US, 1,618 Soviet.
- SLBMs: 656 US, 740 Soviet.
- Bombers: 455 US, 140 Soviet.
- To last five years: SALT II to follow.

Box 3.10 Rise and fall of détente

- 1972 SALT I and ABM agreements are signed. President Nixon visits China.
- 1973 United States helps to overthrow the government in Chile and also pulls out of Vietnam. Egypt and Syria attack Israel (Six-day war).
- 1974 Resignation of President Nixon (succeeded by Gerald Ford).
- 1975 Helsinki accords signed at CSCE. Soviet Union expands activities in Africa (using Cuban troops as proxies). American–Chinese rapprochement.
- 1976 Carter becomes US President.
- 1979 SALT II signed (but never ratified). Soviet Union invades Afghanistan. Iranian revolution overthrows the Shah and American embassy is seized.

America where it assisted a campaign against Chile's Salvadore Allende. Much of this activity took place in the Third World where the potential for the superpowers to become embroiled in conflict was evidenced by the 1973 Arab–Israeli war. The United States was also keen to highlight human rights abuses and was critical of Soviet controls over the emigration of Jews to Israel.

Summary

It should be evident from this chapter that superpower relations during the Cold War were subject to a considerable amount of fluctuation in terms of the potential for conflict. In this sense, although the Cold War did not result in direct conflict between the superpowers, there were instances, such as the Korean War and the Cuban missile crisis, when the potential for war breaking out was greater. Our analysis of this state of affairs is shown in Figure 3.3, which extends into the post-détente period.

As the 1970s came to an end it was evident that the superpowers had different views about the meaning of détente. Neither superpower wanted to give up its ideology and dismantle its alliances. The Soviet Union sought equality of status with the United States, wanted

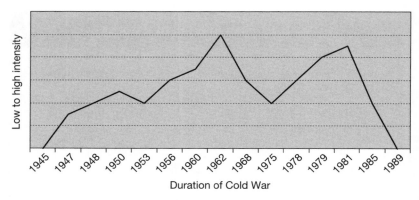

Figure 3.3 Fluctuating intensity of the Cold War

to maintain influence in Eastern Europe and tried to secure agreements on trade and SALT. On the other hand, the United States wanted to restrain Soviet expansionism. The result of these differences, and the reality of the imbalance of the first SALT agreement, was that there emerged greater toughness on the part of the United States when it came to re-negotiating the SALT process in 1979.

Other events conspired against the fruitful resolution of the SALT process. This included the 1979 Iranian revolution, which resulted in the removal of an important Western ally as well as American diplomats being taken hostage in their embassy in Teheran. A few months later the Soviets decided to intervene in Afghanistan and to policy-makers in Washington this was further evidence of Moscow's expansionist policies. The United States reacted through a series of measures that included a decision not to ratify the second SALT agreement, it decided to provide military aid to the mujahideen in Afghanistan, while also boycotting the 1980 Moscow Olympics and rapidly increasing its defence spending. Despite these tough measures, the underlying picture in the late 1970s was that the United States had been disadvantaged in its rivalry with the Soviet Union and that it was losing the Cold War. Much of the blame for these policy outcomes was laid at the feet of President Jimmy Carter who had been unable to stop an increase in Soviet defence spending and Soviet intervention in the Third World. Reflecting on this state of affairs, President Carter's National Security Advisor, Zbigniew

Brzezinski, was able to comment that a major setback for the Carter Administration 'was unquestionably the failure to confront early enough the Soviet policy of combining détente on the Central European front with military expansion (first by proxy and then directly) in areas peripheral to our sensitive geopolitical interests'.[15] Thus, as the 1970s came to a close it was not surprising that many expected the period of détente to give way in the decade ahead to renewed Cold War conflict.

. . . .

What you should have learnt from reading this chapter

- Although the Cold War conflict between the United States and the Soviet Union can be traced back to the 1917 Russian revolution, many commentators place the start of the Cold War in 1947 with the Truman Doctrine and Marshall Plan.

- After the Second World War the Soviet Union wanted to create a buffer zone in Central and Eastern Europe that led to the Berlin blockade.

- American involvement in the Korean War and Vietnam War was influenced by the domino theory.

- Nuclear weapons were a key feature of the Cold War conflict. After the Cuban missile crisis the superpowers recognised the need for closer dialogue and to restrain the growth in the number of nuclear weapons.

- Concern over imbalances in the détente process and the expansionist policies of the Soviet Union in the 1970s were influential factors in the demise of détente and the renewal of the Cold War conflict in the 1980s.

Likely examination questions

What was the significance of the United States' decision to drop atomic bombs on Japan?

Was the Cold War inevitable?

What was the significance of the Truman Doctrine?

What was the United States' policy of containment?

'The weakness of African states is directly attributable to the process of decolonisation in the 1950s and 1960s'. Do you agree?

Is it fair to say that the process of decolonisation created unstable countries?

Why did the United States become heavily involved in Vietnam during the Kennedy and Johnson administrations?

What were the factors which stopped a direct conflict taking place between the superpowers during the Cold War?

To what extent did the end of the Cold War result in ideological conflicts being replaced with nationalist and ethnic rivalries?

Why did détente fail?

 ## Helpful websites

General overview

History in Focus at: www.history.ac.uk/ihr/Focus/cold/websites.html

Speeches

Winston Churchill's Iron Curtain speech at: http://uk.youtube.com/watch?v=P8_wQ-5uxV4

President Kennedy on the Cuban Missile Crisis at: http://uk.youtube.com/watch?v=W50RNAbmy3M

President Richard Nixon's announcement on the SALT agreement at: http://uk.youtube.com/watch?v=ebE2DRr1sVs

Cold War

BBC at: www.bbc.co.uk/history/worldwars/coldwar

CNN at: www.cnn.com/SPECIALS/cold.war

Cold War Museum at: www.coldwar.org

UK Cabinet Papers on the start of the Cold War at: www.nationalarchives.gov.uk/cabinetpapers/themes/start-cold-war.htm

UK Cabinet Papers on Germany and the Marshall Plan at: www.nationalarchives.gov.uk/cabinetpapers/themes/germany-marshall-plan.htm

UK Cabinet Papers on Berlin Blockade and the formation of NATO at: www.nationalarchives.gov.uk/cabinetpapers/themes/berlin-blockade-formation-nato.htm

UK Cabinet Papers on the Berlin Problem and the Cuban Missile Crisis at: www.nationalarchives.gov.uk/cabinetpapers/themes/berlin-problem-cuban-missile-crisis.htm#The%20American%20Blockade

UK National Archives at: www.learningcurve.gov.uk/coldwar/default.htm

Woodrow Wilson International Center for Scholars at: www.wilsoncenter.org/coldwarfiles/index.cfm?fuseaction=home.flash

Cold War International History Project at: www.wilsoncenter.org/index.cfm?fuseaction=topics.home&topic_id=1409

Nuclear weapons at: www.nuclearweaponarchive.org

Korean War

The United States of America Korean War Commemoration at: http://korea50.army.mil/index.html

Suez Canal crisis

UK Public Information Film and Document 'Suez in Perspective' at: www.nationalarchives.gov.uk/films/1951to1964/filmpage_suez.htm

Cuban missile crisis

UK National Archives at: www.learningcurve.gov.uk/heroesvillains/g2/cs1/default.htm

UK Cabinet Papers on Cuban revolution and the American blockade at: www.nationalarchives.gov.uk/cabinetpapers/themes/cuban-revolution-american-blockade.htm

Vietnam

UK National Archives at: www.learningcurve.gov.uk/coldwar/G6/default.htm

Decolonisation

United Nations and Decolonisation at: www.un.org/Depts/dpi/decolonization/main.htm

UK Public Information Film and Document 'Nigeria – The Making of A Nation' at: www.nationalarchives.gov.uk/films/1951to1964/filmpage_nigeria.htm

UK National Archives at: www.learningcurve.gov.uk/empire

UK National Archives at: www.learningcurve.gov.uk/workshops/decolonisation.htm

UK Cabinet Papers on Empire, Commonwealth and decolonisation at: www.nationalarchives.gov.uk/cabinetpapers/themes/empire-commonwealth.htm

Middle East

Avalon Project documentary record of the Middle East at: http://avalon.law.yale.edu/subject_menus/mideast.asp

US Presidential Libraries

Truman at: www.trumanlibrary.org

Eisenhower at: www.eisenhower.archives.gov

Kennedy at: www.jfklibrary.org

Johnson at: www.lbjlib.utexas.edu

Ford at: www.ford.utexas.edu

Carter at: www.jimmycarterlibrary.org

Nixon at: www.nixonlibraryfoundation.org

Suggestions for further reading

Cold War

R. J. Crockatt, *The Fifty Years War: The United States and the Soviet Union in World Politics, 1941–1991* (Routledge, 1996).

M. L. Dockrill and M. F. Hopkins, *The Cold War* (Macmillan, 1988).

J. L. Gaddis, *The Long Peace: Inquiries into the History of the Cold War* (Oxford University Press, 1987).

J. L. Gaddis, *The Cold War* (Penguin, 2005).

J. M. Hanhimaki and O. A. Westad, *The Cold War: A History in Documents and Eyewitness Accounts* (Oxford University Press, 2004).

W. LaFeber, *America, Russia and the Cold War, 1945–2002*, 9th edn (McGraw-Hill, 2003).

M. McCauley, *Russia, America and the Cold War 1949–1991* (Longman, 1998).

R. J. McMahon, *The Cold War: A Very Short Introduction* (Oxford University Press, 2003).

O. A. Westad, *The Global Cold War: Third World Interventions and the Making of Our Times* (Cambridge University Press, 2005).

J. W. Young, *Cold War Europe 1945–1989: A Political History* (Edward Arnold, 1991).

J. W. Young, *The Longman Companion to America, Russia and the Cold War, 1941–1998*, 2nd edn (Longman, 1999).

Orthodox account of the origins of the Cold War

J. L. Gaddis, *The United States and the Origins of the Cold War 1941–47* (Columbia University Press, 1972).

Revisionist account of the Cold War

T. McCormick, *America's Half Century: US Foreign Policy in the Cold War and After*, 2nd edn (Johns Hopkins University Press, 1995).

Colonialism and decolonisation

M. E. Chamberlain, *The Longman Companion to European Decolonisation in the Twentieth Century* (Longman, 1998).

M. E. Chamberlain, *The Scramble for Africa*, 2nd edn (Longman, 1999).

R. F. Holland, *European Decolonisation: an Introductory Survey, 1918– 1981* (Macmillan, 1985).

D. Rothermund, *The Routledge Companion to Decolonization* (Routledge, 2006).

N. J. White, *Decolonisation: The British Experience Since 1945* (Longman, 1999).

Korean War

M. Hickey, *The Korean War: An Overview*, BBC at: www.bbc.co.uk/history/worldwars/coldwar/korea_hickey_01.shtml

Cuban missile crisis

G. Allison and P. Zelikow, *Essence of Decision: Explaining the Cuban Missile Crisis*, 2nd edn (Addison Wesley Longman, 1999).

M. Dobbs, *One Minute to Midnight: Kennedy, Khrushchev, and Castro on the Brink of Nuclear War* (Alfred A. Knopf, 2008).

A. Fursenko and T. Naftali, *'One Hell of a Gamble': Khrushchev, Castro, Kennedy, and the Cuban Missile Crisis 1958–1964* (John Murray, 1997).

E. R. May, *John F. Kennedy and the Cuban Missile Crisis*, BBC at: www.bbc.co.uk/history/worldwars/coldwar/kennedy_cuban_missile_01. shtml

Détente

S. R. Ashton, *In Search of Détente: The Politics of East West Relations since 1945* (Macmillan, 1989).

M. Bowker and P. Williams, *Superpower Détente: A Reappraisal* (Sage, 1988).

R. Garthoff, *Détente and Confrontation: American Soviet relations from Nixon to Reagan*, 2nd edn (Brookings, 1994).

O. A. Westad (ed.), *The Fall of Détente: Soviet–American Relations during the Carter Years* (Scandinavian University Press, 1997).

Memoirs and biographies

S. Ambrose, *Eisenhower, Vol. 2: The President, 1952–1969* (Allen and Unwin, 1984).

Z. Brzezinski, *Power and Principle: Memoirs of the National Security Advisor* (Farrar-Straus-Giroux, 1983).

J. Carter, *Keeping Faith: Memoirs of a President* (Collins, 1982).

A. Dobyrnin, *In Confidence: Moscow's Ambassador to Six Cold War Presidents, 1962–86* (Times Books, 1995).

A. Gromyko, *Memories* (Hutchinson, 1989).

H. Kissinger, *The White House Years* (Little Brown, 1979).

H. Kissinger, *Years of Upheaval* (Little Brown, 1982).

H. Kissinger, *Years of Renewal* (Simon and Schuster, 1989).

R. S. McNamara, *In Retrospect: The Tragedy and Lessons of Vietnam* (Times Books, 1995).

R. Nixon, *RN: the Memoirs of Richard Nixon* (Sidgwick and Jackson, 1978).

End of the Cold War

Contents

Overview

In Chapter 3 we explored the way in which the confrontation of the early Cold War period gradually led to a warming of relations between the superpowers that became known as the era of détente. This chapter looks at the reasons for what became known as the Second Cold War and the personalities that were central to policy developments in this period, particularly America President Ronald Reagan and Soviet leader Mikhail Gorbachev. In time, the relationship between these leaders would result in a further warming in relations between the superpowers and more importantly the defusing of the Cold War conflict at the end of the 1980s.

Key issues to be covered in this chapter

- An examination of the factors that led to the Second Cold War
- A review of the key areas of tension between the superpowers during the 1980s
- The extent to which the end of the Cold War can be attributed to either American or Soviet policies
- Analysis of the end of the Cold War

Second Cold War

Set against a background of a decline in fortunes both at home and abroad, it was not surprising that when, in January 1981, President Reagan took office as the 40th President of the United States it was with 'the explicit intention of restoring our military and political strength',[1] along with the idea of leading America on a new crusade for freedom and **democracy**. In a speech to the British Parliament in 1982 Reagan condemned the Soviet Union to the 'ash heap of history'. One year later he told the National Association of Evangelicals at their Florida meeting that the Soviet Union was the 'focus of evil in the modern world. . . an evil empire'.[2] This reflected Reagan's view that the process of **détente** had failed because it was misguided, seeing it as little more than a Soviet ploy to deceive the United States. He quipped that détente is 'what a farmer has with his turkey – until thanksgiving day'.[3]

The Reagan period witnessed a shift in the ideals of the public who once favoured a policy of moderate **containment**, to a new stance calling for a resurgent America.[4] President Reagan believed that military strength and confidence in American leadership was a prerequisite for peace. This notion of negotiating from strength became known as the Reagan Doctrine. Reagan thus favoured security in strength as opposed to the Carter administration's appearance of weakness. However, it also held a more specific meaning for Reagan: it included the promise of arms reduction negotiations. From the outset, President Reagan called for a reduction in the number of nuclear weapons through what became known as the Strategic Arms Reduction Talks (START), rather than merely imposing ceilings on the number of weapons that could be possessed as had been the case with the Strategic Arms Limitation Talks (SALT), which he regarded as a one-way street in favour of the Soviet Union. In his first press conference as President Reagan spoke of 'Soviet duplicity' and stressed that 'So far détente's been a one-way street that the Soviet Union has used to pursue its own aims.'[5] In a speech at the National Press Club in Washington on 18 November 1981 Reagan proposed the elimination of American and Soviet long-range intermediate weapons under a formula known as the 'zero option', which he liked because of the 'boldness' and 'surprise' of the suggestion.[6] However, in words and deeds, the predominant themes of the Reagan Doctrine centred on 'strength'.

President Reagan rejected the prevailing consensus that the decline of American power was inevitable and saw the problem of America's perceived weakness through the failure of the Nixon, Ford and Carter administrations to devote sufficient resources to the maintenance of American military strength. Between 1970 and 1980 the amount invested in defence had declined by 20 per cent in real terms after inflation.[7] To justify a military build-up Reagan portrayed the United States as being weak. He wanted to overcome the 'Vietnam syndrome', which was the lack of willingness in America for intervention in the Third World, and the 'Carter syndrome', by which he meant a lack of resolve in dealings with the Soviet Union.

Sparked by the Soviet invasion of Afghanistan, Reagan's first term as President witnessed a decisive end to détente, a recommencement of the **arms race** and a refreezing of the **Cold War**. Reagan noted that 'the Soviet Union was engaged in a brutal war in Afghanistan and **communism** was extending its tentacles deep into Central America and Africa'.[8] Many commentators spoke of a **Second Cold War** (see Box 4.1). Indeed, Reagan and some of his

Box 4.1 The stakes are raised, 1980–5

- 1980   The United States boycotts the Moscow Olympics and places an economic embargo on the Soviet Union.
- 1981   Ronald Reagan becomes America president. Commences a policy of increasing defence spending. Crisis in Poland.
- 1982   Soviet leader Brezhnev dies and is succeeded by Andropov.
- 1983   American invasion of Grenada and announcement of Strategic Defence Initiative.
- 1984   Death of Soviet leader Andropov, succeeded by Chernenko.
- 1985   Mikhail Gorbachev becomes leader of the Soviet Union after death of Chernenko. Iran–Contra affair in the United States whereby arms are sold to Iran and the profits are used to support the Contras fighting in Nicaragua.

staff occasionally alluded to the feasibility of winning a nuclear war or limiting a nuclear conflagration to Europe. Opinion polls revealed the greatest fear of nuclear war since the Cuban missile crisis of 1962. Despite the appearance of impending danger, however, there were no flash points – no Berlin blockade, no Korean War, no Cuban missile crisis – that might have ignited superpower conflict. In contrast to the first two decades of the first Cold War, the Second Cold War was largely an exercise in rhetoric and sabre rattling.

Although President Reagan kept up his rhetoric of arms reduction throughout his first term, no negotiations took place with the Soviet Union. This was not all Reagan's fault, as increased repression in Eastern Europe, especially of the Solidarity movement in Poland, would have made it difficult for him to negotiate with the Soviet Union. At the same time, the Soviet Union was crippled by economic and leadership problems. Its failing domestic economy was further burdened by the cost of supporting a growing list of overseas client states that included Afghanistan, Cuba, Ethiopia and Vietnam. The Soviet Union also suffered from a succession of ailing leaders who would die in quick succession: Brezhnev in 1982; Andropov in 1984; and Chernenko in 1985. In contrast, the West presented a strong and united front to the Warsaw Pact: President François Mitterrand of France, Chancellor Helmut Kohl of Germany and Prime Minister Margaret Thatcher of Britain were all committed to the North Atlantic Treaty Organisation (NATO), and all were in office at the end of the Cold War.

According to his biographer, Edmund Morris, after narrowly surviving an assassination attempt in 1981, Reagan began to think in more theological terms and embarked on his crusade against the 'evil empire'.[9] On a visit to the Brandenburg Gate in Berlin on 12 June 1987 he declared 'General Secretary Gorbachev, if you seek peace, if you seek prosperity for the Soviet Union and Eastern Europe, if you seek liberalisation, come here, to this gate. Mr Gorbachev, open this gate. Mr Gorbachev, tear down this wall'.[10] Rather than merely containing the Soviet Union, as had been the stated intention of American presidents since Harry Truman, Reagan spoke of the need to actually 'roll back' its influence. In practice this involved funding 'freedom fighters' who often took the form of anti-Marxist guerrilla fighters in the **Third World**. It also involved supporting the **mujahideen** in Afghanistan as part of an effort to turn back the spread of communism. In Central America the United States sought to overthrow the Marxist Sandinista government by supporting a group of Nicaraguan refugees who were known as the Contras. Yet, apart from America's extremely brief invasion of Grenada in 1983, the its policy of attempting to turn back the spread of communism did not result in the commitment of troops to combat. Instead, the United States offered indirect commitments through the provision of money and arms, which consequently largely distanced US government policy from public scrutiny. A notable exception was Nicaragua when the Reagan administration attempted to bypass a decision by Congress to stop funding the Contras by instead generating the necessary resources through the sale of weapons to Iran. Somewhat inevitably, the public disclosure of the Iran–Contra affair created a backlash against the Reagan administration.

Arms racing and the Strategic Defence Initiative (Star Wars)

A central pillar of American foreign policy in the 1980s was the recommencement of the **arms race**. As Reagan also cut taxes (so-called Reaganomics), the defence build-up placed a huge burden on the US budget. Reagan was not overly concerned about this issue and once told his Cabinet colleagues that 'Defence is not a budget issue. You spend what you need'.[11] Between 1980 and 1985 there was a real increase of 53 per cent in the defence budget. But in terms of tilting the balance in the Cold War struggle with the Soviet Union, it wasn't just a matter of the amount of money that was spent. The United States also outclassed the Soviet Union in the development of new military technologies.

Investment was heavily concentrated on modernising US strategic forces based on the 'window of vulnerability' theory. This stated that Soviet missile technology had improved to an extent whereby they could successfully launch a first-strike against American land-based ICBMs, which were the most vulnerable and yet, at the same time, the most accurate of the US strategic forces. In 1981 the then National Security Advisor, Richard Allen, and Defence Secretary, Caspar Weinberger, stated that the highest priority would be assigned to closing this 'window'.[12] This included increasing the size of the US Navy from 450 to 600 ships. The Reagan administration paid particular attention to the development and deployment of new weaponry, such as his decision to begin work on the supersonic B-1B bomber and the stationing of Cruise and Pershing II nuclear missiles in Western Europe. These were new high-technology weapons with the simple aim of asserting American military and technological superiority over the Soviet Union.

The second element of the recommencement of the arms race was to financially squeeze the ailing Soviet system until it collapsed. This reflected Reagan's fundamental belief that there was an inherent weakness in the Soviet system of government, especially its command economy. In his first press conference as President, he declared communism 'a sad, bizarre chapter in human history whose last pages are now being written'.[13] Whereas both the CIA and most academics predicted moderate Soviet economic growth in the 1980s, Reagan was convinced that this was not possible.

The apotheosis of this high-tech rearmament drive was the Strategic Defence Initiative (SDI) which was first outlined in March 1983. Nicknamed 'Star Wars', it blurred the distinction between the military application of scientific knowledge and science fiction. It underwent various conceptualisations, but in essence consisted of plans for a system of satellites armed with lasers capable of destroying Soviet missiles in flight or even in their silos. This laser astrodome of defence would thus overrule or overcome the core principle of **deterrence** by taking the 'mutual' out of **mutual assured destruction (MAD)**, as it removed the threat of Soviet retaliation. The United States would be able to shelter under a laser umbrella. Reagan announced that nuclear weapons would soon be obsolete. In this sense he wanted to consign nuclear weapons to dustbin of history and in so doing he was able to dampen the protests of the American nuclear disarmament movement.[14]

Whether President Reagan really believed in the feasibility of this project is uncertain, but even so he provided a research budget of $26 billion over five years. He made it his own blueprint for US security and world peace. A great salesman of this and other policies, many commentators referred back to Reagan's acting career. Indeed, in the 1940 B movie *Murder in the Air*, Reagan starred as Brass Bancroft, a secret agent protecting something called an 'inertia projector', a device capable of destroying enemy aircraft in flight.[15] SDI, then, was a case of life imitating bad art! But regardless of whether Star Wars was destined to remain in the realm of science fiction rather than science fact, the Soviets certainly feared it. Such was their concern that the Soviet Union made an end to SDI testing a prerequisite to any arms reduction agreement. The Soviets' prime fear was due not so much to the feasibility of SDI, but rather to the potential technological spin-offs the United States would acquire in the process of research and development. Thus, a combination of not being able to provide the economic means to match the SDI programme and a fear about its potential implications meant that 'US negotiators now had a bargaining chip in dealing with the Soviets'.[16]

A particular low point in American–Soviet relations occurred on 1 September 1983, when a South Korean airliner (KAL007) on flight from New York to Seoul was shot down by a Soviet jet fighter after having inadvertently strayed into Soviet airspace. In his Address to the Nation on 5 September President Reagan spoke of the 'Korean airline massacre' as a 'crime against humanity'. Reagan would later reflect in his memoirs that:

> this was the Soviet Union against the world and the moral precepts which guide human relations among people everywhere. It was an act of barbarism, born of a society which wantonly disregards individual rights and the value of human life and seeks constantly to expand and dominate other nations . . . If the massacre and their subsequent conduct is intended to intimidate, they have failed in their purpose.[17]

But despite this rhetoric, Reagan realised that there was little value in a direct confrontation with the Soviet Union. Having come into office espousing linkage, which meant that arms control progress was dependent on Soviet good behaviour, Reagan realised more than ever that the susceptibility of the American–Soviet relationship to conflict meant that it was even more important that the arms control process continued.[18]

End of the Cold War

When Mikhail Gorbachev assumed the position of General Secretary of the Communist Party of the Soviet Union (CPSU) in March 1985,

Box 4.2 Collapse of the Soviet Union

- In the 1980s few people really expected the Soviet Union to collapse. However, the nature of the command economy limited the ability of the country to deal with key problems, such as poor harvests and the development of new technologies. This meant that key problems of the communist system were increasingly coming to the fore.
- The economic and political changes of glasnost and perestroika created pressure for further change which resulted in questions being asked about the value of communism itself.

the Soviet system was on its last legs, as Reagan had intuited. The communist economic system had failed on its own terms of providing material well-being for all. Economic exhaustion, stagnation in the early 1980s, coupled with the 'overstretch' of the 1970s imperial expansion and the pressure of the renewed arms race, revealed the limitations of a command economy. This was further indicated by the rise of an extensive parallel black market economy and an increase in alcoholism and other social ills. But the Soviet Union was also suffering from a moribund political system with its aged leadership. There was no one with the vitality to deal with domestic reform or with President Reagan's re-energising of American foreign policy. Aged seventy-four, Reagan quipped, 'the reason I haven't negotiated with a Soviet leader is because they all keep dying on me'.[19] Yet, as noted in Box 4.2, despite these problems, few expected that the Soviet Union would itself collapse.

In attempting to grapple with these problems, the two policy keywords of the Gorbachev era were **glasnost** ('openness') – especially after the Chernobyl nuclear accident in 1986, which demonstrated the problems with 'closed' systems of government – and **perestroika** ('restructuring'). These two policies went hand-in-hand: it was not possible to restructure the Soviet economy without free public debate and criticism of existing practice. Despite this emphasis on perestroika, on becoming General Secretary of CPSU Gorbachev declared that his 'First Commandment' was to improve relations with the Soviet satellite states of Central and Eastern Europe (CEE).

Their regimes were imposed and maintained by outside Soviet power, so they lacked the support of their populations as frequent uprisings attested: East Berlin in 1953; Budapest in 1956; and Poland in 1956 and 1981. As a good communist, Gorbachev sought to make the system popular in CEE.

However, Gorbachev was confronted with the tension between the cohesion and the viability of the Soviet bloc. The key issue here was how to hold together the bloc (cohesion), while also making communism a popular system among the peoples of CEE (viability). Previous Soviet leaders had ruled CEE with an iron fist, imposing cohesion at the expense of viability – they sent in the tanks. But Gorbachev was concerned to foster legitimate and popular regimes in CEE. The last previous attempt to make communism popular in CEE was Alexandre Dubček's 'Prague Spring' of 1968 in Czechoslovakia, an attempt to build 'communism with a human face'. Dubček allowed freedom of expression, economic reform (including some market freedoms) and even multi-party elections were countenanced. But the Soviet Union invaded and stamped out his reforms. This was the **Brezhnev Doctrine** of 'limited sovereignty' in action – there could be no threat to the unity of the Warsaw Pact. As we will see below, Gorbachev was far less inclined to control the states of CEE through threats of force, which ultimately led to them going their own way at the end of the 1980s.

Reducing Cold War insecurity

The relationship between Reagan and Gorbachev was extremely important to defusing Cold War tensions. Together they managed to help untie the knot of Cold War insecurity in three key steps. The first of these took place at a summit in Reykjavik, Iceland in November 1986, where they agreed to abolish all nuclear weapons by 1996. The dramatic nature of this announcement was apparently the result of Reagan having dropped his cue cards at the beginning of the meeting; his advisers were shocked with the pronouncement that emerged. Consequently, no full agreement was reached. Reagan was still wedded to SDI research and unwilling to restrict it to the laboratory as the Soviet delegation demanded.

Box 4.3 End of the Cold War, 1986–91

- 1986   American–Soviet summit at Reykjavik.
- 1987   Intermediate Nuclear Forces (INF) Treaty whereby the United States and the Soviet Union agree to remove all medium- and short-range nuclear missiles.
- 1989   Soviet Union rescinds the Brezhnev Doctrine, Soviet forces leave Afghanistan. Poland becomes independent and Berlin Wall comes down. Communist governments fall in Czechoslovakia, Bulgaria and Romania. China puts down protests for democracy.
- 1990   German reunification.
- 1991   Disintegration of the Soviet Union and end of the Warsaw Pact.

The second step was the Intermediate Nuclear Forces (INF) Treaty of December 1987. This was the first agreement which actually reduced the number of nuclear weapons in Europe and removed 2,500 missiles (such as Soviet SS20s and American Cruise missiles) from the equation; it also incorporated an intrusive system of inspections of the dismantling process. Most importantly, it embodied asymmetrical disarmament: 859 American missiles were removed compared with 1,836 Soviet missiles.

The third step was the Soviet Union's unilateral armed forces reduction of December 1988. This decision took place at the UN when Gorbachev surprised everyone (including many in the Red Army) with his announcement of a unilateral reduction in ground forces of half a million men, of which a quarter were stationed in Europe. Once again this was a one-sided reduction in forces and was a clear expression that Gorbachev did not regard NATO forces in European as a threat to the Soviet bloc.

From the Brezhnev Doctrine to the Sinatra Doctrine

A key issue with which Gorbachev wrestled was how to grant freedom to the countries of CEE while at the same time keeping together the Soviet bloc. Gorbachev struggled with this conundrum, but quickly came to the conclusion that he had to grant independence and full sovereignty to the states of CEE. In July 1989 he rescinded the Brezhnev Doctrine, and stressed that it was the business of the peoples of CEE to arrange their own affairs and that the Soviet Union had no right to interfere. Gennadi Gerasimov, press spokesman in the Soviet Foreign Ministry, named the replacement policy the '**Sinatra Doctrine**', implying that the peoples of CEE were 'doing it their way'.[20]

In reflecting on this series of events it is ironic that the **domino theory**, which plagued American policy-makers throughout the Cold War, better fits the spread of democracy in CEE in 1989 than the march of world communism. From reform in Poland and Hungary (where enlightened communist parties introduced democratic procedures), to peaceful protests and strikes in East Germany, Czechoslovakia and Bulgaria, and culminating in the bloody end to the Ceauşescu leadership in Romania on Christmas Day, the states of CEE were swept by what has often been referred to as the 'Velvet Revolution' because of its generally smooth and peaceful nature. Gorbachev reforms were embraced by the peoples of these states and his unwillingness to hold together the Soviet bloc with military force gave them permission to go their own way.

When George H. W. Bush became US President in January 1989 the Cold War was pretty much defused. The symbolic end to the Cold War came on 9 November 1989 when the Berlin Wall was pulled down by the people of Germany themselves, and the reunification of Germany took place on 3 October 1990 (see Box 4.4). At the Malta summit in December 1989, Gerasimov declared that the superpowers had 'buried the Cold War at the bottom of the Mediterranean Sea'.[21]

The implosion of the Soviet Union

Although Gorbachev had good intentions, he unleashed events beyond his control. This particularly applied to the emergence of democratic and nationalist movements inside the Soviet Union itself. Drawing inspiration from the events in CEE, they demanded more regional autonomy, thus threatening the existence of the Soviet state. In August 1991 Gorbachev was briefly ousted by an 'old guard' coup

Box 4.4 Fall of the Berlin Wall

The breach of the Berlin Wall on 9 November 1989 by the people of East Germany signalled the end of the Cold War. The collapse of the Wall took place against a background of increased civil unrest in East Germany throughout 1989. At 7 pm on 9 November 1989 the East German government announced that the border that divided East and West Germany would be opened up immediately. As a consequence crowds started to test this new policy at border crossings and in a matter of a few hours thousands of East Germans had crossed into West Germany, thereby making the border controls redundant. The wall, which had been erected in 1961 to stop people leaving East Germany, was soon subjected to people using hammers to break it up and in so doing their efforts also signalled the crumbling of communist control of Central and Eastern Europe (CEE).

led by senior members of the KGB and Red Army. Boris Yeltsin, the elected president of Russia, stepped in to save him, but wrestled power away from Gorbachev, by then the elected Soviet president, in the process. In Minsk, December 1991, the presidents of Russia, Belarus and Ukraine dissolved the federal Union of Soviet Socialist Republics (USSR) to create a looser Commonwealth of Independent States (CIS). Thus, a popular alternative date for the end of the Cold War is December 1991 when one of the superpowers ceased to exist.

Gorbachev ignored the wisdom of Alexis de Tocqueville who wrote that 'the most dangerous time for a bad regime is when it tries to reform itself'. By embarking on his reforms, Gorbachev unleashed democratic, nationalist, consumer and capitalist forces that the Soviet system could not contain. In due course this resulted in Russia's economic transition to **capitalism**, while former Soviet-dominated countries would in time become members of NATO and the EU. These events led to anti-Western feelings among large segments of the Russian people and these issues were exploited by some politicians, especially Vladimir Zhirinovsky (of the misnamed Liberal Democratic Party), who gave Yeltsin a run for his money in presidential and parliamentary elections in the early to mid-1990s. Zhirinovsky expressed desires for the re-annexation of Finland,

Turkey and the Baltic states. Vladimir Putin played on similar concerns to enhance his popularity as Russian president in the early twenty-first century. Although President Yeltsin tried to impart a westward-oriented inflection to Russian foreign policy in the early post-Cold War era, the country now identifies more with its Eurasian geographical position, and there have been a number of points of contention in Russia's relations with the West.

Unpicking the causes of the Cold War

It is evident that although the American position of bargaining from a position of strength was not sophisticated, it was one that none the less worked. According to historian, John Lewis Gaddis, 'sometimes simple-mindedness wins out'.[22] The Reagan Doctrine offered an assured way of dealing with the Soviet Union, which had broken all previous arms control agreements with the United States. Indeed, even after Gorbachev's reforms, the Soviet army sought to defy the terms of the 1990 Conventional Forces in Europe agreement by transferring tanks to the navy or hiding them behind the Ural Mountains. President Reagan deserves some credit for bringing the Cold War to a close; he carried the American people with him, even if they didn't quite believe everything he said. Probably the most important factor was Reagan's flexibility: his ability to respond to the change in the Soviet leadership, which was not the case with most of his administration.

On the Soviet side of the equation, Gorbachev unpicked the sources of the Cold War one by one, and some authors have even suggested that his actions have made him the dominant figure of the twentieth century.[23] He reversed the arms race by making asymmetrical concessions; he removed ideology as an issue by withdrawing aid from North Vietnam, Cuba, Africa, and withdrawing troops from Afghanistan; and he went to the very source of the Cold War by erasing the division of Europe – he spoke instead of a 'common European home'. In short, whether intentionally or otherwise, Gorbachev resolved each of the problems that the various non-revisionist accounts of the Cold War attribute as its causes.

Looking at these issues in more detail it is noticeable that there are four key points that are worth making. First, Gorbachev released

Box 4.5 Phases of the Cold War

- 1945–49   Cold War emerges.
- 1950–57   Cold War expands.
- 1957–62   Cold War intensifies.
- 1962–72   Cold War stability.
- 1972–79   Rise and fall of détente.
- 1979–85   Second Cold War.
- 1986–91   Cold War ends and the Soviet Union collapses.

CEE from Soviet domination. For those historians who locate the origins of the Cold War in Stalin's mistreatment of the Poles, Czechs and Hungarians, this removed the key point of contention in **East–West** relations. Secondly, he oversaw the end of ideology in Soviet foreign policy. If we attribute the Cold War to the clash of ideologies, Gorbachev's removal of world revolution from the objectives of Soviet external relations, and his termination of aid to regimes antagonistic to the West, eliminated a central cause of Cold War tension. Thirdly, by making asymmetrical concessions in arms control negotiations, Gorbachev set in reverse the arms race, which, if not itself a cause of the Cold War, was to most participants its central motif and most disconcerting dimension. In short, Gorbachev reversed the insecurity spiral that had fuelled the race to acquire nuclear superiority since 1945. Finally, for those **neorealist** writers who find the cause of the Cold War in the bipolar structure of the **international system**, Gorbachev unwittingly set in motion a chain of events that led to the implosion of the USSR and the disappearance of one of the 'poles' of the bipolar Cold War system, thus ending the main source of antagonism.

Did the United States win the Cold War?

As we outline in Table 4.1, a good way of answering the question of who won the Cold War is to consider the causes of the Cold War and to see which superpower prevailed on each point of contention.

From the above discussion it is evident that an account arguing that

Table 4.1 Cold War winners and losers

Cause of Cold War	Resolution	Winner and loser
Division of Germany.	Gorbachev agreed to a reunited Germany in NATO.	A huge concession by the Soviet leader. The West clearly wins on this issue. NATO survived the Cold War, but the Warsaw Pact perished.
Division of Europe.	Gorbachev did nothing to hinder the 'velvet revolutions' of late 1989 in CEE.	The USSR gave up its entire sphere of influence in Europe and elsewhere. It cut aid to Cuba and Vietnam and withdrew from Afghanistan. In Europe, most CEE states are now members of NATO and/or the EU. It is difficult not to read this as a defeat for the USSR.
Ideological conflict.	Gorbachev's reforms led to the spread of capitalism and democracy in the USSR and CEE. This was basically an admission that communism had failed. Moreover, the communist system had been responsible in the USSR alone for the destruction of over forty million people through famine, state terror and purges between 1917 and 1991.	With communism now dead (except for Cuba and North Korea, which are hardly good advertisements), liberal democracy has become the dominant ideology. Planned economies are now frowned upon as inefficient and prone to corruption and the curtailment of liberty.

Table 4.1 *(cont.)*

Cause of Cold War	Resolution	Winner and loser
Tension due to the bipolar nature of the Cold War system.	In December 1991, the USSR was dissolved and ceased to exist. The United States dominates the world as the sole superpower (or 'hyperpower' as some now prefer to call it).	When one of the rivals disappears, how can that not be read as losing the conflict?
The arms race.	Gorbachev made asymmetrical concessions across the board, from intermediate nuclear missiles to troop numbers. Gorbachev reduced the Red Army by half a million men in 1988 with no demand for similar reductions from the West. He permitted the United States to continue with research into the Strategic Defence Initiative.	The United States is now the dominant military power, spending more on arms procurement each year than the next twelve highest defence-spending nations combined.

the United States did not win the Cold War would have to stress the following points: first, the problems the United States has encountered in managing the international system as the sole superpower since the end of the Cold War. To many analysts the bipolar Cold War system had the advantage of containing sources of international instability, as each superpower exerted some control over their allies. A lone superpower seems to find the task of controlling the world a much less manageable proposition. Secondly, the negotiated end to the Cold War and the domestic reforms embarked on by Gorbachev make it difficult to think of the USSR as a loser – it changed its position and transformed superpower relations in the process. For Gorbachev, it was a 'common victory'.[24] As evidence of this point, it is interesting to note that both Presidents Reagan and Bush refused to gloat (at least publicly) over the demise of the Soviet Union. For his role in ending the Cold War Gorbachev was awarded the Nobel Peace Prize in 1990.

Summary

That the Cold War was brought to a close in the 1980s was due to two men. However, many have noted certain historical trends or forces working to tip the balance in favour of the West, implying that something similar would have happened eventually whoever happened to be the leaders of superpowers.

The first of these is **imperial overstretch**, which seems to be a law of world politics that afflicts all **great powers** – they tend to expand their influence beyond their ability to maintain such a position of dominance.[25] Protecting peripheries, excessive ambitions and ideological missions all have costs attached to them. In basic terms the Soviet Union's crippled economy could not fund its international ambitions. Hence, Gorbachev pared back commitments that were not in the national interest, such as ending aid to Cuba and Africa, in an attempt at retrenchment.

The second point is the nature of **post-industrial** development. In this context, while the Soviet command economy was able to produce raw materials, such as coal and steel, it could not compete in the post-industrial world economy which to a large extent requires political freedom. In very basic terms, you cannot force someone to write a computer program at gunpoint in the same way as you can force them to shovel coal. This is a reflection of a broader change in world politics: from the realist image of hostile relations between hermetically-sealed sovereign states to a global interdependent economy, necessitating economic co-operation. The Internet (which incidentally was created to enable communication between survivors of a nuclear holocaust) proffers new potential means of evading state control. According to some commentators, the end of the Cold War should be understood against the background of a shift toward the liberal model of world politics, or as the first momentous change ushered in by the forces of globalisation.

. . . .

✓ What you should have learnt from reading this chapter

- Bipolarity was a key feature of the Cold War international system, defined by two power blocs led by the two superpowers.

- The Cold War can be viewed as an ideological conflict.

- All of the Cold War fighting took place at the periphery, usually in the Third World.

- The end of the Cold War was influenced by the policies pursued by Mikhail Gorbachev and Ronald Reagan.

- The extent to which the Soviet Union and the United States either won or lost the Cold War has been subject to a great deal of debate. However, when the Cold War ended the fact of the matter is that the Soviet Union disintegrated and the United States was left as the only superpower.

? Likely examination questions

Why did the Cold War remain cold?

What was the significance of bipolarity during the Cold War?

In what ways did nuclear weapons help to maintain peace during the Cold War?

What factors led to the end of détente?

Why did the United States pursue a policy of military build up during the 1980s?

What was so significant about Mikhail Gorbachev's decision not to intervene in Central and Eastern Europe in 1989?

What factors brought about the collapse of the communist dominated group of states in Central and Eastern Europe in 1989?

To what extent did the Soviet Union suffer from imperial overstretch?

Evaluate the relative importance of the policies pursued by the United States and the Soviet Union in bringing about the end of the Cold War?

Is it correct to consider that the United States won the Cold War?

Helpful websites

Cold War

Cold War International History Project at: www.coldwarfiles.org

Intute Cold War keyword search at: www.intute.ac.uk/socialsciences/cgi-bin/search.pl?term1=cold+war

Royal Air Force National Cold War Exhibition at: www.nationalcoldwarexhibition.org.uk

Reagan Presidential library at: www.reaganlibrary.com

Gorbachev Foundation at: www.gorby.ru/en/default.asp

A video clip regarding Gorbachev's views about glasnost, perestroika and arms control can be found at: http://uk.youtube.com/watch?v=595W4JJHa2U

End of the Cold War

The Senate Chancellery of Berlin provides a full account of the Berlin Wall at: www.berlin.de/mauer/oeffnung/index.en.html

George Bush Presidential library at: http://bushlibrary.tamu.edu

A video clip of Ronald Reagan's famous 'Tear Down this Wall' speech that he gave at the Brandenburg Gate in Berlin in June 1987 can be found at: http://uk.youtube.com/watch?v=WjWDrTXMgF8. The speech itself can be obtained at: www.reaganlibrary.com/reagan/speeches/wall.asp

Berlin Wall at: www.reaganfoundation.org/programs/lc/berlinwall.asp

 ## Suggestions for further reading

Second Cold War, 1980–5

N. Chomsky, J. Steele and J. Gittings, *Superpowers in Collision* (Penguin, 1982).

F. Halliday, *The Making of the Second Cold War*, 2nd edn (Verso, 1986).

S. Talbott, *Deadly Gambits: The Reagan Administration and the Stalemate in Arms Control* (Picador, 1984).

End of the Cold War

M. Beschloss and S. Talbott, *At the Highest Levels: The Inside Story of the End of the Cold War* (Little Brown, 1993).

M. Brinkworth, *The Soviet Union's Last Stand*, BBC at: www.bbc.co.uk/history/worldwars/coldwar/soviet_stand_01.shtml

A. Brown, *Reform, Coup and Collapse: The End of the Soviet State*, BBC at: www.bbc.co.uk/history/worldwars/coldwar/soviet_end_01.shtml

J. L. Gaddis, *The United States and the End of the Cold War* (Oxford University Press, 1992).

R. L. Garthoff, *The Great Transition: American–Soviet Relations and the End of the Cold War* (Brookings Institute, 1994).

M. J. Hogan (ed.), *The End of the Cold War: Its Meaning and Implications* (Cambridge University Press, 1992).

D. Marples, *The Collapse of the Soviet Union, 1985–1991* (Longman, 2004).

M. Sandle, *Gorbachev: Man of the Twentieth Century?* (Hodder Arnold, 2008).

Memoirs

M. Gorbachev, *Memoirs* (Doubleday, 1996).

R. Reagan, *An American Life* (Hutchinson, 1990).

G. Shultz, *Turmoil and Triumph* (Scribners, 1993).

M. Thatcher, *The Downing Street Years* (HarperCollins, 1993).

The Post-Cold War Order

Contents

Overview

The end of the Cold War was one of the most dramatic and at the same time unexpected events of the twentieth century. In the immediate aftermath of the fall of the Berlin Wall and the collapse of the Soviet Union there was a belief that the new so-called post-Cold War order would be more peaceful than what had been experienced during the Cold War. Yet the very fact that this era was referred to as the post-Cold War order demonstrated that this was a period that had not been shaped by a specific series of events. This lack of definition to the post-Cold War order changed dramatically with the terrorist attacks of 11 September 2001 which resulted in what has now been termed the war on terror. The reality of this changed security environment meant that many commentators have been able to reflect that the Cold War was in fact a period of relative peace rather than one that should be viewed purely in the context of superpower conflict. In this chapter we explore the changes that took place with the end of the Cold War and the impact that the changes have had on international politics.

Key issues to be covered in this chapter

- The post-Cold War order in historical perspective
- The different nature of conflict in the post-Cold War world
- The role of the United States in the post-Cold War order
- The events of 11 September 2001 and their aftermath

The post-Cold War order

The end of the **Cold War**, whenever you date it – either the winter of 1989 when the Berlin Wall came down or December 1991 when the Soviet Union disappeared – was one of the most significant events of the twentieth century. According to then America President, George H. W. Bush, the collapse of the Soviet Union was an event 'of almost Biblical proportions'.[1] The end of the Cold War brought with it considerable speculation about what a post-Cold War world would look like. While some commentators predicted that a period of change would usher in a peaceful 'new world order', others argued that a 'new world disorder' would instead take hold.

Of the scholars who sought to offer analysis of the post-Cold War order, the work of Francis Fukuyama and Samuel Huntington have received particular attention. Writing in the summer of 1989, Fukuyama suggested that 'what we may be witnessing is not just the end of the Cold War, or the passing of post-war history, but the end of history as such: that is, the end point of mankind's ideological evolution and the universalisation of Western liberal democracy as the final form of human government'.[2] Fukuyama's argument was that the end of the Cold War marked the end of an ideologically divided world that had dominated history. In the early days of the post-Cold War order this argument proved to be immediately attractive to academics, policy-makers and the media who inevitably latched onto the 'end of history' theme. Yet the years that have passed have witnessed the continuation of many disruptive historical forces, such as tribalism and nationalism. The implications of these developments are explored in more detail in Chapters 8 and 10.

In contrast to Francis Fukuyama's end of history thesis, Samuel Huntington stressed that the post-Cold War order would be marked by a **clash of civilisations**. Writing in the summer of 1993, he stressed:

> It is my hypothesis that the fundamental source of conflict in this new world will not be primarily ideological or primarily economic. The great divisions among humankind and the dominating source of conflict will be cultural. Nation states will remain the most powerful actors in world affairs, but the principal conflicts of global politics will occur between nations and groups of different civilizations. The

clash of civilizations will dominate global politics. The fault lines between civilizations will be the battle lines of the future.[3]

As with Fukuyama, Huntington's thesis offered a catchy approach to the new world order which ensured that it too gained prominence, and it seemed to account for the conflict between Christians and Muslims in the Bosnian conflict in the mid-1990s. However, Huntington's approach ignored the question of whether ethnic rivalries had been massaged and exacerbated by elites, as Serb leader, Slobodan Milosevic, had certainly done in the former Yugoslavia, and many of the conflicts which have taken place since the end of the Cold War have not always confirmed Huntington's thesis, as they have often been conflicts within rather than between civilisations. For instance, Iraq's invasion of Kuwait in 1990 was a conflict that began within one of Huntington's civilisations rather than between them. At the same time, Western support for Kuwait during the Gulf War and NATO's support for Kosovo against Yugoslavia in 1990 involved alliances that went across civilisations rather than between them.

Despite the ingenuity of Fukuyama's and Huntington's work on the post-Cold War order, much of the discussion in this period focused on the term 'post-Cold War', which in itself highlighted the fact that there was not complete agreement about the nature of world politics in the wake of the Cold War. In reflecting on this term, Richard Haas was able to comment that 'such a label reveals that people know only where they have been, not where they are now, much less where they are heading'.[4] Indeed, writing a decade after the end of the Cold War, Ian Clark noted that although 'there has been no shortage of reflection on the . . . nature of the post-Cold War order . . . we seem to be no closer to having an integrated understanding of the constituents of today's order'.[5] Such a view was influenced by the fact that the years after 1989 were marked by the absence of a stable world order, which in itself led some commentators to note that there was 'a new world disorder' rather than a 'new world order' of peace and stability. In 1994, Eric Hobsbawm reflected that 'for the first time in two centuries, the world of the 1990s entirely lacked any international system or structure'.[6]

One of the most pressing issues in the immediate aftermath of the end of the Cold War was the impact that these events would have on existing security structures. This was a discussion that also affected the governments of Western Europe. Among these governments a key concern was the extent to which a post-Cold War world would bring about a 'peace dividend', as governments would not have to spend as much money on defence issues in the absence of a Soviet threat. For European governments there was also the more specific question as to whether they could continue to rely on the security guarantee that the United States provided via NATO. For some European governments, such as France and Belgium, the post-Cold War environment provided an opportunity for the EU to establish its own defence structures that were independent of the United States. Yet for other European governments, such as Britain, the security guarantee provided by the United States was just as important in the post-Cold War era and as a result it was less willing to see an independent EU security identity develop which would challenge NATO. This was not least because of a concern that even the collective weight of the EU member states was militarily unable to match that of the United States. It can, therefore, be seen that even among the so-called 'victors' of the Cold War there were considerable differences about the nature of the post-Cold War security environment.

The United States and the 'new world order'

With the break up of the Soviet Union, much of the focus of the post-Cold War world fell on the United States, particularly President George H. W. Bush who held office from 1989–92. Bush adopted a pragmatic approach to foreign policy which offered a sense of reassurance. His inaugural speech reinforced this sense of competency by stating that he would offer leadership without 'the sound of trumpets calling'.[7] This conservative approach suggested that Bush had little desire to overturn the world order and, indeed, he hoped that the Soviet Union would stay intact, because he did not want it to split up and create uncertainty. He has been described as 'a post-Cold War King Canute', trying to maintain the familiar **bipolar** international system in the face of demands for radical change.[8]

The first test of the post-Cold War order took place in mid-1990 when Iraq attacked Kuwait on 2 August 1990. This was the first clear act of aggression by one state against another in the post-Cold

War order and brought about a masterpiece of American **diplomacy**, as President Bush was able to form and lead a coalition of thirty-four states to send armed forces to repel Iraq's invasion of Kuwait.[9] This coalition included half of the Arab League states and was supported by a general consensus in the UN through Security Council Resolution No. 678 of 29 November 1990, while China and the Soviet Union were kept on side. As such, this was the first time since the Korean War that the UN worked as it was intended to, as it sought to halt and reverse an act of aggression. This led to frequent discussions about the possible rebirth or renaissance of the UN, as the Security Council, which had been deadlocked for the duration of the Cold War, now appeared to be able to achieve consensus on matters of world order. 'Operation Desert Storm' was launched on 15 January 1991, with the international coalition producing the surrender of the Iraqi army by 28 February 1991.

Although the successful resolution of this conflict gave further emphasis to Bush's claim that a 'new world order' had emerged with states co-operating together along liberal theoretical lines, it could nevertheless be possible to critique the Gulf War from a realist or Marxist perspective. For instance, it could be argued that the Gulf War was in fact shaped by national rather than collective interest, as countries such as the United States used the UN to achieve their own aims. On the other hand, a Marxist interpretation could stress the way in which the conflict was influenced by the interests of the capitalist developed nations that had a dependency on oil.

President Bush first used the 'new world order' phrase in his speech to Congress on 11 September 1990, in which he stated:

> Out of these troubled times . . . a new world order can emerge . . . a world quite different from the one we have known, a world where the rule of law supplants the law of the jungle, a world in which nations recognize the shared responsibility for freedom and justice, a world where the strong respect the rights of the weak.[10]

Yet Bush was unable to give the 'new world order' any real, substantive content. This was despite the fact that he aimed to turn the role of the United States into that of world policeman. In December 1992 he launched 'Operation Restore Hope' in Somalia. He did this not to enhance his popularity – he had already lost the Presidential election to Bill Clinton – but to restore hope and humanitarian aid to a war-torn state. Such action was driven by a purpose, a UN mandate and television images. However, despite committing 28,000 troops, the United States was unable to restore order and instead become embroiled in a **civil war** that ended in disaster when attempting to arrest warlord, General Aideed. The shooting down of two US helicopters and the death of eighteen US military personnel produced a backlash among the American public when pictures were broadcast of an American helicopter pilot's body being dragged through the streets of the Somali capital, Mogadishu. This would directly result in President Clinton pulling American troops out of Somalia within six months. Also, apart from giving rise to a criticism that that the United States lacked commitment direction, the debacle also led to an unwillingness by the United States to provide financial and military contributions to future UN operations. In reflecting on the implication of this state of affairs, some commentators have noted that the lack of American involvement in peacekeeping operations meant that the United States was ill-equipped to undertake interventions as the US military were 'in a state of ignorance' over the requirements of undertaking lightly armed peacekeeping missions.[11]

Bill Clinton won the 1992 Presidential election by focusing debates on economic issues and Bush lost it because he spent too much time focusing on world affairs. The centrality of economic issues to the outcome of the 1992 election was highlighted by the sign 'It's the economy, stupid' that had been put up in Clinton's campaign headquarters. When in office President Clinton tended to hand over foreign policy to subordinates and only became concerned with foreign policy decisions when it boosted his domestic popularity. This

---

Box 5.1 The leadership of President George H. W. Bush, 1989–93

- Pragmatism and conservatism.
- The Gulf War, the 'new world order' and the renaissance of the UN.
- World policeman: 'Operation Restore Hope' (Somalia).

produced an absence of leadership, with policy being dictated by reaction and gave the impression of incoherence. President Chirac of France commented over the Bosnia crisis in 1995 that 'the position of leader of the free world is vacant'.[12] Other commentators spoke of 'Band-Aid diplomacy'.[13] In other words, it appeared that President Clinton was responding to rather than shaping events, merely trying to patch things up after crises had erupted.

Clinton presided over a domestically driven foreign policy that saw the United States being tough on the likes of China in WTO talks and maintaining its interest in resolving the conflict in Northern Ireland. For Clinton, foreign affairs were primarily concerned with America's economic position. In 1994 he stressed that 'we have put our economic competitiveness at the heart of our foreign policy',[14] while he compared the United States with 'a big corporation competing in a global market place'.[15]

Despite turning his back on the world and leaving foreign policy-making to his subordinates (which often resulted in incoherence), something like a coherent doctrine emerged that was suited to the post-Cold War disorder. Clinton asked his advisers for a snappy one-word term, like '**containment**' which we discussed in Chapter 2. This resulted in the suggestion of 'enlargement' – 'of the world's free community of market economies'.[16] In short, a policy aimed at expanding the global reaches of **capitalism** and **democracy**. Enlargement was more complex than containment, since there was not one obvious and overbearing enemy, but lots of small, potentially very disturbing conflicts. There was no longer a dark/light, good/evil dichotomy. In practical terms this resulted in the United States shaping its foreign policy goals depending on the states that it was dealing with, while also attaching emphasis to multilateral policy environments such as the UN and WTO.

As part of his efforts to spread peace and democracy, President Clinton sought to bring stability to the Middle East, most notably resulting in the Oslo Accords of 1993 that were signed by Israel and the Palestinian Liberation Organisation (PLO). Elsewhere the Clinton administration favoured a policy of containing a group of so-called **rogue states** or backlash states, such as North Korea and Iraq, while at the same time offering incentives for good behaviour. Libya's renouncement and dismantling of its nuclear weapons

Box 5.2 The Clinton Doctrine, 1993–2001

- Containment of rogue states (Iraq, North Korea, Libya).
- Engagement with potential rivals (China, Russia), to tie them into the world economy.
- Maintaining relations with trading partners (the EU, Japan).
- Ignoring the periphery (Africa).
- Using military force with only minimal risk to American troops.

programme brought it back into the international community. To contain these states **sanctions** and bombing were deemed necessary to keep each in a 'strategic box'. Yet when dealing with potential rivals of a certain size, namely Russia and China, American policy centred on engagement. Such states were too big to be contained in the fashion of Iraq and hence engagement was deemed to be necessary. This led, of course, to a question of double standards. When Iraq's Saddam Hussein refused to allow UN inspectors to view his chemical weapons programmes, American bombs fell; when Russia abused **human rights** in its war in Chechnya, trade agreements were provided.

In examining the Clinton Doctrine it is evident that it demonstrated an unwillingness by the United States to commit military forces (see Box 5.2). Force was, therefore, dispensed at a distance, with there being a reliance on Cruise missiles and bombing from 15,000 feet due to a fundamental aversion to American casualties. The Clinton Doctrine also largely ignored Africa, despite President Clinton's regular visits to the continent. The 1994 Rwandan genocide, which resulted in 800,000 deaths in just 100 days, was ignored and was not even defined as genocide by the United States, since armed intervention would then have been mandatory under **international law**.

The war on terror

On 11 September 2001, eleven years to the day after President George H. W. Bush had proclaimed a 'new world order', the United

States suffered appalling terrorist attacks that resulted in the collapse of the twin towers of the World Trade Center in New York and structural damage being inflicted on the Pentagon in Washington DC. Known thereafter as 9/11, these events have proved to be the defining feature of the international order of the early twenty-first century and have ushered in what has been referred to as a '**war on terror**'. The American response to these events fell at the feet of President George W. Bush (George H. W. Bush's son) who took office in January 2001.

In examining Bush's election as president it is possible to draw parallels between the 1980 and 2000 presidential elections, in which Ronald Reagan and George W. Bush, respectively, sought to reverse what they perceived to be policy drift in American foreign policy under the preceding presidencies. Within the Bush administration this would result in important positions being taken by supporters of the Project for the New American Century, which had been established in 1997 to provide a platform to challenge the Clinton administration's foreign policy. As an indication of what was to come after 2001, they considered that Clinton had attached too much emphasis on the importance of multilateral policy environments at the expense of directly confronting challenges. The die was, therefore, cast in terms of the future direction of travel of American foreign policy. This would consequently see the Bush administration taking a path towards unilateralism (see Box 5.3).

In the wake of 9/11, the United States took the decision to directly challenge those states who harboured terrorist organisations

---

Box 5.3 The foreign policy of President George W. Bush, 2001–9

- 9/11 was a turning point in American foreign policy.
- The 'Bush Revolution' in foreign policy attached priority to the achievement of security through unconstrained power and preventive war and regime change.
- The war on terror provided the United States with a new global mission.

as well as those that challenged international stability through the development of chemical and nuclear weapons programmes. Thus, whereas President Clinton carved out a strategy of containing rather than confronting rogue states, President Bush sought to face up to and confront the challenge, to tackle threats that might emerge in the future. This led to the preventive war (frequently misnamed a 'pre-emptive war') against Iraq in 2003, to take out one possible source of danger before it could mature. In taking this approach Bush was greatly influenced by the so-called 'hawks' within his administration who favoured a more aggressive policy, in particular Vice President, Dick Cheney, and Secretary of Defense, Donald Rumsfeld. Bush's depiction of the need to tackle the terrorist threat painted a picture of good and evil which, as Reagan had done, conjured up the simplicity of the approach. This straightforward approach became known as 'toothpaste diplomacy' – when reporters asked what he had in common with Britain's Prime Minister, Tony Blair, following the latter's first visit to the new president, Bush answered that they used the same brand of toothpaste (to which Blair responded, 'they're going to wonder how you know that, George!').[17]

In analysing this basic approach to diplomacy, it is evident that 9/11 has proved to be a turning point in American foreign policy, with Bush declaring that Americans now live in a 'new country' facing new threats. A new willingness on the part of the United States to act in an assertive manner abroad saw it leading an invasion of Afghanistan in 2001 with the aim of toppling the Taliban regime and eradicating the al-Qaeda terrorist threat that it protected. This new foreign policy approach also witnessed a shift away from the United States tolerating autocratic regimes that promote radicalisation.

Iraq was a specific case in point. The Bush administration emphasised that an economically crippled Iraq was none the less able to hinder the efforts of UN weapons inspectors who had been forced to leave Iraq in 1998. Although while Iraq agreed to the return of UN weapons inspectors in November 2002,[18] Saddam Hussein's government continued to be less than forthcoming in their co-operation, which meant that the weapons inspectors were unable to confirm to the Security Council that Iraq had acted in accordance with its obligations. As a consequence of these developments the United States,

Britain and other coalition countries started to build up forces in the Gulf.

For US Republican policy-makers the failure of the UN to tackle this threat was further evidence of the pitfalls of the policies pursued by President Clinton, and as such would provide the United States with the justification to invade Iraq on the basis that it possessed weapons of mass destruction (WMD). This meant that after initially defeating the Taliban in Afghanistan the Bush administration shifted its focus towards Iraq where it sought to remove Saddam Hussein from office. However, whereas there was a broad coalition of support for the conflict in Afghanistan (as well as in the previous Gulf conflict), the United States was less able to establish a united coalition over Iraq as consensus could not be achieved in negotiations at the UN. The lack of diplomatic agreement had a number of implications, including a division among NATO allies, as France and Germany were unwilling to support the invasion. By contrast, Britain under the leadership of Tony Blair gave unconditional support to an American policy that resulted in the invasion of Iraq on 20 March 2003. Such was Blair's personal commitment to stand 'shoulder-to-shoulder' with Bush over the war on terror that Iraq has been viewed as being just much 'Blair's War' as 'Bush's War'.[19]

Despite George W. Bush's view that the Iraq war was part of a war on terror that formed the basis of a new global mission for American foreign policy, many commentators viewed this as an ill-conceived adventure.[20] Such a view gained more momentum after the CIA published the Iraq Survey Report on 30 September 2004 that had been authored by Charles Duelfer.[21] This was because the report stressed that Iraq's WMD and nuclear programmes came to an end at the time of the 1991 Gulf War. Consequently, the report undermined the American and British governments who had stressed that the 2003 invasion of Iraq was based on the need to eliminate the threat that Iraq posed by having WMD. This in turn resulted in the American and British governments attaching greater emphasis on the invasion as a democratising process, with both administrations noting the lack of freedom and human rights abuses under Saddam Hussein's regime.

While there are merits in establishing a democratic Iraq, it is none the less evident that rather than extinguishing the potential for terrorist attacks, it has been pointed out by some that the terrorist threat from organisations such as **al-Qaeda** was bolstered by the invasion. Moreover, whatever the rights and wrongs of the arguments that led the Bush administration to invade Afghanistan and Iraq, the reality of the matter is that at the time of writing in 2009 both countries are far from stable and secure, while the conflicts have in themselves created a climate of global insecurity.

In assessing American foreign policy in the post-Cold War era it is noticeable that there has been a tendency for commentators to refer to the emergence of an 'American Empire'. To this end a plethora of books have emerged with the common denominator of 'empire' on the title page.[22] Although much of this focus on empire has been applied in a negative context to the post-9/11 direction of American foreign policy, some commentators have placed this term within a broader historical critique of Cold War revisionism which emphasises the American quest for global domination since 1945.

The very use of the term 'empire' to describe American foreign policy is, of course, extremely problematic because it conflates different concepts – does it relate to the formal control of territories abroad, a hegemonic approach to world domination, or the pursuit of the national interest through unilateral actions? In analysing these issues, it is also evident that the historical landscape provides vastly different examples. For instance, Geir Lundestad has stressed that American leadership of Europe in the post-1945 era can be viewed through the lens of '"empire" by invitation' through the example of NATO. Far from being an American imposition, European allies welcomed and actively encouraged the security blanket that the United States provided.[23]

Many could argue that the spread of American influence has been shaped by the fact that demands exist for an 'American empire'. Such demands have been principally influenced by the fact that the United States is often looked upon as the country most able to provide military security in the world's conflict hot spots, stop the proliferation of nuclear weapons, maintain the safety of navigation of the oceans, fight the drug trade and deal with rogue states. Many would, therefore, argue that such demands position the United States in a role as a provider of 'services' from which all states benefit.

It is also evident that, like the Cold War, this new war on terror could last a very long time. After all, the Cold War policy of **containment** endured from 1947 to 1989. Former US Vice President, Dick Cheney, has said that the war on terror 'may never end. At least, not in our lifetime'.[24] Whatever the rights and wrongs of this approach, the fact of the matter is that such global missions are frequently associated with the problem of **imperial overstretch** – the danger for the United States is that its efforts to combat terrorism across the planet will exceed its ability to maintain such high levels of defence spending along with the human cost in terms of lives lost in combat or to roadside bombs. During the Cold War the United States became embroiled in protracted wars in Korea and Vietnam, and many analysts today point to the similarities of American losses in Iraq with the latter conflict.

Mapping the contours of the post-Cold War order

Even though the Cold War ended almost twenty years ago, we cannot discern with any certainty the main features of the post-Cold War order. The events of 9/11 and their aftermath have compounded the uncertainty that already existed following the collapse of the USSR. However, we can say that there are three central questions we can ask that should allow us to begin to chart the emerging contours of the post-Cold War order. First, will the post-Cold War **international system** be more peaceful? Secondly, will it be a unipolar system with one **superpower** or will we see a return to a multipolar system with three or more main powers as existed during the nineteenth century and early twentieth century? Thirdly, what foreign policy orientation will be adopted by the United States, militarily the most powerful state in the international system?

The end of the Cold War led many to hope that the international system would become more peaceful, as they saw superpower rivalry as the main source of conflict in world politics. The ability of the Soviet Union and the United States to co-operate in the UN Security Council following Saddam Hussein's invasion of Kuwait fuelled a belief that a 'new world order' had dawned. Many conflicts which had previously been intractable seemed, in the early 1990s, to be in the process of being solved. Nelson Mandela's release from prison in South Africa in February 1990 led relatively smoothly to the first multi-racial elections in the country in 1994 with the election of Mandela as the country's first black president, while in the Middle East there was movement toward a peace settlement between the Israelis and Palestinians following the Oslo Accords of 1993. However, a different story was told by the violence attending the break-up of the former Yugoslavia, especially the civil war which erupted in Bosnia. This account of a post-Cold War disorder, as bloody ethnic conflict seemed to replace ideological rivalry and was further illustrated by conflicts in Africa and elsewhere, most notably the genocide in Rwanda in 1994. The danger of rogue states also became an issue, with North Korea's nuclear weapons programme being particular unsettling. Therefore, initial hopes for a 'new world order' were swiftly replaced with talk of a 'new world disorder'. Paradoxically, it seems that the Cold War division of the planet might have been more conducive to world order. The end of the Cold War signalled the end of the restraining influence of the superpowers. The rising disorder and uncertainty led President Clinton to comment in October 1993, 'Gosh! I miss the Cold War'.[25]

The emergence of al-Qaeda as a major threat from the mid-1990s heightened this perception of a world of disorder. Former CIA Director, James Woolsey, captured this feeling well, when he said that following the slaying of the Soviet 'dragon' 'we now live in a jungle filled with a bewildering variety of poisonous snakes, and in many ways the dragon was easier to keep track of'.[26] Or as George W. Bush put it in the presidential election campaign of 2000: 'When I was coming up, it was a dangerous world, and we knew exactly who the "they" were. It was us versus them and it was clear who "them" was. Today, we're not so sure who the "they" are, but we know they're there.'[27] Therefore, the post-Cold War world seems be less manageable, with more threats to security from a wider variety of sources, many of which we do not anticipate. Donald Rumsfeld referred to these things as 'unknown unknowns' – the threats 'we don't know we don't know' about.[28]

For a number of commentators, the end of the Cold War heralded the emergence of a multipolar world of three or four major economic powers. The initial hopes for a more peaceful world were coupled with a belief that military might was less important than economic power. David Halberstam captured this is his claim that 'The Cold War is over: Japan won', by which he meant that the superpower **arms race** had been a waste of money and that countries like Japan and Germany that focused primarily on their economic development were going to emerge as the new leading states.[29] However, the emergence of sources of conflict and disorder across the world soon led to a recognition that military force remained a vital element of statecraft: it was the United States that led the coalition to liberate Kuwait in 1991. In fact, in terms of military power the United States is more dominant than ever before, accounting for more than 40 per cent of world military expenditure. Therefore, we seem to now live in a world of military unipolarity and economic multipolarity. The United States is the sole superpower, able to project its military power across the globe, but the EU, Japan and China have emerged as sizeable economic rivals. Russia's economic influence has also increased as a result of the dependency of many countries on it for their gas supply, which in the case of the EU represents about a quarter of its gas.

Joseph Nye went one step further in depicting the post-Cold War order as a three-level chessboard: on the military level, the United States is supreme; on the economic level, it shares influence with Japan, the EU and China; while on the third level of 'transnational relations', which includes the influence of **Multinational corporations**, **Non-governmental organisations** and terrorist groups, power is much more diffused across a range of international actors, many of which evade the control of states.[30] If we follow Nye's argument about the increasing importance of the third level in a world of **globalisation**, then it is questionable whether it makes sense to think of the world in terms of poles of power any longer.

Finally, we return to the central theme of this chapter: the role that the United States will carve out for itself. As we have seen, the three post-Cold War presidents faced different challenges and had contrasting visions about the role that the United States should play. The key issue centres on the question of whether the United States will adopt a unilateralist stance, pursuing its national interest with little regard for the interests of other states, or whether it will co-operate with others in multilateral efforts. While this distinction is often overdrawn – the Clinton administration frequently put America's interests first, while George W. Bush rarely acted without the support of at least some allies – as the world's most militarily powerful state, how the United States behaves will have significant implications for the nature of the post-Cold War order.

Summary

Although the post-Cold War environment was initially shaped by an absence of a dominating issue, the terrorist attacks of 9/11 resulted in the emergence of a theme that centred on the war on terror. Central to this theme was the willingness of the United States to undertake military intervention to eradicate the terrorist threat, as well as a willingness to challenge so-called rogue states. Such a course of action resulted in the United States adopting what became a foreign policy agenda that was increasingly set within a unilateral context and which as a result bypassed multilateral policy environments such as the UN. This has, however, proved to be a costly policy decision by the United States, both in terms of the loss of human life and the international backlash that has emerged against US policies, such as the detainment of alleged terrorists without trial and the use of extradition procedures. As a result the United States has ended the first decade of the twenty-first century having experienced a dramatic decline in international support for its policies. Moreover, rather than eliminating the threat from al-Qaeda, US policies have potentially had the opposite effect.

• •

✔ What you should have learnt from reading this chapter

- The end of the Cold War offered grounds for both optimistic and pessimistic speculation.

- Hopes for a 'new world order' were soon dashed following the emergence of a 'new world disorder'.

- The Clinton administration arrived at a workable doctrine for dealing with the post-Cold War order.

- The key defining feature of the post-Cold War order was the 9/11 terrorist attacks which in turn resulted in the war on terror.

? Likely examination questions

Why did George H. W. Bush's vision of a 'new world order' not come to pass?

What are the main security preoccupations of the United States?

'The world after the end of the Cold War is a unipolar world.' Critically assess this statement with reference to the role of the United States since 1990.

In what ways is the 'war on terror' a new type of war?

Is it correct to refer to the events of 11 September 2001 as representing a 'clash of civilisations'?

To what extent were the American-led invasions of Afghanistan and Iraq inevitable after the terrorist attacks of 11 September 2001?

To what extent has the end of the Cold War replaced ideological conflicts with nationalist and ethnic rivalries?

To what extent is the 'war on terror' a confirmation of the accuracy of Huntington's predictions in his clash of civilisations thesis?

How does the war on terror differ from the Cold War?

Why is the threat from rogue states greater in the post-Cold War world than it was during the Cold War?

 ## Helpful websites

Post-Cold War order

Information that is relevant to the post-Cold War world can be found in many of the websites that are listed in Chapters 3 and 4.

International Committee of the Red Cross at: www.icrc.org

Médecins Sans Frontiers at: www.msf.org

New World Order speech by President George H. Bush at: http://uk.youtube.com/watch?v=7a9Syi12RJo

1991 Gulf War speech by President George H. Bush at: http://uk.youtube.com/watch?v=IFrnQHaQWoA&feature=related

Information on boundaries and borders

National borders at: www.nicolette.dk/borderbase/index.php

International Boundaries Research Unit at Durham University at: www.dur.ac.uk/ibru

 ## Suggestions for further reading

Post-Cold War order

I. Clark, *The Post-Cold War Order* (Oxford University Press, 2001).

M. Cox, *US Foreign Policy after the Cold War* (Pinter, 1995).

War on terror

J. Burke, *Al-Qaeda: The True Story of Radical Islam*, 2nd revised edn (Penguin, 2004).

N. Chomsky, *Failed States: The Abuse of Power and the Assault on Democracy* (Penguin, 2007).

D. Coates and J. Krieger, *Blair's War* (Polity Press, 2004).

M. Cox, 'From the cold war to the war on terror', in J. Baylis, S. Smith and P. Owens (eds) *The Globalization of World Politics*, 4th edn (Oxford University Press, 2008), pp. 70–89.

I. Daalder and J. Lindsay, *America Unbound: The Bush Revolution in Foreign Policy* (Brookings, 2003).

F. Halliday, *Two Hours that Shook the World: September 11, 2001 – Causes and Consequences* (Saqi Books, 2001).

G. Kepel, *The War for Muslim Minds: Islam and the West* (Belknap Press, 2004).

W. Laqueur, *No End to War: Terrorism in the Twenty-First Century* (Continuum, 2004).

P. Rogers, *Why We're Losing the War on Terror* (Polity Press, 2008).

B. Woodward, *Bush at War* (Simon and Schuster, 2002).

B. Woodward, *Plan of Attack* (Simon and Schuster, 2004).

B. Woodward, *State of Denial: Bush at War, Part III* (Simon and Schuster, 2006).

B. Woodward, *The War Within: A Secret White House History 2006–2008* (Simon and Schuster, 2008).

US foreign policy in the post-Cold War period

T. Ali, *Bush in Babylon: The Recolonisation of Iraq* (Verso, 2004).

W. Blum, *Freeing the World to Death: Essays on the American Empire* (Common Courage Press, 2004).

N. Ferguson, *Colossus: The Price of America's Empire* (Penguin, 2004).

L. Gardner and M. B. Young, *The New American Empire: A 21st Century Teach-in on US Foreign Policy* (The New Press, 2005).

C. Johnson, *Blowback: The Costs and Consequences of American Empire* (Time Warner, 2002).

C. Johnson, *The Sorrows of Empire: Militarism, Secrecy and the End of the Republic* (Verso, 2006).

C. Johnson, *Nemesis: The Last Days of the American Republic* (Henry Holt, 2008).

Memoirs

M. K. Albright, *Madam Secretary: A Memoir* (Random House, 2003).

G. Bush and B. Scowcroft, *A World Transformed* (Alfred A. Knopf, 1998).

A. Campbell, *The Blair Years* (Arrow Books, 2008).

B. Clinton, *My Life* (Arrow Books, 2005).

Theories of International Politics

Contents

Overview

So far we have explored the historical development of international politics since the start of the twentieth century. An essential part of the study of IR is the body of theoretical approaches that have been developed to explain how the international system operates. In this chapter we demonstrate the relevance of IR theory to explaining international politics and outline four of the most important theoretical approaches: Realism; Liberalism; Marxism; and Constructivism. While each of these theories offers a different approach to the analysis of international affairs, Realism has been the most dominant theory for most of the period since 1945, largely shaping and setting the theoretical agenda to which the other theories have responded.

Key issues to be covered in this chapter

- The relevance of theory to the study of international politics
- The context of theory in a historical perspective
- The nation-state and the relevance of Realism
- Interdependence and the application of Liberalism
- The radical approaches of Marxism and Constructivism

The importance of theory

Theory is important and inescapable. What do we mean by this remark? It is meant to indicate that while many students of international politics (including academics) shy away from more abstract theory, preferring to concentrate on historical and empirical analyses, all of us always already have theories about how the world works, even if we deny that we do or neglect to reflect upon them, and even if these theories turn out at a later date to be false. Indeed, such theories are a requirement of the ability to apprehend and interpret reality in the first place, since they allow us to prejudge which factors, actors, processes and events are important and which we can safely filter out as irrelevant to an exploration of the issues with which we are concerned. This is true – and necessary – for both academic study and day to day existence, otherwise we would find ourselves rudderless and overwhelmed by a world of constant flux with no apparent structure or regularities.

Without theories about how the world around us works, we would be like the protagonist in the film *Memento* who lacks a short-term memory and who stumbles from one scenario to another, constantly revising his interpretations of events and losing his grasp on reality – without such theories, most of us wouldn't get out of bed in the morning! The same is true, in a more limited and less threatening sense, for academic study: without some form of theory guiding us, we wouldn't know where to start. The philosopher of science Sir Karl Popper (1902–94) once told his students to go out and 'observe'.[1] Their response was, 'observe *what*?' This was Popper's means of demonstrating that we need theories to guide our observations, to focus our attention and to filter out extraneous phenomena before we can commence our studies, even if we subsequently revise or reject those theories as a result of our investigations. Richard Rorty went one step further when he rejected the idea that the world is naturally divided into 'sentence-shaped chunks', which implies that what we take to be the building blocks of the world are already concepts in a theoretical system. In short, theoretical models precede and enable any attempt to understand the world.[2]

Theories are important to us for a number of other reasons. They allow us to provide deeper explanations and richer analyses of international politics. Rather than just describing an event, theories allow us to explain it in more general terms and to examine and compare the explanations of competing theories. They also help us to explain regularities and the appearance of patterned behaviour in world politics. For example, as we will see below, both Realist and Marxist theories of international politics provide explanations for why the **balance of power** has been a recurrent feature of the **international system**, while **Liberalism** provides a general explanation for why it appears to have been of less importance or has even ceased to operate in the last two decades. Therefore, theory allows us to move beyond descriptions of individual events and processes toward more general explanations.

Theory is also important for policy-makers, with theorists providing policy prescriptions and advice. This is especially true in the United States, where there is a very close relationship between the policy and academic worlds. One prominent illustration of this relationship is the tendency, from the Kennedy administration onward, for American presidents to select their **national security advisors** from the ranks of leading IR academics, from McGeorge Bundy through Henry Kissinger and Zbigwiew Brzezinski to Condoleezza Rice. And many more academics have left their 'ivory towers' for stints in the State Department and Pentagon.

An important reason for American involvement in the Vietnam War is that policy-makers in Washington DC laboured under false theories about the Cold War international system, in particular the domino theory (the belief that one country falling to **communism** would set off a chain reaction, as more and more states toppled under communist forms of government) and the theory of a monolithic communist bloc (the belief that all communist states were controlled from Moscow). As the Vietnam War and its aftermath demonstrated, these theories were false: no other countries in southeast Asia fell to communism, except for Laos and Cambodia (the latter undoubtedly due to President Nixon's illegal bombing and invasion of this neutral country, rather than as a result of the fall of South Vietnam), and the communist 'bloc' frequently experienced severe divisions, which led to military conflict between China and the Soviet Union in the late 1960s, the Vietnamese invasion of Cambodia and the Chinese invasion of Vietnam in the mid- to late 1970s. America's war in Vietnam

Box 6.1 The importance of theory

- Theories make the interpretation of events possible.
- They provide deeper and more general explanations for events and processes.
- Theories can guide policy – but not always in the right direction.

was a tragedy because it was unnecessary for the maintenance of US security and could have been avoided.

A good demonstration of how theory can inform practice is the contrasting approaches to international politics displayed by the administrations of Bill Clinton (1993–2001) and George W. Bush (2001–9). Although the difference can be overstated, President Clinton was more concerned than President Bush to co-operate and act in concert with other states in order to regulate cross-border processes and tackle global issues (in his speech to the 2002 UK Labour Party Conference, Clinton used the Liberal keyword 'interdependence' nine times); Bush was more concerned to assert America's **national interest**, even before the events of 9/11, guided to some extent by the Realists, 'assertive nationalists' and **neoconservatives** in his administration. Critics of Bush's foreign policy have argued that his underlying theory of how the world works led to counterproductive policies, such as an over-reliance on military power in the war on terror which further alienated the Muslim world and boosted the recruitment of terrorist groups and the insurgencies in Iraq and Afghanistan.[3]

International history and the history of international theory

Our move to the study of theories of international politics may seem to mark a significant departure from the international history of the preceding chapters, but we should note the important connections between the way in which the international system has evolved and more abstract attempts to capture these developments in thought. While it would be a mistake to posit a one-way connection between international history and IR theory, theories are none the less influenced and conditioned by the era in which they are situated.

The thoughts and theories of the broad and diverse group of scholars writing in the inter-war period, which were subsequently collectively labelled – and dismissed – as **Idealism**, were closely connected to the attempts to establish a **collective security** system through the League of Nations. For example, Sir Alfred Zimmern, one of the most significant IR professors in this period, helped to draft the Covenant of the League of Nations in 1919. Similarly, the ascendancy of the Realist approach must be understood against the background of the rise of **fascism** and authoritarian imperialism in the 1930s, the global convulsion of the Second World War and the long, tense standoff of the Cold War. When war and security were pushed to the top of the agenda, **Realism** became the predominant theory adopted by students of IR.

In this sense, it is not accidental that the Liberal approach, indicating that peaceful co-operation between states might be possible, emerged with such force in the early to mid-1970s – a more relaxed period of superpower détente – when other international issues, such as human rights and the environment were shunted up the international agenda. The collapse of détente following the Soviet invasion of Afghanistan in 1979 and the emergence of the so-called Second Cold War seemed to provide verification for Kenneth Waltz's (1924–) reassertion of the central tenets of Realism through his Structural Realist approach, which formed the centre of theoretical debates in the early to mid-1980s as Realists fought off the criticisms of their Liberal and Marxists contenders.[4]

The failure of any approach to predict and explain the momentous events bound up with the peaceful and negotiated end to the Cold War and its aftermath plunged the discipline of IR into flux. Since the early 1990s we have seen a proliferation of theoretical approaches to the study of world politics, including Critical Theory, Feminism, Postmodernism or Poststructuralism, **Constructivism** and Green theory approaches, to name the most prominent. Each of these schools of thought contains within it intense debates between rival conceptions. For example, Feminist IR theory comprises Liberal, Marxist, Critical Theory, Socialist, Radical and Postmodern-Feminist variants, among others.

Many of the most intense and protracted debates now take place within rather than between rival theories of the international system. What was called 'the **interparadigm debate**' of the 1980s, between the three main rival theories (or paradigms) of Realism, Liberalism and **Marxism**, has evolved into the co-existence of many theoretical approaches. It can no longer be said, as it could be said of Realism between 1945 and 1970, that the study of international politics is dominated by one theoretical approach, as, for example, the Neoclassical approach dominates the study of economics. And in contrast to the 1980s, when Realism, Liberalism and Marxism vied for the theoretical centre ground of the discipline, today many theorists are happy to sit on the margins or periphery of the discipline, renouncing any hegemonic ambitions and content to criticise theoretical developments in their own and other approaches.

This development points to a key distinction between different forms of IR theory. On one side are the conventional approaches of Realism and Liberalism, which seek to explain how the international system operates in a dispassionate and objective manner. Many of the authors representing these approaches explicitly and proudly adopt the methods of natural science by testing their hypotheses through the use of statistics. This is especially the case in the United States. In Britain a more discursive, historical methodology still holds sway. This is what Hedley Bull in the 1960s called the 'classical approach'.[5] None the less, we shall define Realism and Liberalism as 'mainstream' approaches to the study of world politics, since they are concerned with explaining how the international system works as it is, often seeking to advise policy-makers to prevent them from making mistakes.

On the other side stand the wide range of more critical approaches, comprising a diversity of internally diverse theories, which are generally less concerned with explaining how the international system operates than with attempting to analyse how the state and interstate system are constituted. We will describe these theories as 'radical' approaches, although it must be recognised that their radicalism varies enormously, from Marxists seeking a global revolution to establish a world socialist state for planetary economic redistribution, on one the hand, to Postmodernists intervening in abstract theoretical debates to open conceptual space for alternative forms of political practice, on the other hand. None the less, these approaches share a common concern to understanding how the existing reality of world politics is constituted, usually married to a commitment to change or transform it in some way or other. In this chapter we do not have space to examine all of these theories in turn, so we will concentrate on the broad schools of Marxism and Constructivism, which have many adherents and boast many significant and important texts on IR theory.

Before we proceed to examine these theories in more detail, it is important to make one further distinction: between general and partial theories of international politics. Partial theories are attempts to explain certain regularities and patterns of behaviour in specific areas of world politics. Take, for example, theories of nuclear deterrence which seek to explain how states with nuclear weapons devise their strategies and maintain international order through threats to respond to a nuclear attack in the same fashion. These are partial theories, focusing on one specific issue. While such theories are important for explaining key events and processes in world politics, in this chapter we will concentrate on grand theories of IR, which are concerned with the development of the international system as a whole and within which partial theories often sit.

Mainstream approaches

The story of mainstream IR theory since the foundation of the discipline is one of rivalry between the two broad approaches, with one central issue at the heart of the contest: whether progressive change is possible in the international system. Realists paint a very pessimistic picture of the world, in which states are locked in perpetual power struggles with each other, with frequent recourse to warfare, in an attempt to gain the security which almost always eludes them. For Realists, attempts to theorise international politics should focus on the continuities we can observe in relations between states across the past centuries and even millennia. By contrast, Liberals present a more optimistic view of the potential for progressive developments in international affairs. By focusing variously on the emergence of international organisations, the integration of the world economy, sometimes successful attempts to deal with global problems, such as the hole in the ozone layer, and the global spread of democracy, Liberals argue that the international system is amenable to reform and that change has in fact occurred.

Realism

Realism is a fairly broad church comprising scholars with differing perspectives and theoretical premises. However, although they may start out from different foundational assumptions, they all arrive at a very similar conclusion concerning the nature of the international politics. As we outline in Box 6.2, for Realists IR is a realm of constant struggle between states for their own security and, if possible, for supremacy over the others, frequently involving the use of military force. It is possible to identify a number of reasons for Realists' pessimism concerning the possibility of progress in the international system, which we have grouped under three headings: history, human nature and the structure of the international system.

Realists draw on history to support their arguments in a number of ways. In order to assert the unchanging nature of relations between states, many Realists refer back to past events to demonstrate continuities. The ancient Greek historian Thucydides (460–404 BC) is often presented as the first Realist writer or a precursor for Realist thinking through his *History of the Peloponnesian War* (431–404 BC).[6] During the Cold War it became popular to draw parallels between the superpower rivalry following the Second World War

---

Box 6.2 Key assumptions of the Realist perspective

- There is no overarching world government or accepted authority, which results in a state of affairs that is referred to as international anarchy (the absence of a world government).
- States seek to protect and pursue their own national interests, which leads them to compete against each other rather than working together.
- Power is central to Realist thinking, especially military power which states often resort to using in their struggles with each other.

and the events documented by Thucydides in the conflict between Athens (a democracy and naval power, like the United States) and Sparta (a dictatorship with land-based military forces, like the USSR). By pointing to similarities between the contemporary and ancient worlds, Realists make their case for the timeless nature of international politics.

Realists also often draw on the history of political thought, especially the works of Thomas Hobbes (1588–1679) and Niccolò Machiavelli (1469–1537). Writing shortly after the end of the English Civil War, Hobbes argued in his *Leviathan* that, in the absence of a strong overarching authority maintaining peace, society dissolves into a 'war of all against all'.[7] As we will see below, Realists emphasise the anarchical nature of the international system, defined as the absence of a world government able to maintain international peace and order, and often refer to Hobbes' depiction of the violent 'state of nature' in a country without a state. Machiavelli's advice in *The Prince* to sacrifice what is morally required in order to undertake what is politically expedient or necessary for success makes him an early Realist of sorts, although many twentieth- and twenty-first-century Realists would be unhappy with his apparently complete rejection of moral concerns.[8]

Finally, the history of the inter-war period is of central importance to understanding Realism, not least because Realism emerged as a distinct approach to international politics following the convulsions of the 1930s. We have already noted in Chapters 1 and 2 that the failure of the League of Nations' bid to outlaw war and to maintain international order in the face of German and Japanese aggression signalled the demise of the theory of collective security which self-proclaimed Realists subsequently derided as Idealist. One of the founding texts of Realist theory, E. H. Carr's (1892–1982) *The Twenty Years' Crisis*, bases its analysis on the failure of international law and the League of Nations to regulate international politics, arguing instead for the necessity of paying attention to power realities.[9] In this book Carr argues that it would be foolish for policy-makers to ignore 'the unpalatable fact of a divergence of interest between nations desirous of maintaining the status-quo and nations desirous of changing it'.[10] Rather ironically at the time of publication in 1939 Carr held the position of Woodrow Wilson Professor of International

Relations, which had, of course, been named after the very person who had championed the cause of Liberalism.

While nearly all Realists have recourse to history in one way or another to support their arguments, there is a clear division between those who privilege a particular understanding of human nature in developing their theories (frequently referred to as Classical Realists) and those who focus on the structure of the international system (Structural Realists or Neorealists). Classical Realists derive their pessimistic view of international politics – and politics generally – from their assumptions about human nature, which they deem to be deeply flawed and driven by permanent natural drives. These drives include the desire to dominate others, which, unlike the drives to eat and to reproduce, can never be even temporarily satisfied. Thus, for Classical Realists, all politics is concerned with the struggle for power and this state of affairs is unchanging because it is rooted in human nature.

By contrast, Structural Realists derive their pessimistic model of international politics purely from the structure of the international system, which they deem to be anarchic due to the absence of a world government. The word '**anarchy**' derives from the ancient Greek words denoting absence of rule, so to speak of international anarchy is to refer to the lack of a world authority able to maintain order. Hence, as the leading Structural Realist, Kenneth Waltz, has argued, wars happen because there is nothing to stop them – there is no higher authority to step in when states' national interests clash and to prevent war from breaking out.[11] Arnold Wolfers famously likened states in the international system to billiard balls, which collide with each other when their trajectories cross.[12] This resulted in the coining of the term the 'billiard ball model'. Likewise, Realists view states as 'hard-shelled' entities with clearly defined national interests that will frequently lead them to go to war to defend or promote those interests. Therefore, states go to war for any number of reasons, from concerns to define, defend or extend their borders (for example, the 1962 border war between China and India), to World Cup qualifying football matches (the 1969 Football or Soccer War between El Salvador and Honduras, although it should be noted that the match exacerbated more enduring sources of tension between the countries).

Structural Realists reach the same pessimistic conclusion as Classical Realists without having to make assumptions about human nature – the anarchic structure of the international system is the determining factor in their account. But all Realists accord some importance to the absence of world government when analysing the conflict-prone nature of the international system. This is not to say, however, that Realists would prefer to see the creation of a world government, since they usually argue that it would result in world tyranny (with one leader or ethnic group using the world state to dominate the others) or world civil war (as ethnic groups fight in a bid to wrest control of the world state from the others in order to dominate them).

From this image of states in international anarchy, two key logics, which appear to be inevitable and irresistible, come to the fore: the **security dilemma** and the balance of power. The security dilemma refers to the simple consequences of the fact that states have to arm themselves in order to protect themselves under conditions of international anarchy. In the absence of a world government able to defend them, states are required to provide for their own security; as Waltz puts it, the international system is a 'self-help' system.[13] However, by arming to defend themselves, states frequently pose security threats to their neighbours, regardless of their intentions – an armed state is a potential threat, if not today, then at some point in the future.

The upshot of this is a tendency toward insecurity spirals and **arms races**, even if this is not what any of the states intended.[14] For example, in the run up to the First World War Britain and Germany engaged in the very costly 'boat race' as each sought to build more battleships than the other. At the time Winston Churchill realised how irrational it was to keep producing more battleships than were needed to defend Britain's interests, yet he also recognised that Britain had no choice but to try to keep its nose ahead in this arms race.[15] Likewise, between the 1950s and the 1970s the superpowers accumulated nuclear weapons stockpiles sufficient to destroy life on the planet many times over; none the less, each side sought to acquire still more warheads in order to achieve the security which always seemed to be beyond their grasp.

The second logic of an anarchical international system is the balance of power. As Realists contend that international law and international organisations are incapable of dealing with threats to international peace and order, the only means states have at their disposal for dealing with powerful rivals is to form alliances to restrain them. Realists present different views about how a balance of power is formed. Classical Realists tend to suggest that balance is something to be created or brought about by skilful statesmen and as such Martin Wight described the balance of power as 'the masterpiece of international politics'.[16] By contrast, Structural Realists seem to suggest the balance of power has an almost automatic quality similar to a law of nature, much as a level surface always forms on still water.

Realists also differ among themselves over whether a **bipolar** balance of power (an international system dominated by two powers or 'poles') is preferable to a multipolar system of four to six great powers. Structural Realists tend to argue that bipolar systems are better because they are more stable (in a system dominated by two states, each is clearly aware of the main threat to its security), whereas Classical Realists tend to prefer a multipolar system in which alliances are more flexible and fluid as states switch sides to balance against now this, now that threat to their security. For Classical Realists a bipolar system, with each great power focusing intently on the activities of the other, is a recipe for over-reaction and lacks the room for judgement and freedom for action of a well-oiled multipolar balance of power.

While Realists argue that war is a permanent feature of international life, which is sometimes necessary and justifiable in matters of defence or maintaining or correcting the balance of power, it is important to recognise that they are not pro-war. Indeed, some prominent Realists have been vocal critics of particular wars which they viewed as unnecessary. So, for example, Hans Morgenthau and George Kennan were forthright critics of American involvement in the Vietnam War, which they viewed as unnecessary and counter-productive crusading (demonstrating the tendency to over-react in a bipolar system), rather than the rational defence of the national interest.[17] Similarly John Mearshemier and Stephen Walt came out against the invasion of Iraq in 2003, arguing that Iraq was not a direct threat to American national interests.[18] In contrast to how it is frequently caricatured, Realism is not without a critical dimension.

Liberalism

As we noted in the introduction to this chapter, Realism was the dominant approach to the study of IR from the Second World War until the 1970s, when Liberalism emerged as a major challenger. Although Liberalism can be traced to the writings of John Locke (1632–1704), Jean Jacques Rousseau (1712–78) and Immanuel Kant (1724–1804), the rise of Liberalism in the study of IR can be charted by the enthusiastic response to Robert Keohane and Joseph Nye's *Power and Interdependence*, first published in 1977.[19] As is suggested by the word 'interdependence' in the title of their book, Keohane and Nye emphasised the existence of multiple connections between states involving a variety of actors, such as MNCs, NGOs and international organisations.

A number of events and factors emerged in the 1960s and 1970s which seemed to confound Realism, confronting its ability to explain developments in the international system. For example, the rise of many large MNCs and influential NGOs challenged the Realist assumption that states are the only important actors in international politics. Similarly, the decision of the Organisation of Petroleum Exporting Countries (OPEC) to seriously restrict the supply of oil to world markets in 1973, along with America's defeat in the Vietnam War, raised doubts about the emphasis that Realism places on military power, as militarily weak states were able to wield considerable power over the world economy and a largely agrarian nation was able to defeat the leading superpower. These events suggested that something new was happening in international politics. Taking advantage of the relaxation in Cold War hostilities during this period of détente, Liberalism emerged as a significant rival to the Realist approach.

Much more than is the case with Realism, Liberalism comprises a broad group of theorists presenting a diverse range of arguments. Many scholars prefer to write on Liberal themes rather than develop a clearly defined approach as such. This situation is not helped by the tendency of Liberals to fashion their own labels. Whereas nearly all Realists call themselves Realists, Liberals have adopted the terms World Society, Complex Interdependence, Neoliberal Institutionalism and Post-International Politics among others to refer

Box 6.3 Key assumptions of the Liberal perspective

- States will often seek to co-operate with each other and acknowledge the limits of military force, especially in relations between states which share many economic ties.
- Non-state actors, such as NGOs and MNCs, are able to exert considerable power and influence.
- Democracy is a key ingredient in maintaining stability.

to their theories. [20] Moreover, further confusion is sown as Liberalism is one of the most significant political ideologies. However, as we note in Box 6.3, it is possible to discern three key arguments at the heart of Liberal approaches to IR: international interdependence and the reduced utility of military force; the emergence of many influential non-state actors in world politics; and the seemingly robust peace which exists between democratic states.

Although it is often neglected in textbook accounts of Liberal IR theory, the main challenge posed to the Realist model of international politics is the Liberal image of the international system as one of complex networks between myriad forms of organisations. In contrast to the billiard-ball model mentioned above, John Burton proposed in the early 1970s that world politics resembled more a cobweb model with multiple, if often fragile, connections between a wide variety of actors. [21] Hence, rather than talk of international politics, with its emphasis on inter-nation relations, Liberals usually prefer to speak in more inclusive terms, such as world politics or world society. As a result of various modernisation processes, such as the growth of transnational **capitalism** and new information technologies, Liberals argue that world politics has been transformed through the emergence of various forms of interdependence as the destinies of nations are linked, making them mutually dependent. Since the early 1990s it has become more popular to refer to processes of **globalisation**, which can be thought of as the strengthening, lengthening and intensification of patterns of interdependence.

Liberals usually accord primary importance to economic interdependence, with the emergence of a globally integrated economy forging connections between national economies; but they also often stress the importance of social and political forms of interdependence. The point is that, to paraphrase John Donne, no state is an island – even these which are in fact islands. No state which wishes to benefit from global trade can shut itself off and try to insulate itself from the rest of the world – or it can, but not without doing much damage to its own economy and international reputation. A fine example of this was provided by the fate of Swiss Air, the national airline of Switzerland, a country which for centuries has prided itself on its neutrality and independence to the extent of remaining outside even the United Nations until the early twenty-first century. Swiss Air was the first airline that went bankrupt following the sharp decline in air travel following the events of 9/11. We will examine the impact of interdependence and globalisation on states in more detail in Chapter 7. However, in terms of its challenge to Realism, Liberalism draws the conclusion that war between states becomes increasingly unlikely as their level of interdependence rises. States will find it difficult to issue threats of force against target states when their economies are significantly dependent on each other.

As indicated above, Keohane and Nye produced the most influential account of this strand of Liberal thinking in IR. They developed a model of complex interdependence by reversing the key assumptions of Realism. Where Realism views the world as populated solely or mainly by nation-states, their model recognises other types of actor with multiple connections linking them. Realism's firm assumption that there is a clear national interest defined in terms of state security is relaxed, so that other issues, such as trade and environmental degradation, can become the most pressing concern. Finally, this model argues that the use of military power is significantly devalued, as states are no longer able to continue the practice of gunboat diplomacy (issuing demands backed by threats or the use of force) without endangering the economic, social and political interconnections which bind them. Therefore, Liberals are able to conceive of progress in relations between states, as military violence becomes an increasingly costly tool of statecraft and states learn to co-operate in order to deal with problems that they face in common. It seems possible to identify such progressive change in world politics when we consider the relations between the most developed states, which, in contrast to world politics before 1945, seem to be largely peaceful, with threats of force almost entirely absent.

It is important to note that the model of complex interdependence is not a global theory, although it is frequently mistaken as such. Instead, it is an ideal type which can be approximated in certain geographical regions or issue areas. Therefore, while the model seems to fit the history of Western Europe since 1945 as we will see in Chapter 11, or the relationship between the United States and Canada (between whom military conflict is only imaginable to the makers of the film *South Park: Bigger, Longer and Uncut*), it does not apply everywhere at all times. Hence, states will still employ military force at the periphery of networks of interdependence, in regions which are not closely integrated into the world economy. For example, the Clinton administration was a forceful advocate for the bombing of Serbia in 1999 over the human rights abuses perpetrated by that state's security and paramilitary forces in the province of Kosovo, as there was little danger of damaging the US economy – Serbia at that time was effectively a pariah state with few economic connections to the West.

The fact that military power is devalued in relations between interdependent states (it can be employed only with costly and counter-productive consequences) should not lead us to think that power is no longer at play. Other forms of power, such as economic power (the use of aid or threats of economic sanctions), will not inflict such high levels of damage on networks of interdependence. However, Joseph Nye has argued that 'soft power', the influence of attraction, is a more appropriate and successful means of achieving objectives under contemporary conditions.[22] In short, if a state's culture, institutions and policies are attractive to other states, they will follow its lead and emulate its policies without threats or the use of military and economic sanctions and, therefore, without upsetting global economic processes. As we noted above, Nye and others have been critical of the Bush administration's war on terror for undermining America's soft power reserves through what they see as the excessive use of military force, which tends to alienate rather than attract young Muslims.

The other key arguments of Liberalism are premised on two developments which are explored in more detail later on and which are only briefly stated here. The first development, which is the subject of Chapter 8, is the increasing prominence of non-state actors, such as international organisations, NGOs and MNCs, in world politics. These transnational and global actors are the carriers or channels of processes of interdependence between states. For example, since the mid-1960s, the number and economic strength of MNCs has increased markedly. Liberals argue that these actors must, therefore, appear in any realistic theory of world politics. The second development, which we will return to in Chapter 12, is the transition to democracy of many formerly authoritarian regimes in the last forty years. Since the 1980s Liberals have revived Immanuel Kant's notion of a 'perpetual peace' between democratic states.[23] As democracies tend not to go to war with each other, the spread of democracy around the globe holds out the prospect of entire regions based on purely peaceful relations between states and, ultimately, the Idealist dream of a world without war. On the basis of these themes of interdependence, non-state actors and peaceful relations between democracies, Liberals assert that change has taken place in the international system and that further progress in world politics is possible.

Radical approaches

In contrast to Liberals, who hold out the potential for reform and modernisation of the international system, radical approaches propose that more fundamental change in the nature of world politics is possible. Indeed, many radical IR scholars go so far as to imply the desirability and potential for the revolutionary transformation of international politics; some even indicate that the interstate system can be overcome or replaced by some form of world political community.

As we noted above, there are many forms of radical IR theory presenting a wide variety of concerns and modes of analysis. However, what they all have in common is a critical attitude toward the core assumptions of more mainstream approaches. Radical approaches take one step back to examine the constitution of the units of world politics which Realism and Liberalism tend to take for granted or presuppose. In particular, radical approaches trace the emergence and development of the sovereign state in world history, whether through a confluence of certain material and economic conditions and/or through certain developments in political ideas and organisation.

This recognition that states are not an immutable feature of the political world raises the possibility that new and novel forms of political organisation, with greater scope for freedom and social justice, might be possible. Rather than starting with the assumption of an international system comprising nation-states (as do Realists and most Liberals), radicals are more concerned with how the sovereign state came into existence and how it might be replaced with other forms of political organisation. For example, for Marxists, the existence and actions of states and MNCs must be set against the backdrop of the capitalist economic system in which they are embedded and which, to one degree or another, helped constitute and shape them; transforming the nature of the world economy would, therefore, imply and require a far-reaching reordering of international politics. Alternatively, Postmodern theorists tend to trace the emergence of the modern state through developments in political ideas and practices. What is common to both approaches is the notion that the state emerged in history and, therefore, may also be transformed or replaced by other forms of political community in the future.

To conclude, whereas mainstream approaches are concerned with explanation, such as explaining why wars occur or how co-operation between states is possible, radical approaches focus instead on how the state and international politics are constituted and how they may be transformed. The remainder of this chapter will examine two of the most significant radical approaches: Marxism and Constructivism.

Marxism and its offspring

Marxist IR theorists are critical of Realists and Liberals for their ahistorical approach – their tendency to assume that the state is an unchanging fact of international life. While Liberal IR theorists are primarily concerned with certain changes that have occurred since the end of the Second World War and since the 1960s in particular, they often confirm the accuracy of the Realist account of world politics before the impact of various forms of modernisation was felt in the last sixty years or so. Marxists, by contrast, view historical developments against a much more extended timeframe. They are concerned with the emergence of modernity, which is primarily constituted by the capitalist market economy, the sovereign state and enlightenment forms of knowledge. According to this account, the modern state appeared following the profound transformations and upheavals that Western Europe experienced from the fourteenth century onwards. Marxists argue that this process cannot be understood without placing it within the context of the transition from medieval feudalism to modern capitalist society.

Rather than viewing the state as a largely autonomous actor, Karl Marx (1818–83) saw it as an institution rooted in society and performing a specific function regarding the fundamental conflict between capitalist owners of the means of production (the bourgeoisie) and the workers they exploited (the proletariat). Marx argued that the state protected the interests of the capitalist class and, therefore, preserved the unjust capitalist economic system. Marx and his colleague, Friedrich Engels (1820–95), wrote at the start of the *Communist Manifesto* that 'The history of all hitherto existing society is the history of the class struggle.' To this end they predicted that when the workers became fully conscious of their exploitation by the less numerous capitalist class, a revolution would ensue which would replace capitalism with communism, a society without class divisions where people collectively manage the economy in their common interest; consequently the state would wither away.

Marx wrote his most important texts in the mid- to late nineteenth century, which has often been described as 'the century of peace' due to the general absence of major wars between the great powers in this era (domestic upheavals may have seemed more frequent and more momentous). Perhaps as a consequence of this, Marx did not develop a sustained and systematic account of international politics. However, since the late 1960s a number of IR theorists have attempted to extend Marxist analysis of one form or another to the international system and the global capitalist economy. There is a great deal of variety within the Marxist camp, but in this section we will concentrate on the world-systems theory of Immanuel Wallerstein,[24] which is loosely based on but shares many affinities with Marxism, and Justin Rosenberg's critique of Realism, which follows similar lines.[25]

For all their differences, both Wallerstein and Rosenberg set their analyses of international politics within the broader social context of the development of capitalism as a global economic system. Wallerstein dates the emergence of the capitalist world economy – a global system of trade between independent territorial units – back to 1500. Both analysts are concerned with how the more developed states exploit the poorer, less developed countries in the international system. Wallerstein uses the words 'core' and 'periphery' to denote the groups of developed and less developed states, respectively, and documents in great historical detail the economic processes through which the core exploits the periphery through practices and processes of unfair exchange.

The key point for the study of international politics is that we come to see the state system in a new light. A system of independent, sovereign states is no longer just the main ordering principle of international politics, it is the political counterpart to the underlying capitalist world economy. The latter would cease to exist if the state system was replaced by some form of global empire imposing economic decisions from the centre. The state system also plays an ideological function, concealing or justifying economic inequalities. Just as Marxists have argued that notions of human rights conceal great differences in life opportunities between individuals of different social classes, so the idea that all states are sovereign conceals their often vastly different positions in the structure of the world economy, which determines their current and future levels of wealth and autonomy or **dependency**. Finally, the balance of power should be reinterpreted: it is not only, or even primarily, the mechanism by which states defend themselves against more powerful and threatening states, but should be seen instead as a device by which the capitalist world economy is protected against its possible replacement by a world empire. Therefore, the state system is the political counterpart to global capitalism. The Realist claim that states have great freedom of action in the international system ignores the fact that states are embedded in, and their actions are conditioned if not determined by, the capitalist world economy.

Through their depiction of states as entities which have emerged within history and their concern with the exploitative nature of the world capitalist economy, Marxist IR theorists have promoted the possibility and desirability of the revolutionary transformation of both the global economy and the state system. In a manner analogous to Marx's account of revolution, Wallerstein has argued that increasing inequality between core and periphery, along with the recurring depressions and economic crises of global capitalism, will lead to a worldwide social revolution, sweeping away both global capitalism and the interstate system and replacing them with a socialist world government.[26] Although Wallerstein's writings on this subject are necessarily somewhat vague, a socialist world state would make economic and redistributive decisions in the collective interests of the population of the planet, unlike global capitalism which is beyond the control of any single centre of authority and operates in the interest of one class of states. Rosenberg also shares this vision of the simultaneous replacement of both capitalism and international politics by a more just and equitable socialist world government. Communist revolution in one state, such as the Russian Revolution of 1917, is doomed to failure on this account, since it replaces neither global capitalism nor the competitive military rivalry of the international system. The USSR found it necessary to trade with non-communist states and was forced to engage in arms races with the United States which it could not afford and which distracted its resources away from domestic social development.

Not all Marxist IR theorists would go this far, however, with many shying away from talk of a global revolution. Historically social revolutions have displayed a tendency to descend rapidly into totalitarian dictatorships which dominate, persecute and often decimate whole populations. The communist experiments in the USSR and China alone cost an estimate 100 million lives through terror, state-manufactured famines, executions and purges – the loss of life following a global communist revolution might be even more catastrophic. Hence, some Marxist IR theorists have followed the pattern of Western Marxist thought since the failure of the Russian Revolution to live up to its own ideals, and have adopted a more reformist approach.

Rather than calling for the dissolution of global capitalism and replacement of the interstate system, these theorists focus instead on means of reducing social inequalities within these structures. Many

Box 6.4 Key assumptions of the Marxist perspective

- Marxists focus on the potential for transforming or overthrowing the global capitalist economy.
- Within the Marxist theoretical school there are notable differences of thought. While some Marxists advocate a global revolution of the capitalist system, others focus on reducing inequalities within existing social structures.
- Despite the failure of the communist experiment in the USSR, the Marxist theory of IR is important because of its analysis of the capitalist system.

of these theorists, such as Robert Cox, transpose to the international system the approach to class struggle developed by the Italian Marxist Antonio Gramsci.[27] Gramscian theorists tend to be concerned with the way in which the global capitalist economy is ordered. Borrowing Gramsci's use of the word 'hegemony', they see the world economy as dominated by a neoliberal 'hegemonic bloc', forged and led by the transnational capitalist class, and advocate the need for workers across the world to form a 'counter-hegemonic bloc' to more force-fully represent the interests of those most exploited in free market economies and to work for a more socially just ordering of the world economy. Other theorists, drawing on the ideas of another branch of Western Marxism, the Frankfurt School of Critical Theory, are even less concerned with replacing or transforming the global capitalist economy and focus instead on the way in which state sovereignty acts as a form of exclusion, dividing citizens from non-citizens. This Critical International Relations Theory applauds the emergence of more progressive and more inclusionary regional, transnational and even global forms of political community.[28]

Constructivism

Whereas Marxists are predominantly concerned with the material economic conditions within which the interstate system was formed and is embedded, Constructivists by contrast are more interested in the role of ideas and with how world politics is socially constructed. They, none the less, share with Marxists and other radical theorists a concern with the possibility of the fundamental transformation of world politics. Constructivism is the newest approach to the study of IR of the four we have explored in this chapter, emerging most forcefully following the end of the Cold War. The failure of Realists – and other approaches, for that matter – to adequately explain, let alone predict, the momentous yet peaceful transformation of international politics between 1989 and 1991 gave a great boost to Constructivism which is able to explain developments of this sort.

As we saw above, Realists and Liberals take the national interests of states for granted – this is their starting point. Constructivists, however, take one step back and inquire into how the interests of states are shaped and examine the possibility that they are subject to change. Therefore, Constructivists tend to be more interested in questions of identity. If a state's identity – that is, the image it has and wishes to promote of itself – changes, then it will either interpret its interests in a new light or may even fundamentally revise and redefine its national interests. Gorbachev's reform and redirection of the USSR in the late 1980s is a good case in point. To some extent he transformed the Soviet Union's identity, making possible the peaceful resolution of the Cold War confrontation with the United States. For Constructivists, identities precede and largely define interests.

Exploring how identities are formed and reformed opens up the possibility that states and other actors might behave differently and that the nature of the international system may be transformed. To borrow the title of Alexander Wendt's seminal article on this subject, 'anarchy is what states make of it'.[29] The absence of a world government does not determine that relations between sovereign states will necessarily be war prone and dominated by security concerns. For Constructivists, the latter is a contingent outcome dependent on states' identities and their interpretations of the nature of the international system and, therefore, it is amenable to change; states residing in international anarchy might achieve greater levels of co-operation and peaceful interaction.

More than any of the other approaches we have looked at so far in this chapter, Constructivism is a very broad church. Indeed, compared with Realism, Liberalism and Marxism, Constructivism

Box 6.5 Key assumptions of the Constructivist perspective

- Emphasis is placed on the world being socially constructed.
- Human agreements are central to the way in which we accept issues such as sovereignty and human rights.
- Constructivists focus on the potential for global change because they stress that the world is socially constructed.

is not really a theory of international politics at all – it is more of a worldview or framework. Consequently Constructivist analyses can proceed in a wide range of directions. Some Constructivists are much more radical than Wendt, exploring how states themselves are socially constructed entities and proposing the possibility of a radically different mode of political organisation for the world. Postmodernist IR theorists are often subsumed under the Constructivist heading due to their concern with the formation of personal and collective identities in relation to developments in world politics. On some accounts, Critical International Relations Theory should also been brought under this heading by virtue of its emphasis on the construction of new forms of transnational society. But all of these approaches share the view that the international system is socially constructed to one extent or another, and is not the immutable sphere of conflict that Realism depicts.

Summary

The issue of continuity and change in world politics is, therefore, one which divides not only Realists and Liberals, but also the mainstream and radical approaches more generally. As we have seen, Realists stand alone in asserting the unchanging nature of the international system. Liberals claim that progress is a distinct possibility, even in the absence of a world government. By contrast, radical approaches hold out the potential for more far-reaching transformation of world politics and are more concerned with analysing how the international system is constituted rather than explaining how international politics is conducted within that system.

. . . .

✔ What you should have learnt from reading this chapter

- IR theories provide a framework for understanding events that have happened in the past as well as providing a framework for making broad predictions about the future. Theories provide a basis upon which we can start our studies.

- Theories help us to move beyond merely describing events to instead providing a stronger analysis and explanation.

- The ascendancy of one particular theory of international politics over another is often linked to the historical context. The Realist approach was prominent in the late 1930s, the Second World War and for most of the Cold War. By contrast, the Liberal approach gained influence in the 1970s when there was a relaxation of tension between the superpowers.

- While there are key differences and debates between the main IR theories, it is also the case that there are significant debates within theoretical camps.

- The mainstream approaches to the study of IR are Realism and Liberalism.

- The two most significant radical approaches to the study of IR are Marxism and Constructivism.

- Whereas mainstream approaches are concerned with explanation, such as explaining why wars occur or how co-operation between states is possible, radical approaches focus instead on how the state and international politics are constituted and how they may be transformed.

? Likely examination questions

Of what value is theory in the study of international relations?

Why are Realism and Liberalism regarded as conventional theoretical approaches?

What is the security dilemma?

Why has Realism been the dominant theory of international relations?

Why does Marxism continue to be relevant?

In what ways does Marxist theory offer an important means of understanding international politics?

'Liberal ideas are no longer appropriate for the twenty-first century.'
Discuss.

In what ways does Realism offer the most appropriate means of explaining
the war on terror?

To what extent is Constructivism a useful theory for understanding
international politics?

In what ways does Liberalism challenge the Realist model of international
politics?

Helpful websites

Whereas there are websites that are of specific relevance to many of the
points that have been raised in this book, there are by contrast relatively
few websites that are dedicated to the study of IR theory.

A useful source of information is the IR Theory website at: www.irtheory.com.

Suggestions for further reading

General overview

J. Baylis, S. Smith and P. Owens (eds), *The Globalization of World Politics:
An Introduction to International Relations*, 4th edn (Oxford University
Press, 2008), chs 5–10.

D. Boucher, *Political Theories of International Relations* (Oxford University
Press, 1998).

C. Brown with K. Ainley, *Understanding International Relations*, 3rd edn
(Palgrave Macmillan, 2005).

R. Little and M. Smith (eds), *Perspectives on World Politics*, 3rd edn
(Routledge, 2006).

J. Steans and L. Pettiford with T. Diez, *Introduction to International
Relations: Perspectives and Themes*, 2nd edn (Pearson Education, 2005).

Advanced introductions

S. Burchill, A. Linklater, R. Devetak, J. Donnelly, M. Paterson, C. Reus-
Smit and J. True, *Theories of International Relations*, 3rd edn (Palgrave
Macmillan, 2005).

T. Dunne, M. Kurki and S. Smith (eds), *International Relations Theory:
Discipline and Diversity* (Oxford University Press, 2007).

J. M. Hobson, *The State and International Relations* (Cambridge University
Press, 2000).

R. Jackson and G. Sørensen, *Introduction to International Relations: Theories and Approaches*, 3rd edn (Oxford University Press, 2007).

C. Reus-Smit and D. Snidal (eds), *The Oxford Handbook of International Relations* (Oxford University Press, 2008).

Realism

M. E. Brown, S. M. Lynn-Jones and S. Miller (eds), *The Perils of Anarchy: Contemporary Realism and International Security* (MIT Press, 1995).

S. Guzzini, *Realism in International Relations and International Political Economy* (Routledge, 1998).

J. Mearsheimer, *The Tragedy of Great Power Politics* (Norton, 2001).

H. Morgenthau, *Politics Among Nations: The Struggle for Power and Peace*, 5th edn (McGraw-Hill, 1985).

Liberalism

R. O. Keohane and J. S. Nye, *Power and Interdependence: World Politics in Transition*, 3rd edn (Longman, 2001).

J. N. Rosenau, *Turbulence in World Politics: A Theory of Change and Continuity* (Harvester Wheatsheaf, 1990).

Marxism

A. Linklater, *Beyond Realism and Marxism: Critical Theory and International Relations* (Macmillan, 1990).

I. Wallerstein, *World-Systems Analysis: An Introduction* (Duke University Press, 2004).

Constructivism

C. Reus-Smit, *The Moral Purpose of the State: Culture, Social Identity, and Institutional Rationality in International Relations* (Princeton University Press, 1999).

A. Wendt, *Social Theory of International Politics* (Cambridge University Press, 1999).

The State in International Politics

Contents

Overview

As we saw in Chapter 6, for Realists the state is the main or only unit of analysis in international politics due to its control of armed forces. They follow Max Weber in defining the state as the entity which has the monopoly on the legitimate use of force. In the dangerous world of international anarchy depicted by Realists, only military power allows states to defend themselves and to act in any meaningful sense on the world stage. Our attention in this chapter is focused on analysing the role of nation-states in more detail. The relationships between states cover a whole range of issues, including diplomacy, war, regional co-operation and trade negotiations. Today there are around 200 independent states in the world and together these states form the international system. The international system refers to the relationships that take place among states and the way in which these relationships have resulted in certain 'rules of the game'. These rules apply to the way in which the actions of a state are kept in check by the influence of another state. This balance of power refers to the way in which actions are counter-balanced in the international system and this has particularly applied to role of alliances.

Key issues to be covered in this chapter

- Sovereignty and the nation-state
- The nation-state and national communities
- The significance of resources to nation-states
- Nation-states and the impact of globalisation

The emergence of the modern sovereign state

Throughout every historical epoch the world has consisted of a variety of political forms. These have included the **city-states** of ancient Greece and Renaissance Italy, the empires of Rome, China, Holland and Britain and the nomadic cultures found in parts of Africa and Asia Minor. Indeed, even during the first half of the twentieth century, the states of Europe and the Americas co-existed with colonies, mandated territories and protectorates. The nation-state is originally a Western form of political organisation, emerging in Western Europe in the seventeenth century and reaching maturity following the French Revolution in 1789. The concept of the nation-state began in Europe and subsequently spread throughout the world. Much of the increase in the number of nation-states and the consolidation of its status as a global norm has taken place since 1945.

The states that comprise the international system are in theory independent of each other because they are regarded as sovereign states and the notion of **sovereignty** is a cornerstone which underpins the international system. Sovereignty basically means the ability of a state to exercise control over its own territory which refers to an autonomous right to pursue its own interests. The importance of sovereignty is emphasised in the Realist approach to international politics, whereby states seek to secure their own security (see Chapter 6). It is a view that has been influenced by the work of such political theorists as Thucydides, Machiavelli and Hobbes. Writing in the seventeenth century against a background of conflict at the end of the Middle Ages, Hobbes argued that state sovereignty was the only alternative to insecurity and **anarchy**. In his best-known book, *Leviathan*, Hobbes contended that conflict was a 'state of nature' and that states had to protect their own interests because of the absence of a higher power.[1]

The notion of state sovereignty was formally expressed in the 1648 Treaty of Westphalia which ended the Thirty Years' War 1618–48. This was a ruinous religious war between Catholics and Protestants that was fought principally in Germany. The Peace of Westphalia marked a turning point in the development of a European state system and a move away from the dominance within Europe of the

Catholic Church and Holy Roman Empire. It laid the foundations for the two key principles that govern the relationship between states. First, the principle of internal sovereignty which means that the ruler of a state should have control over power within the state. Secondly, the principle of external sovereignty which means that a state should not intervene in the internal affairs of another state, and the key point here is one of equality between states in terms of their sovereignty irrespective of how large or small, or how weak or powerful a state is. The very significance of these developments is reflected in the fact that the modern-day state system is often referred to as the Westphalian system.[2]

However, while such a picture of sovereignty is inevitably linked to notions of authority and legitimacy, it is nevertheless the case that this is a view that is not always adhered to by states. As we have already noted in earlier chapters, there have been many occasions when states have taken decisions that have in effect not recognised the sovereignty of other states. For instance, consider the US invasion of Grenada in 1983. The reality of this state of affairs for Stephen Krasner is that the Realist view of sovereignty can basically be referred to as 'organised hypocrisy' because states follow the rules only when its suits their own interests.[3]

The rise of nationalism

Although the sovereign territorial state emerged in Western Europe in the seventeenth century, the formation of the modern nation-state did not take place until the nineteenth century following the developments and international impact of the American Revolution of 1776 and the French Revolution of 1789. Central to the revolutions was the idea of the nation. William Doyle has written that 'The revolution began as an assertion of national sovereignty. Nations – not kings, not hereditary elites, not churches – were the supreme source of authority in human affairs.'[4] Marx described the events of 1789 as 'a gigantic broom', sweeping away the 'relics of bygone times', primarily the antiquated and complex state administration and class structures.[5] In their place the French Revolution left behind a direct relationship between the citizen and the state, supposedly unmediated by class differences. The idea of equality and fraternity between citizens provided the basis for the idea of the national community. Through the wars that followed the French Revolution, the idea of **nationalism** spread across much of the rest of Europe and encouraged national independence movements in South America following the French invasions of Spain and Portugal. It is more than coincidental that Jeremy Bentham coined the term 'international' in the 1780s to refer to the relations between states.[6]

The French Revolution, largely through Napoleon's reforms, was also important in leading to the development of many features of the state that we now take for granted, such as conscription for service in standing armies, a national system of taxation to provide for defence budgets, and the structures of modern state administration. The revolution was also instrumental in spreading the French language among the new citizens, most of whom spoke other languages or dialects. A national system of education emerged to produce and maintain the new national culture.

Since 1789 there have been roughly four waves of nationalism which have significantly reshaped the international system. The first wave, affecting Western Europe, grew out of the French Revolutionary and Napoleonic Wars. The second wave emerged in Central and Eastern Europe following the end of the First World War, as demands for national **self-determination** arose following the collapse of the Austro-Hungarian and Ottoman empires. The third wave was composed of the national independence movements in the **Third World** following the Second World War, as subject peoples demanded independence from the empires of Britain, France, Belgium, Holland and Portugal. Finally, the fourth wave of nationalism followed the collapse of communism in Central and Eastern Europe as well as the former Soviet Union. Following each wave of nationalism, new independent states emerged. The third wave was particularly significant, as the process of decolonisation led directly to the globalisation of the nation-state as the only recognised form of political community. We will revisit this theme in the concluding chapter to this book. However, the most recent wave has often been referred to as the 'new nationalism' or 'ethno-nationalism' and, due to its emphasis on ethnicity, has been identified as the main cause of bloody civil wars in the Balkans and elsewhere.[7]

The nation-state is now generally used as shorthand for the main form of political organisation in IR. For many, this relates to important elements of statehood, such as having exclusive control of territory with clearly defined borders and a defined and stable population. Just as important as these physical attributes of states is the recognition conferred on states by other states and international organisations. Of course, the state is in many ways a physical entity, but in many important respects a state is only a state if it is recognised as such by other states. Taiwan has all of the physical and tangible trappings of statehood, but it is only recognised as an independent state by twenty-three states. Alongside President Nixon's opening to the People's Republic of China (PRC) in the early 1970s, which the United States had refused to recognise as the official representative of mainland China, Taiwan was ejected from the UN in 1971 so that the PRC could assume the seat in the General Assembly and Security Council. Since its recognition of the PRC in 1979, even the United States, which has repeatedly committed itself to defending the island from threats from the PRC, no longer recognises Taiwan as a state and relations with the province have been conducted through the American Institute in Taiwan instead of an embassy. Likewise, Taiwan has established economic and cultural offices in over sixty states around the world in place of full diplomatic missions. Moreover, Taiwan is not a member of international organisations such as the WHO, which has created difficulties with the emergence of transnational health issues such as bird flu outbreaks and the SARS virus.

It is also important to note that most states do not correspond neatly, if at all, to national communities. States which have borders that precisely fit the boundaries of clearly defined and discrete nations are a rarity in world politics. While Japan is a good example of a state whose borders follow fairly closely the boundaries of the Japanese nation, this is much more the exception rather than the rule. More frequently states will contain two or more national communities (for example, Britain comprises three nations, English, Scottish and Welsh, along with representatives of many other ethnic communities in an increasingly multicultural society), or a national group may find itself spread across two or more states (for example, the Kurds lack their own state and straddle the borders of Turkey, Iran, Iraq and Syria).

Providing nations within states with a degree of national autonomy through some form of **devolution** is often sufficient to deal with any tensions that might emerge with the mismatch between nations and states. Federal systems of governments, with significant powers accorded to regional government, have worked well in states containing diverse communities such as India. This is just as well, since if the principle of national self-determination was applied to every **ethnic group** across the globe, there would be thousands of states and international politics would become unworkable. But elsewhere, often where attempts to accommodate national differences have been denied or revoked, conflict is a distinct possibility and a frequent occurrence. Movements for **secessionism** (where ethnic groups seek to break away from states) and **irredentism** (where ethnic groups seek to redraw state boundaries to incorporate fellow nationals who currently reside in neighbouring states) have been a frequent source of, or justification for, conflict in world politics. For example, the breakaway Ibo tribe's failed attempted to declare an independent state of Biafra plunged Nigeria into three years of civil war in the late 1960s, while Somalia went to war with both Ethiopia and Kenya in the 1970s partly in a bid to redraw boundaries to bring ethnic Somalis within the state. But it is important to note that the principle of self-determination can often be employed to mask ulterior motives, such as Hitler's justification for Germany's invasion of the Sudetenland in Czechoslovakia. These issues are examined in more depth in the concluding chapter.

Just as states face challenges in terms of responding to the demands of nationalism, so they also face the pressure of the impact of external forces. Later in the chapter we highlight the impact that globalisation has on the ability of a state to manage its own economy. For the moment, however, we will address the way in which **supra-national** organisations can impact on nation-states. In the case of the EU it is noticeable that the member states have had to give up an element of their own national sovereignty because decisions are regularly taken by all the member states on a majority basis. What this means in practice is that a member state has to comply with a decision on a particular policy even though it may not have supported such a policy. This provides critics of the EU (so-called Eurosceptics) with the ammunition with which they can criticise

European decisions for impacting too much on national life. This has been particularly evident in Britain. Yet, it is also the case that EU membership can enhance the influence of individual member states because they are now able to exercise greater influence in a collective organisation at a global level. This is an issue that we will examine in more detail in Chapter 11.

Military power

When examining the influence of states it is also important to consider the impact of military power. Some states are able to have a particularly influential voice in the international system because they possess significant military resources (see Box 7.1). Military power is a relative concept and thus some states are able to exercise a dominant role in a regional context although they are unable to exercise considerable influence in a global context. We need, therefore, to be aware of the concept of a regional power just as we are of a **superpower**. When examining military power we also need to be aware of the 'security dilemma'. This refers to the fact that while a nation may feel greater security by acquiring military capability, this very process does, of course, make it a threat to its neighbours who will then in turn seek to match the other state's military capability. This security dilemma has often resulted in arms races as states seek to match and surpass military build-ups in other countries.

The most potent example of military power is the possession of nuclear weapons. The move to develop a nuclear bomb took place during the Second World War because the United States was concerned that if Nazi Germany developed such a weapon then it would have the potential to win the war and destroy its enemies. As a result the United States invested a great deal of effort and resources in developing an atomic bomb in what became known as the 'Manhattan Project'. The advent of the nuclear age was marked by the United States being the first country to test a nuclear bomb on 16 July 1945 when it exploded a device in the Alamogordo desert in New Mexico. The sheer destructive force of this explosion shocked everyone, although by that stage the Nazi threat no longer existed as Germany had surrendered. The Second World War was still going on with Japan and to bring about the end of that conflict as quickly

Box 7.1 What makes a powerful state?

Throughout history some states have been more powerful than others. This has been the result of various factors, such as technological innovation and access to raw materials. In Chapter 2 we noted the move away from the great powers of Austria, Russia, Prussia, Britain and France which dominated the nineteenth century to the emergence of superpowers in the twentieth century. At the end of the Second World War Britain was referred to as being one of the 'Big Three' states alongside the Soviet Union and the United States even though Britain was not equal to the other two. When the United Nations was founded, five countries were given the status of permanent members of the Security Council (the United States, the Soviet Union, China, France and Britain) and in so doing conferred the status of a great power on each of the states. These states were equal and while all would in time become nuclear powers, only the United States was a nuclear power in 1945. It is none the less the case that because these five countries are the recognised nuclear powers they do have special influence (Russia has replaced the Soviet Union as the permanent member of the Security Council). However, other factors are also important in determining the influence of states.

Some states, such as China and India, have very large populations and with size comes influence. Other states have great wealth in terms of their resources. The most notable example here is the way in which wealth, influence and status has been conferred on those states that have significant natural resources, in particular oil and gas. This has been mainly evident in the Middle Eastern countries of the Gulf which have accumulated considerable financial wealth (budget surpluses) that has in turn often been invested in other countries through what are often referred to as Sovereign Wealth Funds. In our understanding of the influence of states it is often the case that the majority of people give little thought to the power of these state-owned financial funds. Yet, these funds have considerable power on global financial markets which in many ways gives them more influence than if they were to possess a nuclear weapon.

as possible American President Harry Truman ordered the use of the atomic bomb to force Japan's surrender. Atomic bombs were, therefore, dropped on Hiroshima and Nagasaki on 6 and 9 August 1945 which directly led to the Japanese surrender on 15 August.

Some scholars have suggested that the use of the atomic bomb by the United States was not so much about forcing Japan's surrender as it was about demonstrating to the Soviet Union the military strength that the United States now had. By 1945 the American–Soviet alliance that defeated Nazi Germany was crumbling and a new Cold War was emerging. With the advent of the atomic bomb, a nuclear arms race commenced with the Soviet Union, which in turn obtained a nuclear capability in 1949. This was followed by Britain (1952), France (1960) and China (1964) becoming nuclear powers and to this day they are the five recognised nuclear powers, albeit with Russia replacing the Soviet Union as a result of the latter's dissolution. But the spread of nuclear weapons has not rested with these five countries as there are three illegitimate nuclear powers, namely India, Pakistan and Israel. There are in addition a number of rogue states who have sought to develop nuclear weapons, of which North Korea and Iran are of particular note. We explore this issue in more detail in the concluding chapter.

It has been suggested by some that the very possession of nuclear weapons helps to deter aggression and students could rightly be asked to analyse the role that nuclear weapons have played in helping to maintain peace. This was a point that was made during the Cold War when the capability of the Soviet Union and the United States to destroy each other meant that a bizarre form of stability came about through the possession of nuclear weapons. This was referred to as **Mutual Assured Destruction (MAD)**. Even today, the recognised nuclear powers are unwilling to get rid of all of their weapons, not least because the threat of a conflict in the twenty-first century comes from rogue states and non-state actors such as terrorist organisations. The persistence of such tensions raises an important question: is **Realism** the most appropriate theory of IR?

Strong and weak states

Despite the principle of state sovereignty, it is true that states are not equal. Some are able to exercise great influence while others are relatively weak. Distinctions between strong and weak states are partly influenced by the historical development of the states system and the resources that are available to an individual state. Such resources might include raw materials like oil, as in the case of Saudi Arabia, or the fact that a state has a large population, as in the case of the PRC. Some states possess considerable raw materials and have sizeable populations and yet are not able to exercise influence that is equivalent to these resources. This is particularly apparent in Africa and is a notable concern to global economic and political stability. Although Nigeria is an oil-rich nation with a relatively large population of 140 million people, it is a relatively impoverished state with the vast majority of the nation's wealth being concentrated in the hands of a small political and military elite. The presence of an unrepresentative political system in Nigeria is of particular concern, given that Nigeria is an important oil producer; were Nigeria to experience significant domestic political problems, the potential impact on the global economy would be substantial. This does, of course, show that the impact of unrest within states can vary considerably.

In answering a question on the factors that have contributed to the weakness of many African states, students might point to such issues as political leadership, ethnic and civil rivalries, levels of corruption, natural problems of draught and famine, underdeveloped state infrastructure and poor levels of education. It is a list of factors that was been added to in recent years by the spread of the HIV/AIDS virus which has infected in excess of twenty million people in Africa. Over and above all of these factors, the legacy of **colonialism** is widely acknowledged to have been of particular importance in affecting Africa's development. As we examined in Chapter 3, the process of decolonisation which gathered pace in the post-1945 era often resulted in a swift transfer of power to new states that had no tradition of pluralism with regard to their political institutions, and were from the very outset ill-prepared to act as a parliamentary **democracy**. This often resulted in power in the new state being concentrated in a relatively small group of people who tended to enrich themselves with corruption becoming a normal part of political activity.

Drawing on the theories that we examined in Chapter 6 it is evident that where a student sits theoretically can determine how they view the factors that have impacted on Africa's development. Africa's recent history of conflict and power struggles can, for instance, be analysed from a Realist perspective which emphasises states protecting their own interests. Yet the student of international politics also has to examine the impact that colonialism has had on Africa. While it is true that many African states have been ill-served by poor leadership, these states were themselves ill-prepared for independence. In this sense, there are notable structural factors which have underpinned Africa's weakness. It is a view which is reflected in Marxist thinking and is reinforced by contemporary trading relationships that often exploit **developing countries**. This latter point will be explored in more detail in Chapter 9.

There are other consequences that derive from the lack of correspondence between boundaries of states and nations. The concept of 'weak states' or '**quasi-states**' has been developed by Robert Jackson to help us understand the situation of predominantly post-colonial Third World states which emerged from the hurried process of decolonisation after the Second World War.[8] In these regions of the world, state structures have often been unsuccessfully grafted on to pre-existing tribal and ethnic communities, with the frequent result that individuals will identify more closely with their tribes than with the nation-state. This was a state of affairs that was often encouraged during the Cold War as the superpowers sought to gain influence in the Third World by supporting rival groups, which in turn created a climate of instability, such as in Angola and Mozambique.

These states are, therefore, said to be weak not only because they lack economic resources and military and political power, but also because they suffer from a lack of national cohesion. In Robert Jackson's phrase, many states in Africa are 'quasi-states' that exist more through the international recognition they are accorded in international organisations rather than by virtue of their internal coherence. Hence, the danger that these states will be plunged into civil war, as ethnic groups that have been excluded from positions of power revolt or attempt to secede.

Since the end of the Cold War, with the wealthy states more reluctant to provide resources to other states to maintain them as allies, there have been problems of political instability in a number of countries. In Europe in the 1990s this was most noticeably evident through the break up of Yugoslavia, while today there remain a number of flashpoints on Russia's borders, such as in the case of Chechnya. But it is particularly in the Third World that a number of formerly weak states have collapsed or imploded, resulting in what are generally called '**failed states**'. For Mark Leonard, this is reflective of a broader trend whereby 'the Cold War dichotomy of freedom versus communism has been replaced with a new organising principle: order versus disorder'.[9] Failed states occur where the central state authority dissolves and order breaks down. Without a central state to provide any form of stability and protection, the domestic situation descends into anarchy, with armed groups frequently organised by warlords fighting each other and among themselves and preying on the civilian population. Somalia was the first state to be described as a failed state in the early 1990s and is the most enduring example of this phenomenon. Today it tops the global index as the world's weakest state and over the last seventeen years it has lacked any form of central government (see Box 7.2 and Table 7.1). Somalia also demonstrates the centrality of recognition to states' existence, as even though it has been without a sovereign government for nearly two decades, Somalia still exists as a state, in name if not in reality.

Following 9/11 failed states have been seen as major security threats. This is because they can provide safe havens for terrorist groups to operate beyond the reach of **international law**, while other security threats can emanate from them, such as organised crime. The reality of this threat was emphasised in the 2002 *National Security Strategy of the United States*[10] as well as in the 2003 *European Security Strategy*.[11] In 2008 the US-based Brookings Institution ranked all 141 developing countries against four key criteria of being a state, namely: the provision of security; the maintenance of legitimate political structures; the capacity to develop economic growth; and the ability to meet the basic needs of their population. As we show in Table 7.1, the outcome of this survey was that just under sixty countries were unable to undertake these four key criteria, with the vast majority of the thirty weakest states in the world being located in Africa, with Somalia, Afghanistan and the Democratic Republic of the Congo being regarded as failed states. It is noticeable that many weak states border on other weak states, thereby creating a climate of instability.

In reviewing this section on the role of nation-states we can see that it is a story which is rooted in such concepts as the quest for security, the nature of security dilemmas as evidenced by the arms

Box 7.2 Somalia: a failed state

In 1991, following the cessation of American aid to its Cold War ally, the regime of Colonel Said Barre collapse and Somalia descended into a state of civil war between competing clans leading to a humanitarian crisis. The UN Security Council took an unprecedented step in December 1992 when it passed Resolution No. 794. This was the first time the Security Council had interfered directly in the internal affairs of a state without that state's formal consent. On this occasion that was largely because there was no state to represent Somalia.

UN efforts to restore order in the country quickly failed; with the Clinton administration pulling out its peacekeepers following the death of nineteen US soldiers in the capital city of Mogadishu in 1993 (these events are the subject of the Ridley Scott film *Blackhawk Down*). For most of the time since the collapse of the state in 1991, Somalia's parliament has held its sessions outside the country in the neighbouring states of Djibouti and Kenya.

The absence of a central authority in Somalia and the economic difficulties faced by its population has resulted in many Somali fishermen abandoning their traditional role to become pirates. Because the borders of Somalia are strategically located near the Gulf of Aden which forms the route to the Suez Canal, Somali pirates have in recent years hijacked dozens of ships and demanded a ransom from the ship owners. Such local action, fuelled by the lack of authority in Somalia, has had global implications that have ranged from re-routing of shipping away from the Suez Canal to the deployment of warships to protect the shipping lanes. The latter has seen ships deployed from the United States, the EU and even the PRC.

race, the reality of the balance of power and the presence of conflict between and within states. This is a story of international politics which is akin to the Realist interpretation that emphasises that the primary objective of all states is survival. Yet, it is an approach to international politics which does not reflect other centres of power in the form of non-state actors.

Sovereign statehood: conformity and diversity

As we have seen above, through the process of decolonisation from the late 1940s onward, the sovereign nation-state has become the

Rank	Country	Rank	Country
	Table 7.1 The world's thirty weakest states[12]		
1.	Somalia	16.	Chad
2.	Afghanistan	17.	Burma
3.	Democratic Republic of the Congo	18.	Guinea-Bissau
4.	Iraq	19.	Ethiopia
5.	Burundi	20.	Republic of Congo
6.	Sudan	21.	Niger
7.	Central African Republic	22.	Nepal
8.	Zimbabwe	23.	Guinea
9.	Liberia	24.	Rwanda
10.	Côte D'Ivore	25.	Equatorial Guinea
11.	Angola	26.	Togo
12.	Haiti	27.	Uganda
13.	Sierra Leone	28.	Nigeria
14.	Eritrea	29.	Cameroon
15.	North Korea	30.	Yemen

predominant form of organisation of political community in the international system, while other forms of organisation, such as empire, have been robbed of the legitimacy they once possessed. However, within this conformity to the norm of sovereign statehood there exists a great deal of diversity. Even though states are formally equal (for example, all 192 members of the UN have only one vote each in the General Assembly), in many other respects states are anything but equal.

In terms of the size of their territories, states range from Russia, the largest state in the international system at 6.59 million square miles, to a **microstate** such as Singapore, which covers only 240 square miles and in many ways resembles the city-states of ancient

Table 7.2 The world's top ten economies in 2007[13]

Rank	Country	GDP in US$ trillions
1.	United States	13.8
2.	Japan	4.4
3.	Germany	3.3
4.	China	3.3
5.	United Kingdom	2.7
6.	France	2.6
7.	Italy	2.1
8.	California	1.8
9.	Spain	1.4
10.	Canada	1.3

Greece or Renaissance Italy. In terms of population, the PRC is at one end of the spectrum with over 1.3 billion people, with states such as the Gambia toward the other end with just over a million citizens. In this regard, it is interesting to note that just two states – the PRC and India – together make up over one-third of the world's population. There are also great disparities in terms of wealth, with **Gross Domestic Product (GDP)** per capita varying between $100,000 for the average citizen of Luxembourg and $100 for the average citizen of Burundi. Traditionally distinctions have been drawn between states in terms of their relative power, with states ranked as **great powers**, medium powers and small powers.

A further point to note is that wealth is not always evenly distributed within a nation-state. In Britain the wealth that is generated from the City of London is approximately equivalent to 10 per cent of the total wealth of Britain. As we show in Table 7.2, the situation in the United States is even more stark in the case of California, which being home to 'Silicon Valley' and huge companies such as Microsoft, has an economic wealth that would rank it independently as the eighth wealthiest economy in the world.

The state and globalisation

To many analysts, the processes of globalisation spell the end of the sovereign nation-state, a point that we explore in more detail in Chapter 9. Indeed, Susan Strange went so far as to describe the contemporary state system as the 'Westfailure system', with the integration of the world economy, transnational environmental problems such as acid rain and global warming, increasing migration flows and the promotion of international **human rights** as examples of processes which are eroding state borders and reducing their ability to manage successfully what happens on their territory.[14] As we show in Box 7.3, one of the aspects of globalisation that seems to spell the death of sovereign control of territory is the World Wide Web.

A neat example of states' loss of control over their economic destiny in an age of economic interdependence is the U-turn imposed on President Mitterrand's attempt to implement his socialist economic agenda in the early 1980s (see Box 7.4). The increasing globalisation of the world economy since the end of the Cold War has

Box 7.3 Sovereignty in the Internet age

One of the aspects of globalisation that seems to spell the death of sovereign control of territory is the World Wide Web. Even though states retain legal authority over their land, when it comes to attempts to control information, the ability to meaningfully maintain this capacity is severely eroded by the Internet, which allows information to cross state borders with great ease.

However, there are counter-examples where states less concerned with liberal freedoms of information have attempted to assert their sovereign authority over even the Internet. For example, the PRC developed 'the Great Firewall of China' in order to block access to Google until the company kowtowed and revised the Chinese version of its search engine to find websites that provided sympathetic accounts of former leaders such as Deng Xiaoping. Similarly, Iran has banned fast broadband access to make it more difficult for Iranians to access online materials of opposition movements. Authoritarian states, it seems, have fewer qualms about controlling the information available online in their countries.

led to claims that we now live in a 'borderless world'. According to this view, states are engaged in a 'race to the bottom' as social welfare provisions and economic regulations are slashed in order to attract highly mobile investment capital. While this view certainly accords with the emphasis on flexible labour markets and the reduction of state involvement in the economy in British and American politics in recent decades, critics point to the fact that European states such as Denmark and Belgium have been able to maintain their levels of social welfare spending without losing inward flows of foreign

---

Box 7.4 Sovereignty at bay? Mitterrand's 'break with capitalism' and U-turn, 1981–2

A powerful illustration of the inability of states to conduct domestic policy as they choose, without regard to international conditions and the constraints imposed by both economic interdependence between states and transnational economic forces, is provided by the first two years of the Mitterrand administration in France in the early 1980s.

François Mitterrand was elected on a socialist platform to 'break with capitalism' in the presidential elections of 1981. Immediately on assuming office he began to implement far-reaching reforms, including significant increases in the minimum wage and state pensions, along with a wide-ranging programme of nationalisation – even the 132 largest banks in France were bought by the state and brought under state control.

However, far from stimulating growth and reducing unemployment in the French economy as had been his intention, Mitterrand's reforms led to the flight of capital investment out of the country and a severely worsened balance of payments deficit as lower-paid workers and pensioners spent their additional income on goods manufactured abroad. Mitterrand quickly admitted defeat and reversed his socialist policies, adopting instead neoliberal economic policies not dissimilar to those of Margaret Thatcher's Conservative government across the English Channel.

This case study demonstrates that even in the early 1980s, more than a decade before globalisation became a buzzword, the economic policies of developed states were seriously constrained by economic interdependence. As global capital and financial markets have become increasingly more integrated since the early 1990s, these constraints have become ever more binding.

direct investment. Seen in this light, arguments about the necessity of rolling back state intervention in the economy and society in an age of globalisation are a means of disciplining labour movements and the economy more generally, rather than an imperative imposed from outside. For some, the idea of the powerless state is a myth.[15]

It should be recognised that this is not just a case of developments in the international system transforming the state, as these changes at the international level are as much a consequence of a change in the nature of the developed states. The twentieth century witnessed significant developments in the administrative scope of states and their ability to intervene in their societies. This development is usually characterised as a shift from the classical liberal conception of the 'security' or 'night-watchman state', which had the sole function of maintaining the security of state borders and domestic order, to the welfare state, which plays a much more active role in the management of the economy and the education, health and welfare of its citizens. Therefore, it can be argued that the emergence of the welfare state is 'dissolving international politics' as the increasing importance of international negotiations on economic, development, environmental and social matters has made the international system resemble domestic politics to a greater extent than ever before.[16]

Some have gone so far as to argue that these processes have led to the fundamental transformation of the state, at least in the West. Developed states' disinterest in the traditional state concerns of expanding territorial control and their increasing concern with their relative share of the global economy has led to the emergence of concepts such as the 'trading state', 'market state' or 'post-modern state'. This new type of state rejects the traditional Realist agenda of applying military force to meet its national interests in favour of a more open, engaged approach to world politics.

Hand-in-hand with this redefinition of the state have gone attempts to redefine state sovereignty. Rather than thinking of sovereignty in Westphalian terms, as the complete, comprehensive and unrivalled control of territory, new approaches to sovereignty tend to think of it as a resource that states can share, pool or trade to better obtain their objectives or as the ticket that permits access to international negotiations that attempt to deal with transnational and global concerns. This more flexible approach to sovereignty is more

appropriate to a globalised world than the more traditional understanding which views it as analogous to virginity – something that is
either intact or has been lost.

Summary

It appears that states are being pulled in opposite directions. On the
one hand, many states face **subnational** demands for autonomy by
ethnic groups within the state. On the other hand, there are often
pressing issues at the regional or global level demanding co-operation
between states and the integration of their activities. This has led to
descriptions of the 'hollowing out' of the state, as many of the state's
functions are either devolved to subnational, local government or
handed upwards to regional and international organisations. Such
changes have been presented in the context of multi-level governance,
with policies being decided on at different levels of decision-making.
For some this is best viewed in the context of a layered cake model,
ranging from the supranational level at the top to the subnational level
at the bottom, a point that we emphasise in Figure 7.1.

Spain provides a fascinating case of this process with foreign and
defence policy placed largely in the hands of the EU's Common
Foreign and Security Policy (CFSP) and NATO, respectively, monetary policy controlled by the European Central Bank (ECB), border
controls evaporating due to the Schengen agreement between continental EU states, and many policing, taxation, health, education and
social policy powers devolved to the regions within Spain such as the
Basque Country, Navarra and Catalonia. The state in Spain is thus

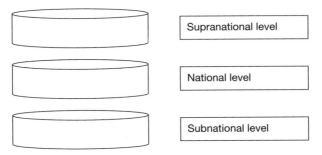

Figure 7.1 Multi-level governance

just one point of authority among others – subnational, international and supranational. It has lost its unique status.

• •

 ## What you should have learnt from reading this chapter

- There are around 200 states in the world and together they form what is known as the international system. The relationships that take place between states are influenced by the relative strength of states and any alliances of which a state is part. This can be viewed in the context of the balance of power.

- Sovereignty is a key concept that relates to nation-states and the notion of state sovereignty was formally expressed in the 1648 Treaty of Westphalia.

- The nation-state is the main form of political organisation in international politics.

- Although states are theoretically independent of each other and each state has national sovereignty, states are not always in full control of their affairs. This is particularly evident with economic issues whereby globalisation has meant that states often have to respond to events and pressures that take place on distant shores.

- Since the end of the Second World War there has been a dramatic increase in the number of nation-states which has had a significant impact on the international system. This has gone hand-in-hand with demands for nationalism and has been noticeable with demands for independence from colonial powers after 1945. After the end of the Cold War and the collapse of the Soviet Union there emerged new nation-states.

- States also have to deal with external pressures, such as globalisation, and in some cases supranational organisations, such as the EU.

- Some states are more powerful than others and power is relative to context that can be influenced by the possession of economic and military resources as well as the geographical location and size of a state. In recent years there has been some focus on the notion of weak and failed states. Failed states occur when there is an absence of central state authority with Somalia being the most notable example.

- IR theories provide important analytical tools to investigate state power and the role that states play in the international system. Realist theories stress the centrality and importance of nation-states, while Liberal theories emphasise that states are part of a broader network of relationships that include non-state actors.

Likely examination questions

To what extent is it still possible to refer to the sovereignty of nation-states?

Does sovereignty matter?

What are failed states?

To what extent is Realism merely just a means of analysing the way in which powerful states are able to get what they want?

'Rather than being a threat to the nation-state, nationalism helps to strengthen it'. Discuss.

How relevant is international relations theory to analysing failed states?

To what extent has globalisation eroded the sovereignty of nation-states?

What is nationalism?

What factors account for the spread of nationalism?

 Helpful websites

S. E. Rice and S. Patrick, *Index of State Weakness in the Developing World*, The Brookings Institution, 2008, at: www.brookings.edu/reports/2008/~/media/Files/rc/reports/2008/02_weak_states_index/02_weak_states_index.pdf

Suggestions for further reading

Overview

H. Bull, *The Anarchical Society: A Study of Order in World Politics* (Macmillan, 1977).

C. Hay, M. Lister and D. Marsh (eds), *The State: Theories and Issues* (Palgrave, 2005).

A. Hurrelmann, S. Liebfried, K. Martens and P. Mayer (eds), *Transforming the Golden-Age Nation State* (Palgrave, 2007).

B. Jessop, *State Power* (Polity, 2007).

J. Mayall, *Nationalism and International Society* (Cambridge University Press, 1990).

M. Van Creveld, *The Rise and Decline of the State* (Cambridge University Press, 1999).

Statehood and sovereignty

S. D. Krasner, *Sovereignty: Organized Hypocrisy* (Princeton University Press, 1999).

R. Jackson, *Sovereignty* (Polity, 2007).

Multi-level governance

I. Bache and M. Flinders (eds), *Multi-level Governance* (Oxford University Press, 2004).

The state and IR theory

J. M. Hobson, *The State and International Relations* (Cambridge University Press, 2000).

Failed and quasi-states

R. Cooper, *The Breaking of Nations: Order and Chaos in the Twenty-First Century* (Atlantic Monthly Press, 2004).

R. Jackson, *Quasi-States: Sovereignty, International Relations and the Third World* (Cambridge University Press, 1991).

Non-State Actors

Contents

Overview

Although states are key actors in world politics it is important to go beyond the state to pay attention to the influence of non-state actors in international politics. This focus beyond the state directly challenges the Realist assumption of international politics as the Liberal view contends that there are a plethora of actors that are all capable of exercising influence. These actors vary in power and size, from important regional organisations such as the EU to global organisations such as the IMF. There are in addition many non-state actors, such as MNCs and NGOs. This group of non-state actors also includes terrorist and religious groups. In this chapter we will explore the activities of two of the most important groups of legitimate non-state actors on the world stage: MNCs and NGOs. Some of these actors will be considered in other chapters of this book. For instance, international organisations such as the UN and terrorist groups will be considered in Chapter 10.

Key issues to be covered in this chapter

The rise of non-state actors in international politics

Theoretical approaches to understanding the role of non-state actors

An understanding of the various types of non-state actors that range from MNCs to IGOs

The way in which the activities of non-state actors impact on nation-states

The sources of influence that allow non-state actors to exert influence in international politics

The rise of non-state actors

As we saw in Chapter 6, one of the key differences between **Realism** and **Liberalism** is the importance they accord to non-state actors. Realists argue that to be an actor on the world stage requires sovereign control of territory, a resident population overseen by a government and control of armed forces to provide security. Consequently, on the Realist account, **non-state actors** can safely be left out of any analysis, as they will not affect the distribution of power in the international system. By contrast, Liberals tend to give a prominent place to non-state actors, as in certain issue areas, such as the environment, non-state actors can play defining roles which determine, or help to determine, outcomes in contemporary world politics.

While it may be the case that the impact of non-state actors in the area of international security is fairly limited – although analyses of so-called 'new wars' recognise the role of non-state actors, such as informal militias, diaspora networks and terrorist organisations as we will see in Chapter 10 – their role can be much more pronounced in issue areas such as the environment, trade and development. Indeed, the UN World Summit on the Information Society, held in Tunis on 16–18 November 2005, marked a watershed in the emergence of non-state actors, as **non-governmental organisations (NGOs)**, **multinational corporations (MNCs)** and other civil society and business groups concerned with the management and use of the World Wide Web were accorded formal equality with states in the Working Group on Internet Governance for the very first time in such a forum.[1] This reflected a general recognition that, when it comes to controlling the Internet, states lack the capacity and the know-how to achieve this alone. Moreover, as is shown in Table 8.1, non-state actors were the major source of representatives at the Tunis summit.

While there are differences of opinion regarding the impact of non-state actors on the conduct of international affairs among the approaches to IR explored in Chapter 6, there is general agreement that the number and size of non-state actors has increased markedly in recent decades. Large business corporations operating in more than one continent and transnational voluntary organisations have

Table 8.1 Number of participants and entities at the UN World Summit on the Information Society, held in Tunis, 16–18 November 2005[2]

Representative	Number of participants	Number of entities represented
States and the EU	5,857	174
International Organisations	1,508	92
NGOs and civil society entities	6,241	606
Business sector entities	4,816	226
Media	979	642
Total	19,401	1,740

existed for centuries. The East India Company was founded in 1600 and was granted a state-licensed monopoly to trade with that particular region of the world, and in the early 1800s the British and Foreign Anti-Slavery Society exerted a great deal of influence over British foreign policy, culminating in the Royal Navy's policing of the ban on the slave trade on the high seas. What is new, however, since the late 1960s in particular, is the sheer number of such organisations in the international system and the networks that have formed between them. In 1948 only forty-one NGOs were given consultative status by the Economic and Social Council (ECOSOC) of the UN. By 1998 their number had increased to over 1,500.[3] The end of the **Cold War** appears to have had a great unleashing effect on the development of NGOs in the international system. Within the first decade following the fall of the Berlin Wall the number of NGOs with pronounced international activities swelled from 6,000 to 26,000, and it is generally recognised that the number of voluntary organisations operating in the world today runs into the millions.

As Box 8.1 demonstrates, non-state actors encompass a wide variety of organisations which play many diverse roles on the world stage and this chapter does not have space to consider all of them in detail. It is common in analyses of non-state actors to make a

Box 8.1 Types and examples of non-state actors

IGOs: International organisations created by states to help them regulate international processes, such as trade, and to deal with global problems, and within which states are the primary or usually the only members. Examples include the UN, the WTO, the IMF, the Commonwealth, the League of Arab States and the EU.

Sub-state government bodies: regional and local government bodies will often establish external relations. For example, even though the US Constitution prohibits individual states from conducting their own foreign policies, state governors travel abroad frequently in order to promote the industries of their states. This is particularly apparent in the case of California which is the richest state in the United States, and if it were an independent country would be eighth richest country in the world. Similarly, London's mayor tours the world promoting London as a global city. Even British city councils often establish connections with counterparts in other EU countries as well as the EU's institutions in Brussels. These are examples of what came to be known, somewhat paradoxically, as local foreign policy. In recent years the interaction between policy development at a local level and globalisation has resulted in the coining of a new term, 'glocalisation'.

MNCs: despite the name, MNCs are generally defined as profit-making companies which have factories or outlets in more than one continent. Examples include car manufacturers such as General Motors, cigarette producers such as Philip Morris and oil companies such as Shell.

NGOs: non-profit making bodies which usually focus their activities in one or two issue areas in an attempt to set or change the agenda of world politics. Examples in the area of human rights include Amnesty International, Global Witness and Human Rights Watch. In the area of environmental issues, Greenpeace is the most high-profile example.

Social movements: protest, workers' and peoples' movements frequently play an important role in world politics. For example, the protests against the 2003 Iraq War demonstrated a significant level of coordination across state borders.

Individuals: cheaper air travel and the Internet have enabled private individuals to play a more significant role in world politics, including celebrities.[4] Examples include Jody Williams, winner of the 1997 Nobel Peace Prize who successfully campaigned for the banning of landmines, and Mother Teresa who, depending on your perspective, was either a force for moral improvement in the world or the wizened cheerleader for conservative dictatorships in Latin America.[5]

Terrorists: also benefiting from less expensive global transportation and communication, terrorist groups and networks have found it increasingly easy to conduct campaigns of violence internationally. Since 9/11 the most noted example is Al-Qaeda.

Transnational organised crime: criminal groups, families, gangs and networks that operate across territorial borders and increasingly between continents. Examples of such activities include people trafficking and the trade in narcotics, which in terms of value is second only to the trade in petroleum.

distinction between legitimate and illegitimate forms of organisation. The former operate within the law (both domestic and **international law**) and are generally recognised as having a right to voice their concerns in international affairs. Legitimate non-state actors include MNCs, NGOs, **intergovernmental organisations (IGOs)**, **subnational** governments and individuals. By contrast, illegitimate non-state actors operate outside or beyond the law and are frequently categorised as threats to state security and world order more generally.

Intergovernmental organisations

One of the most common forms of non-state actors is IGOs. They exist to serve the interests of the member states and are characterised by having formal structures that usually include a secretariat to provide a continuous point of contact. While IGOs started to develop from the late nineteenth century onwards, the great expansion in their number took place after 1945 with their work embracing

Table 8.2 Comparison of IGOs		
	Single purpose	**Multiple purpose**
Universal	• International Atomic Energy Agency (IAEA) • International Labour Organisation (ILO)	• United Nations (UN)
Regional	• North Atlantic Treaty Organisation (NATO) • Australian, New Zealand and US Alliance (ANZUS)	• European Union (EU) • African Union (AU)

such concerns as education, health, the environment, **human rights** and security.

Although there are a plethora of IGOs, their individual remits vary considerably. IGOs such as the African Union have a regional focus that covers a multitude of issues, including security concerns, social cohesion and economic development. Others, like NATO and the Australian, New Zealand and US Alliance (ANZUS), have a regional focus which in both cases relates to security concerns. In a different vein, some have a global focus with a single purpose, such as the WTO and World Health Organisation (WHO), while others have a global focus with multiple purposes like the UN (see Table 8.2). Others have particular ideologies or values, such as the **Non-Aligned Movement (NAM)**, which emerged in the 1950s as a direct response to the threat of superpower domination. The existence of these organisations is reflected in the Liberal approach to international politics which places great emphasis on the emergence of international economic institutions such as the IMF and WTO, regional economic integration in the form of the EU and the North American Free Trade Agreement (NAFTA), and in the creation and growth of the UN.

In looking in more detail at the form of these organisations, it is evident that there are notable distinctions between the commitment and costs that they impose on their members. For instance, while some organisations have a permanent commitment and require a financial contribution, such as the UN, others do not have the same type of permanent structure, such as the NAM. In another way, NATO has the ability to draw on the defence resources of its members and has a commitment in Article 5 of the North Atlantic Treaty that an external attack on any one member is an attack on all members. Finally, the EU has the ability to make laws and take decisions that are binding on its member states.

One of the more interesting features of IGOs is the way in which they provide a forum for multilateral negotiations, whereby it is possible to note the decline of traditional patterns of individual state-to-state negotiations. The very ability of IGOs to operate on a multilateral basis has been assisted by developments in air travel and communication technology which mean that it is relatively easier for negotiations to take place. Yet, even in a globalised world it is noticeable that some states have greater ease of access to where the negotiations take place than others. For example, in the case of the EU it is interesting that the member state with one of the biggest groupings of staff in its permanent representation in Brussels has traditionally been Greece and not one of the largest member states such as France, Germany or Britain. This has been principally because Greece lies further away from the key EU institutions and has less regular flights to Brussels than some other member states.

It is also important to note that it is not only the member states that have an interest in IGO activities. Rather, one of the more fascinating developments has been the way in which other actors such as MNCs, NGOs and non-member states regularly focus their lobbying efforts on IGOs, principally because these organisations have the ability to make decisions that impact at a global level. In some instances, such as the EU, this can result in groups within the member states taking a conscious decision to lobby decision-makers at the EU level rather than their own domestic government, so as to affect change at an EU rather than a domestic level. Within Britain it was, for instance, noticeable during the eighteen-year period of Conservative government from 1979–97 that trades unions sought to promote the importance of social issues at the European level by lobbying the **European Commission** because they were unable to affect change at the domestic level.

Of the various IGOs, the UN, along with its agencies, is the one with a global focus that is the most well known (see Figure 8.1).

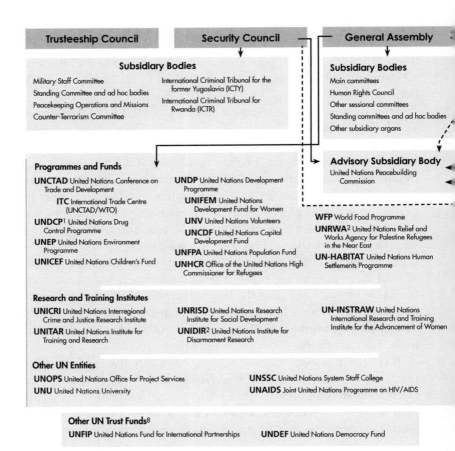

NOTES: Solid lines from a Principal Organ indicate a direct reporting relationship; dashes indicate a non-subsidiary relationship.
1 The UN Drug Control Programme is part of the UN Office on Drugs and Crime.
2 UNRWA and UNIDIR report only to the GA.
3 The United Nations Ethics Office, the United Nations Ombudsman's Office, and the Chief Information Technology Officer report directly to the Secretary-General.
4 In an exceptional arrangement, the Under-Secretary-General for Field Support reports directly to the Under-Secretary-General for Peacekeeping Operations.
5 IAEA reports to the Security Council and the General Assembly (GA).
6 The CTBTO Prep.Com and OPCW report to the GA.
7 Specialized agencies are autonomous organizations working with the UN and each other through the coordinating machinery of the ECOSOC at the intergovernmental level, and through the Chief Executives Board for coordination (CEB) at the inter-secretariat level.
8 UNFIP is an autonomous trust fund operating under the leadership of the United Nations Deputy Secretary-General. UNDEF's advisory board recommends funding proposals for approval by the Secretary-General.

Source: UN Department of Public Information at: http://www.un.org/aboutun/chart_en.pdf.

Figure 8.1 The principal organs of the UN

Economic and Social Council

Functional Commissions

Commissions on:
Narcotic Drugs
Crime Prevention and Criminal Justice
Science and Technology for Development
Sustainable Development
Status of Women
Population and Development
Commission for Social Development
Statistical Commission

Regional Commissions

Economic Commission for Africa (ECA)

Economic Commission for Europe (ECE)

Economic Commission for Latin America and the Caribbean (ECLAC)

Economic and Social Commission for Asia and the Pacific (ESCAP)

Economic and Social Commission for Western Asia (ESCWA)

Other Bodies

Permanent Forum on Indigenous Issues

United Nations Forum on Forests

Sessional and standing committees

Expert, ad hoc and related bodies

Related Organizations

WTO World Trade Organization

IAEA[5] International Atomic Energy Agency

CTBTO Prep.Com[6] PrepCom for the Nuclear-Test-Ban Treaty Organization

OPCW[6] Organization for the Prohibition of Chemical Weapons

International Court of Justice

Specialized Agencies[7]

ILO International Labour Organization

FAO Food and Agriculture Organization of the United Nations

UNESCO United Nations Educational, Scientific and Cultural Organization

WHO World Health Organization

World Bank Group

IBRD International Bank for Reconstruction and Development

IDA International Development Association

IFC International Finance Corporation

MIGA Multilateral Investment Guarantee Agency

ICSID International Centre for Settlement of Investment Disputes

IMF International Monetary Fund

ICAO International Civil Aviation Organization

IMO International Maritime Organization

ITU International Telecommunication Union

UPU Universal Postal Union

WMO World Meteorological Organization

WIPO World Intellectual Property Organization

IFAD International Fund for Agricultural Development

UNIDO United Nations Industrial Development Organization

UNWTO World Tourism Organization

Secretariat

Departments and Offices

OSG[3] Office of the Secretary-General

OIOS Office of Internal Oversight Services

OLA Office of Legal Affairs

DPA Department of Political Affairs

UNODA Office for Disarmament Affairs

DPKO Department of Peacekeeping Operations

DFS[4] Department of Field Support

OCHA Office for the Coordination of Humanitarian Affairs

DESA Department of Economic and Social Affairs

DGACM Department for General Assembly and Conference Management

DPI Department of Public Information

DM Department of Management

UN-OHRLLS Office of the High Representative for the Least Developed Countries, Landlocked Developing Countries and Small Island Developing States

OHCHR Office of the United Nations High Commissioner for Human Rights

UNODC United Nations Office on Drugs and Crime

DSS Department of Safety and Security

ℭℜ𝔒

UNOG UN Office at Geneva

UNOV UN Office at Vienna

UNON UN Office at Nairobi

Published by the United Nations Department of Public Information

DPI/2470—07-49950—December 2007—3M

Box 8.2 The evolution of the UN

The concept of a UN developed during the Second World War and negotiations started in October 1944 at Dumbarton Oaks, a mansion near Washington DC. The main negotiators were the United States, the Soviet Union and Britain, while China was also represented. The end product was agreement on a blueprint of a UN that would consist of a Security Council with permanent and non-permanent members and a General Assembly. The UN Charter was then formally signed in San Francisco on 26 June 1945. From a relatively small group of member states, the UN membership expanded rapidly throughout the 1950s and 1960s as a result of the process of decolonisation. During the Cold War the UN was greatly affected by the power struggle between the superpowers, while the end of the Cold War resulted in the UN being faced with many new challenges, such as state fragmentation, terrorism, HIV/AIDS and questions being raised about the UN's capacity to respond to these challenges.

Negotiations that led to the creation of the UN emerged towards the end of the Second World War, and it formally come into existence on 24 October 1945 (see Box 8.2)

The idea for the UN emerged out of a desire to provide a framework to control aggression between states as well as to establish such principles as national **self-determination**, **sovereignty** and universal human rights. In this context the aim of national self-determination provided a spur towards decolonisation, although at a time of Cold War conflict moves towards the granting of independence to colonies was often set within the context of superpower rivalry. Thus, as we saw in Chapter 3, while the United States was a great champion of national self-determination, it none the less intervened in the Vietnam War to thwart the independence movements that they perceived to be part of the global spread of **communism**. This particular example highlights a broader trend whereby the effectiveness of the UN during the Cold War was often hampered by superpower rivalry. This is a point that we will return to in more detail in Chapter 10, but it is worth noting that to outside observers one of the most frustrating concerns has been the way in which

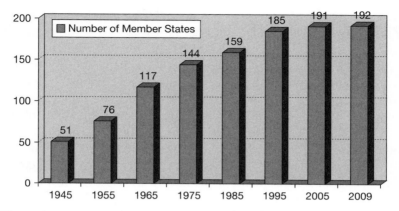

Figure 8.2 Number of UN member states, 1945–2009

IGOs have often failed to live up to the expectations that are laid down in their mandates. For instance, although Article 39 of the UN Charter specifically gives the UN Security Council the responsibility for maintaining international peace and security, this is a task that it has regularly failed to meet.

From an original UN membership of fifty-one nation states, there were by 2009 some 192 members (see Figure 8.2). This expansion in membership reflects the significant changes that have taken place in the second half of the twentieth century, most notably the end of **colonialism** (see Chapter 3). But while the world has itself undergone significant change, the structure of the UN has not been radically altered. As we will examine in more detail in Chapter 10, our analysis of the UN can be viewed in the context of its effectiveness in dealing with the post-Cold War challenges and the way in which it was subject to superpower manipulation during the Cold War. In this sense, while the establishment of the UN recognised the equality of states and helped to create an understanding of international order that was grounded in such notions as respect for human rights and the role of international law, the UN has none the less not been without its critics.

This partly relates to the fact that any state can join the UN. Whereas the EU, ASEAN, NATO and NAFTA all have membership criteria, the UN is home to a range of countries. The failed states of Somalia, Afghanistan and the Democratic Republic of the Congo that we examined in Chapter 7 are all UN members. Similarly, Zimbabwe led by the intolerable regime of Robert Mugabwe is a UN member, so too is Burma and North Korea. The UN is, therefore, an organisation which provides a home to all willing countries irrespective of their records on human rights abuses or attempts to develop weapons of mass destruction. Moreover, each of these member countries is provided with a vote. For some analysts this ability of the UN to include all countries is, of course, one of its strengths, but for others it is one of its principal weaknesses because of the UN's inability to respond effectively to crises in Iran, North Korea and Darfur. This led to the advancement of the idea of the creation of a League of Democracies by Senator John McCain during the 2008 US presidential election campaign. However, the problem with this idea is that it has the potential to divide the world into two blocs of countries as was the case during the Cold War. Moreover, it is also unlikely that a League of Democracies would be able to deal with problems such as the repressive regime in Burma because, as recent examples have shown, it is not an easy process to just march into a country and sort out perceived problems.

If the League of Democracies idea has limited potential, then in what way can the UN be made to be more effective? One area of thought is that the Security Council, which is the key decision-making body of the UN, needs to be reformed. Such a view rests on the fact that the Security Council has the same five permanent members today as it had originally: the United States, Russia (formerly the Soviet Union), China, France and Britain – otherwise known as the P5. These countries are incidentally the five recognised nuclear powers. The Security Council contains an additional ten member states that are rotated among nations on a two-year basis. The permanent members do, however, possess a key influence in that they have a veto power on decisions and as such the non-permanent members are second-class citizens within the Security Council. This state of affairs has led to a discussion about how best to reform the Security Council. One option might be to enlarge the permanent membership to include such countries as Brazil, Germany, Japan and India. This does, however, beg the question whether an enlarged permanent membership would make the Security Council more effective, while the existing P5 countries are less than enthusiastic about seeing their influence diluted. This has led to some people suggesting that the Security Council could be reformed by creating a second category of permanent members who would not have a veto power. But while this would widen the geographical and population representation and therefore tackle a major criticism of the Security Council, it would none the less create three categories of membership (permanent with veto, permanent without veto and rotating members) and in the end might not make the Security Council more effective.

But the UN is about more than just the membership of the Security Council. It is an organisation which covers a multitude of tasks, of which some of the most important include the promotion of human rights and the provision of economic and development assistance. UN agencies such as the WHO and the United Nations International Children's Emergency Fund (UNICEF) seek to tackle specific problems. Much of the work that these agencies undertake highlights the inequalities between nations, with many countries of the world experiencing considerable poverty. The emergence of critical diseases, such as HIV/AIDS, and the concentration of these in **less developed countries (LDCs)** brings further to the fore the challenges that exist in the contemporary world.

The importance of these issues are reflected in the eight UN Millennium Development Goals that world leaders agreed to at the UN Millennium Summit of September 2000 (Box 8.3).[6] While it is noticeable that these challenges are considerably different from the threat of global conflict that dominated world politics during the Cold War, it is, of course, the case that problems of poverty, disease and gender inequality existed during the Cold War as well as for centuries before. Crucially, however, these issues have gained greater prominence on the international stage, helped in part by the decline in ideological tension as well as advances in technology which bring the reality of malnutrition direct to the population in a way that was not evident in previous years. One of the most notable examples of this linkage between technology, globalisation and the desire to combat poverty and malnutrition was the Live Aid concert of 13 July 1985 that was organised to raise funds to tackle the famine that was devastating Ethiopia at that time.

Whereas the UN has near universal membership, some IGOs

Box 8.3 UN Millennium Development Goals

Goal 1   Eradicate extreme hunger and poverty.
Goal 2   Achieve universal primary education.
Goal 3   Promote gender equality and empower women.
Goal 4   Reduce child mortality.
Goal 5   Improve maternal health.
Goal 6   Combat HIV/AIDS, malaria and other diseases.
Goal 7   Ensure environmental sustainability.
Goal 8   Develop a global partnership for development.

are restricted to a specific group of countries. This applies to the EU. The membership of the EU has expanded considerably from an initial six member states to twenty-seven member states by 2008, with this dramatic change being influenced by the end of the Cold War and the collapse of Soviet domination of Eastern Europe. The EU is a different form of IGO because it is a **supranational** organisation. As we will see in more detail in Chapter 11, this means that the member states have agreed to take joint decisions in a number of policy areas and to accept the decisions made by institutions above the nation-state. EU member states have agreed to surrender some national sovereignty to the EU, while EU law has primacy over domestic law. The EU has also obtained the status of an actor in the international political arena, in many instances having the same level of influence as nation-states. This has in turn increasingly focused attention on whether it is possible to categorise the EU in the same way as other IGOs, or whether it is indeed possible to continue to refer to the EU as an IGO at all. A central point of this argument is that the EU can no longer be viewed as an IGO because 'it no longer pursues just – or even primarily – the common interest of the membership but more the common interest of the Union'.[7]

But while an expansion in the membership of the EU has taken place, with more and more policies being dealt with at the EU level, it is nevertheless the case that there have been significant tensions in the EU's history over the extent to which individual member states should surrender their sovereignty to a collective organisation (see

Chapter 11). One might, therefore, ask the question about the extent to which IGOs such as the EU have challenged traditional views of state authority.

Multinational corporations

MNCs are profit-making business enterprises with significant economic activities in more than one country and often in two or more continents. Many individuals tend to view MNCs as having their origins in developed countries and as such when asked to name an MNC will often refer to examples such as General Motors, BP, Coca-Cola, Ford Motor Company, Volkswagen and ExxonMobil. Interestingly, few people in the United Kingdom would probably regard the supermarket chain ASDA as an MNC, and yet as we show below in Table 8.3 it is part of the Wal-Mart group which is the world's largest economic corporation in terms of annual turnover. When looking at MNCs from developing nations it is somewhat to be expected that given the tendency for such countries to have a high proportion of their wealth based in raw materials and extractive industries that many of the examples do not have the same global resonance as say Coca-Cola. Yet, there are plenty of well-known examples of MNCs from former developing countries, but it is often the case that many people do not view these companies in this light. This includes the Hyundai Motor Group and Kia Motors, both of which are based in South Korea. Samsung is another good example of an MNC from a former developing country – and which is incidentally also based in South Korea – and is best known in the United Kingdom for its sponsorship of Chelsea Football Club.

Although these examples show that there are many notable examples of MNCs from former developing countries, we show in Figure 8.3 that it is developed countries that continue to account for the greatest MNC activity, as evidenced by the total foreign direct investment (FDI) flows over the period from 1995–2006. This is further highlighted by the fact that there were only seven MNCs from developing countries in the top 100 largest non-financial MNCs in 2005 (the latest year for which data is available).

MNCs often have political as well as economic objectives. In many instances their financial resources are greater than those of Third

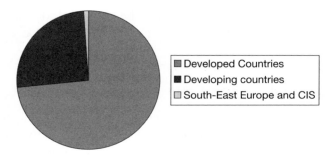

Source: United Nations Conference on Trade and Development, *World Investment Report 2007: Transnational Corporations, Extractive Industries and Development*, New York and Geneva, 2007, at: www.unctad.org/en/docs/wir2007overview_en.pdf.

Figure 8.3 FDI flows, 1995–2006

World countries, and it is not surprising that questions are raised over the degree of their influence. This influence is, however, not just seen within poorer countries where the discrepancy between the wealth of MNCs and the countries concerned is particularly evident. Even in the most developed countries these companies are able to influence the decisions of government. For instance, there can be little doubt that the 2001 decision by American President George W. Bush to abandon the commitment given by the previous Clinton administration to the **Kyoto Protocol** on **climate change** was significantly influenced by companies (particularly the US oil giant ExxonMobil) arguing that adherence to the protocol would have a negative impact on American competitiveness and employment.

Through their global economic activities, MNCs are justifiably seen as one of the main driving forces behind the processes of **globalisation**, although there is a great deal of debate about just how global and just how independent of states such corporations are. For example, Realists tend to interpret the activities of large MNCs, when they pay them any heed at all, as extensions of the economic power of their home states. What is not disputed is the size of many of these corporations – their individual annual turnovers often compare favourably with the national incomes of major developed states. As Table 8.3 demonstrates, only twenty-six of the 192 member states of the UN have a **gross domestic product (GDP)** greater

Table 8.3 The world's sixty largest economic entities

Rank	Country/company	GDP/revenue US$ millions
1.	United States	13,811,200
2.	Japan	4,376,705
3.	Germany	3,297,233
4.	China	3,280,053
5.	United Kingdom	2,727,806
6.	France	2,562,288
7.	Italy	2,107,481
8.	Spain	1,429,226
9.	Canada	1,326,376
10.	Brazil	1,314,170
11.	Russian Federation	1,291,011
12.	India	1,170,968
13.	South Korea	969,795
14.	Mexico	893,364
15.	Australia	821,716
16.	The Netherlands	754,203
17.	Turkey	657,091
18.	Belgium	448,560
19.	Sweden	444,443
20.	Indonesia	432,817
21.	Poland	420,321
22.	Switzerland	415,516
23.	Norway	381,951
24.	Saudi Arabia	381,683
25.	Austria	377,028
26.	Greece	360,031
27.	Wal-Mart Stores	351,139

Table 8.3 (cont.)

Rank	Country/company	GDP/revenue US$ millions
28.	ExxonMobil	347,254
29.	Royal Dutch Shell	318,845
30.	Denmark	308,093
31.	South Africa	277,581
32.	BP	274,316
33.	Iran	270,937
34.	Argentina	262,331
35.	Ireland	254,970
36.	Finland	246,020
37.	Thailand	245,818
38.	Venezuela	228,071
39.	Portugal	220,241
40.	General Motors	207,349
41.	Hong Kong	206,706
42.	Toyota Motors	204,746
43.	Chevron	200,567
44.	DaimlerChrysler	190,191
45.	Malaysia	180,714
46.	ConocoPhillips	172,451
47.	Colombia	171,979
48.	Total	168,357
49.	General Electric	168,307
50.	Czech Republic	168,142
51.	Romania	165,980
52.	Nigeria	165,690
53.	Chile	163,915
54.	Israel	161,822

Table 8.3 (cont.)		
Rank	Country/company	GDP/revenue US$ millions
55.	Singapore	161,347
56.	Ford Motors	160,126
57.	ING Group	158,274
58.	Citigroup	146,777
59.	Philippines	144,129
60.	Pakistan	143,597

This table lists the sixty largest economic entities in terms of GDP and total revenue. Figures are drawn from World Bank figures for GDP and Fortune 500 figures for revenue. (Sources: http://siteresources.worldbank.org/ DATASTATISTICS/Resources/GDP.pdf; http://money.cnn.com/magazines/fortune/ global500/2007/full_list/index.html).

than the annual revenue of Wal-Mart, the corporation conducting the most economic activity. Of course, the size of corporations can be measured in a number of ways. If we compare the GDP of states with the value-added by MNCs rather than their turnover, a less impressive image emerges of forty-three states with larger economies than Wal-Mart.[8] In terms of level of investment around the world, Table 8.4 shows us that General Electric and Vodafone emerge as the largest corporations. Table 8.4 also demonstrates that the world's top twenty-five non-financial MNCs are headquartered in only seven countries, with Hutchinson Whampoa being the only MNC that is from a former developing country. It is, therefore, evident that MNCs based in a small group of developed countries exercise a considerable degree of influence on global economic developments. Whatever measurements one employs, the figures demonstrate why Liberal and Marxist approaches to world politics accord such an important place to the activities of these economic giants.

By virtue of undertaking production and distribution in more than one country, MNCs are often able to avoid or evade states' attempts to tax or control their activities through a variety of means. One-third of all trade in manufactured goods is accounted for by the

Table 8.4 The world's top twenty-five non-financial MNCs, ranked by foreign assets, 2005

Rank	MNC	Home economy	Industry	Total assets (US$ millions)
1.	General Electric	United States	Electrical and electronic equipment	673,342
2.	Vodafone Group	United Kingdom	Telecommunications	220,499
3.	General Motors	United States	Motor vehicles	175,254
4.	BP	United Kingdom	Petroleum	161,914
5.	Shell	United Kingdom / Netherlands	Petroleum	151,324
6.	ExxonMobil	United States	Petroleum	143,860
7.	Toyota	Japan	Motor vehicles	131,676
8.	Ford	United States	Motor vehicles	119,131
9.	Total	France	Petroleum	108,098
10.	Eléctricité de France	France	Electricity, gas and water	91,478
11.	France Télécom	France	Telecommunications	87,186
12.	Volkswagen	Germany	Motor vehicles	82,579
13.	RWE Group	Germany	Electricity, gas and water	82,569
14.	Chevron	United States	Petroleum	81,225
15.	E.ON	Germany	Electricity, gas and water	80,941
16.	Suez	France	Electricity, gas and water	78,400
17.	Deutsche Telekom	Germany	Telecommunications	78,378
18.	Siemens	Germany	Electrical	66,854
19.	Honda	Japan	Motor vehicles	66,682
20.	Hutchinson Whampoa	Hong Kong	Diversified	61,607
21.	Procter & Gamble	United States	Diversified	60,251

Table 8.4 (cont.)

Rank	MNC	Home economy	Industry	Total assets (US$ millions)
22.	Sanofi-Aventis	France	Pharmaceuticals	58,999
23.	ConocoPhilips	United States	Petroleum	55,906
24.	BMW	Germany	Motor vehicles	55,308
25.	Nissan	Japan	Motor vehicles	53,747

Source: United Nations Conference on Trade and Development, World Investment Report 2007: Transnational Corporations, Extractive Industries and Development, New York and Geneva, 2007, at: www.unctad.org/en/docs/wir2007overview_en.pdf.

movement of components of products between subsidiaries of the same companies. This allows MNCs to engage in transfer pricing, that is, the setting of prices of components to exploit lower levels of corporation tax in certain countries.

Because their economic activities are so sizeable, MNCs are frequently in a position to negotiate generous terms with states in which they consider locating, and the latter will view them as an important means of stimulating economic growth and importing advanced technologies. This is often seen as a problem for **developing countries**, where state revenues pale in comparison to the economic resources wielded by the larger MNCs, with additional concerns that MNCs may do deals with corrupt leaders against the general economic interests of the populations of those countries. But this is often an issue for developed countries as well. In the late 1980s Margaret Thatcher was very keen to entice Nissan to set up a car-producing plant in the northeast of England to alleviate the economic depression in that region.

Critics of MNCs argue that their freedom to locate their production and distribution facilities wherever is most profitable enables them to exert a great deal of leverage over states, forcing the latter to make concessions in terms of tax breaks and relaxed health and safety and environmental protection standards. This potential for companies to obtain unfair competitive advantages because of support from national governments led the EU to impose restrictions on the level of support that EU member states can give to companies within their own country. This is known as State Aid Rules and they were introduced by the EU to ensure fair competition across all member states, and as such restrict the ability of governments to support industries that would distort the market and harm business competitiveness.

Non-governmental organisations

NGOs are non-profit making, voluntary organisations which are usually focused on a single issue of concern. Traditionally, a distinction was made between NGOs operating solely at the domestic level, where they frequently lobbied national and local governments, and international NGOs (or INGOs), which played an active role beyond state borders. Examples of 'domestic' NGOs or **interest groups** include the American-Israeli Public Affairs Committee, which lobbies American politicians to support policies and generous aid packages favouring the state of Israel, and the British Medical Association (BMA), which represents the interests of doctors in the United Kingdom. Examples of 'international' NGOs include the European Movement, which aims to develop a pan-European political identity conforming to the borders of the EU; Greenpeace, which is concerned with global environmental issues; and Amnesty International, which monitors and promotes the protection of human rights across the planet.

However, globalisation is rendering the distinction between 'domestic' and 'international' NGOs increasingly redundant, with the BMA and other 'domestic' organisations frequently lobbying on issues that have international consequences and vice versa. For example, in the late 1990s, the BMA called for a moratorium on the testing of genetically modified crops, which had ramifications for American 'life-sciences' MNCs such as Monsanto, and the 2007 annual conference of the University and College Union, which represents the interests of its members among British lecturers in higher and further education institutions, decided that it had something to say on the Israel–Palestine situation.

More recently other distinctions between types of NGOs

have been drawn. Following the categories defined by Amnesty International at the 1995 Beijing UN Conference on Women, analysts frequently distinguish between GRINGOs or GONGOs (government financed or organised NGOs, which critics view as mere extensions of the state and lacking independence), BONGOs (business organised NGOs, which work to present the human face of multinational enterprise) and MANGOs (male controlled NGOs, criticised by feminists). The critics who draw such distinctions are keen to separate those NGOs which they view to have 'sold out' to powerful interests from those which jealously guard their independence. A prime example of the latter is Greenpeace, which will only accept donations from private individuals.

Steve Coogan's comedy TV character, Alan Partridge, dismissed Amnesty International as 'five bitter men with beards'. However NGOs have come a long way from their old image of cardigans and musty charity shops. The non-profit voluntary sector is now the fasting growing sector of employment in Western economies. In the United States, for example, over 7 per cent of the workforce is employed by non-profit organisations, which is greater than the percentage which works in federal and state government offices.[9] And NGO executives are now paid salaries not too dissimilar to those found in large corporations. The voluntary sector, it seems, is now big business. Certainly, NGOs are capable of exerting considerable influence on international politics. As we show in Figure

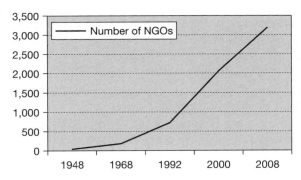

Source: http://www.un.org/esa/coordination/ngo.

Figure 8.4 The growth in the number of NGOs at the UN

8.4, there has been a dramatic growth in the number of NGOs that have consultative status at the UN, with the most significant increase occurring in the post-Cold War era, with 3,184 NGOs represented at the UN by 2008.

NGOs have been particularly prominent in the area of human rights, where organisations such as Amnesty International and World Vision have been vocal campaigners in highlighting the cause of children. As we will see in Chapter 10, one of the grim aspects of globalisation is the way in which a new slavery has emerged, which in the twenty-first century primarily relates to the sale of children and adults to work in the sex industry and/or to work as domestic servants. Thus, while organisations like the UN exist to protect the human rights that are set down in the 1948 Declaration on Human Rights, more than sixty years later slavery continues to exist in the world. As much of this exploitation is at the expense of women, it is notable that a considerable focus has been attached to the rights of women. Indeed, at the 1995 UN World Conference on Women's Rights in Beijing the majority of the 35,000 participants were from NGOs. One of the oldest organisations representing the rights of women is the Women's International League for Peace and Freedom (WILPF). Since its establishment in 1915, the WILPF has played an active role campaigning on behalf of women which has included lobbying governments around the world and monitoring the work of the UN.

In analysing NGOs it is possible to identify three possible positions that they may adopt toward other actors in the international system, although it must be said that their main targets tend to be states, MNCs and IGOs. We can define these positions as 'the three Cs': co-operation; co-option; and confrontation. If they view it as an effective means of advancing their goals, NGOs can co-operate with other actors on a particular issue. For example, from the late 1990s Oxfam and Friends of the Earth have advised the World Bank on the issue of Third World development. However, critics would see such activity as an example of co-option, with the independence of the NGOs in question thrown into doubt. It is possible that the acquiescence of NGOs may be bought through funding and incorporation into the policy process. A large proportion of British and EU aid to the developing world is now administered by NGOs, many of which are funded entirely by government donations, again raising questions about their autonomy. The third possibility is that NGOs will directly confront MNCs and states over issues such as environmental degradation or human rights abuses. In this case the mobilisation of public protest is the main strategy adopted, which has been greatly facilitated in recent years by the Internet and email. For example, the WTO's meeting in December 1999 was subsequently dubbed 'the Battle for Seattle', as protestors clashed with police outside the venue. Of course, these three modes of interaction are not mutually exclusive and we can observe NGOs adopting two approaches simultaneously. For example, at the Gleneagles summit of the G-8 in 2005, Bob Geldof both engaged in talks with heads of state and organised a popular music festival outside the venue to apply pressure on negotiators.

Although NGOs lack the military power of states and frequently do not have the huge economic resources of MNCs at their disposal, they none the less exert a significant impact on the conduct of world politics through the use of media to whip up publicity for their causes. NGOs and other civil society groups often form complex transnational networks to help and support each other and to advance their causes.[10] Contentious issues in world politics are frequently focal points for NGO 'swarms', as likeminded organisations and groups congregate around a certain issue and create such a storm of publicity that states and other organisations come under great pressure to change their policies.[11] While the swarming of NGOs around an issue can often be decisive for outcomes in world politics, it is very difficult to predict which issues will provoke such a response and which will develop with little or no protest activities.

A good example of an NGO swarm is the protests which surrounded the issue of genetically modified (GM) foods in the late 1990s. NGOs from a variety of countries and backgrounds with complementary interests gathered around issues related to the testing of GM crops and the development of various food technologies and the patenting of the DNA of foodstuffs such as basmati rice. NGOs as diverse as Indian farmers' groups, medical associations, European consumer groups and environmental and development NGOs swarmed around this cluster of issues, forcing the EU to halt GM crop testing and to introduce proper labelling on all food packages to indicate whether GM produce is among the ingredients.

In the United Kingdom, supermarket chain Iceland pre-empted legislation by becoming the first retailer to market foods entirely free of GM ingredients. This is a clear instance of NGOs and social movements forcing powerful corporations to change their practices and pressuring states and the EU to reverse their policies. However, this series of events was completely unpredictable, as was evidenced by the sharp decline in the share price of Monsanto and other life-sciences MNCs.

The sources of non-state actors' influence

Although they do not control territory and generally lack their own military forces, non-state actors are often able to exert significant influence on the world's stage. In direct contrast to the Realist position, James Rosenau argues that the influence of non-state actors stems largely from the fact that they are not tied to specific parcels of territory for which they are responsible. Rosenau argues that non-state actors are 'sovereignty free' – that is, they are not tied down in space and time to a particular chunk of land with its resident population, but instead benefit from their freedom of movement and autonomy. Whereas Realists define the absence of sovereign state-hood as disqualifying an actor from importance in world politics, Liberals can find in this supposed lack of sovereignty a source of strength. Non-state actors are free to relocate, as we saw in the case of MNCs above, giving them significant leverage in their dealings with land-bound, immobile states.

Non-state actors can also exert significant influence over states and other entities through their representation of sizeable numbers of people. The membership of some NGOs is greater than that of many of the smaller states in the international system. Amnesty International has 2.2 million members worldwide, Greenpeace has 2.8 million members, and the World Wildlife Fund (WWF) boasts 5 million members – equivalent to the population of Denmark. It is clear, therefore, that sheer numbers adds weight to the voices of these organisations in international affairs. Moreover, members of such organisations also tend to be of above average education and are generally highly engaged citizens, making it difficult for state representatives to ignore their concerns.

Non-state actors also wield a number of resources which enable them to achieve their objectives in world politics. These resources can be broken down into financial, technical and knowledge categories. As we have seen above, MNCs often have annual turnovers larger than many states, but sizeable NGOs can also compete with states and IGOs in this area. For instance, Greenpeace has a very healthy research budget compared with that of the United Nations Environment Programme (UNEP), the body created by states to examine global environmental problems, while the head of the UN Centre for Human Rights observed in 1993 that his centre had less money and resources at his disposal than Amnesty International.

Non-state actors may also have access to new technologies, which enhances their influence in world affairs. For example, MNCs are frequently placed in an advantageous position vis-à-vis developing states by fact that the latter have no other means of access to new technologies. Finally, non-state actors exert a great deal of influence over states and other actors by virtue of their specialist knowledge of specific issue areas. For instance, Amnesty International operates in almost every country in the world and provides an unrivalled account of human rights globally.

From the foregoing information we can see that with their broader concerns, states could not hope to acquire such a body of information and, therefore, they become reliant on non-state actors where the latter possess relevant knowledge. To take another example, in a technical issue area such as the regulation of civil aviation, aircraft manufactures will need to be consulted before any meaningful regulations can be produced by states and IGOs. Groups of scientists working in particular areas, such as the depletion of the ozone layer, are said to form 'epistemic communities' which exert influence over decision-makers purely through their superior knowledge. Therefore, the resources non-state actors possess will give them credibility, influence and access to policy-makers on the world stage.

The ability of non-state actors, especially NGOs, to generate and manipulate publicity is a very important source of influence which should not be overlooked. NGOs have become increasingly media-savvy over recent decades and have exploited the emergence of new communications technologies, such as rolling news broadcasts, satellite television and the Internet, to maximum effect. Box 8.4 outlines

Box 8.4 The power of publicity: the case of Greenpeace and the *Brent Spar* oil platform

In the early to mid-1990s, the question of how best to dispose of Shell UK's redundant *Brent Spar* oil platform became a very controversial issue, not least through the activities of Greenpeace. This episode provides a fascinating and informative case study of the power that NGOs can exert through their use and manipulation of publicity in their interactions and contests with states and MNCs.

When Shell UK considered how best to dispose of the oil platform, it was swayed by the findings of an independent study which concluded the deep-sea disposal of the metal and concrete structure was preferable to dismantling it on shore. The study concluded that sinking the platform was six times safer and four times cheaper than the other option, and would have a minimal impact on the environment. These conclusions were confirmed and supported by the Conservative government of John Major and the Department of Trade and Industry (which granted Shell a disposal licence in May 1995), an independent study conducted by Aberdeen University and Det Norske Veritas in Norway, the signatories to the Oslo Convention on Maritime Environment and the UK scientific community generally.

However, Greenpeace disputed these findings. In April 1995 its activists stormed and occupied the platform, and publicised its actions through its sophisticated media department, which provided film footage to the major news broadcasters. On news programmes on the BBC and ITV, Greenpeace representatives claimed that sinking the platform in the North Sea would set a 'toxic time bomb', as they claimed that the platform contained 5,550 tonnes of oil on board. Through the use of the 'toxic time bomb' sound bite, Greenpeace quickly took the lead in the publicity war and the governments of Britain and Norway found themselves isolated. In Germany, where the environment is generally treated as a more serious issue than in Britain, fifty Shell oil stations were attacked and damaged, with two stations firebombed and one shot at. German Chancellor Helmut Kohl, along with other European leaders, exerted pressure on John Major to resolve the issue in order to end such worrying forms of ecological activism. Consequently, one of the world's most powerful states and one of its wealthiest MNCs backed down and shelved their plans for deep-sea disposal of the platform. In January 1998, following reconstructive work, the platform reopened as part of a roll-on/roll-off car ferry quay in Norway.

> What makes this case especially interesting is that Greenpeace subsequently apologised, admitting that the scientific findings on which the British Government and Shell UK had based their initial disposal plans were in fact correct. This case study demonstrates the pressure that NGOs can bring to bear on states and non-state actors alike, even when their arguments lack credence.

the case study of Greenpeace's campaign against the sinking of the *Brent Spar* oil platform in the early 1990s. Even though the arguments and information it presented were false, Greenpeace was still able to prevail over Shell UK and the British government through its manipulation of the news media.

The enduring importance of states

Despite the impressive record that non-state actors have in shaping contemporary world politics in certain issue areas, we shouldn't jump to the conclusion that the nation-state is in radical decline or is obsolete. As we discussed in Chapter 7, there are certain things that only states can do and certain functions that only they can fulfil.

It is frequently forgotten that the environment within which MNCs and NGOs function and flourish is provided and maintained by states. As practically every square inch of territory in the world is under the sovereign jurisdiction of one state or another, non-state actors rely on states to provide the security and freedom they require in order to operate. In a liberal **democracy** these preconditions for the existence and successful operation of MNCs and NGOs are taken for granted. However, some states jealously guard the sovereign control of their territories and place constraints on the ability of non-state actors to function. For example, the Russian state has imposed restrictions on the operation of human rights NGOs such as Amnesty International and Human Rights Watch, making it virtually impossible for them to operate in the country. The state in Russia has also used its sovereign authority to support powerful economic interests in the country, forcing even powerful MNCs such as BP into making significant concessions. The Chinese state first curtailed the ability of Google to operate in the country and then did a deal with the Internet company, so that truths unpalatable to the Communist regime will not be thrown up by the company's Chinese version of the search engine. In another example, following the cyclone that hit Burma in June 2008, the Burmese regime flexed its sovereign authority by first prohibiting and then severely limiting the attempts of NGOs and aid agencies to reach the afflicted population. In an important sense, non-state actors are parasitic on the liberal freedoms of association, speech and movement that are provided and sustained by the less restrictive states. If every state in the international system was ruled by communist dictatorships, there would be no MNCs or NGOs.

Moreover, only states can provide democratic accountability and representation for entire communities over the whole range of issues. Non-state actors represent exclusive groups of people in one particular issue area. For example, MNCs represent first and foremost the interests of their shareholders, who are concerned primarily with profit margins, and NGOs represent the interests and concerns of their members usually in one particular issue area, such as human rights or the environment. Only states can represent the interests of their whole societies across a wide range of issue areas. In a sense, the ability to focus activity in one area is a luxury that states do not have. Of course, not every state has a democratic form of government and not every state is governed in the best interests of its people; none the less, adequately functioning democratic states provide the only form of organisation in world politics which can be said to meaningfully represent the interests of entire communities and can be held to account through regular elections. By contrast, many NGOs lack the internal transparency and democratic procedures of the most successful democratic states.

Finally, as we saw in Chapter 7, states still retain the legitimate monopoly over the means of violence, despite some moves toward the privatisation of military affairs in contemporary world politics. The international suspicion generated by the operation of mercenary organisations such as Sandline International and Executive Outcomes in Sierra Leone in the late 1990s or the excesses of private military companies (PMCs) such as Blackwater in post-Saddam Iraq, have led many to conclude that only states should possess and use the means of violence in IR, as non-state actors wielding military force often seem to be beyond accountability.

Summary

In reviewing this section on the role of non-state actors we can see that it reflects a Liberal approach to international politics. This is, therefore, a story which highlights the importance of such MNCs as Wal-Mart and General Motors as well as the role of NGOs like Amnesty International. We are also made aware of the extent to which the Liberal approach to international politics emphasises attempts to deal with global issues that include such examples as **global warming** through the Kyoto Protocol. Yet we need to consider the extent to which non-state actors reflect Western values rather than global values. Is it the case that IGOs, like the IMF and World Bank, as well as such notable MNCs as Exxon Mobil are shaping a world that represents their interests? It is an argument that would certainly be made by Marxist theorists who would stress that these non-state actors are in effect creating a new wave of colonialism whereby many Third World countries are being subjugated to rules and norms that are outwith their influence and control.

. . . .

✅ What you should have learnt from reading this chapter

- While nation-states are the principal actors in international relations, other non-state actors have become increasingly influential. The focus beyond the state challenges the Realist view of IR because the Liberal view considers that there are a number of actors that are capable of exerting influence.

- Types of non-state actors include IGOs, sub-state government bodies, MNCs, NGOs, social movements, individuals, as well as terrorists and transnational organised crime networks.

- Non-state actors vary in size and influence. Some focus on a single issue, others focus on multiple issues.

- The UN is the most well known of IGOs that have a global focus.

- MNCs are able to exercise considerable influence as non-state actors.

This can be particularly apparent in less developed countries, where they often have wealth that is greater than the state in which they are operating. Even in developed nations MNCs can exert influence as governments are keen to attract business investment and this can result in MNCs obtaining preferential treatment.

? Likely examination questions

Discuss the influence of the United Nations in the contemporary international system.

To what extent do non-state actors challenge the ability of states to manage international affairs?

Are nation-states or international governmental organisations (IGOs) the most appropriate actors to deal with complex international issues?

To what extent has power been diffused throughout the international system?

What are the sources of influence of non-governmental organisations (NGOs)?

How is Amnesty International able to exercise influence on policies relating to human rights?

Is sovereignty irrelevant to non-state actors?

To what extent are multinational corporations (MNCs) able to exercise greater influence on developing than developed countries?

'States in all but name.' Is this a correct view of MNCs?

What are the differences between Realist and Liberal interpretations of non-state actors?

Helpful websites

United Nations

United Nations at: www.un.org

UN Security Council Reform at: www.globalpolicy.org/security/reform/index.htm

Intergovernmental organisations

International Monetary Fund (IMF) at: www.imf.org/external/index.htm

European Union at: http://europa.eu

African Union at: www.africa-union.org

The Commonwealth at: www.thecommonwealth.org

Association of South East Asian Nations at: www.aseansec.org

World Trade Organisation at: www.wto.org

North Atlantic Treaty Organisation at: www.nato.int

North American Free Trade Agreement at: www.nafta-sec-alena.org/ DefaultSite/index_e.aspx

International Atomic Energy Agency at: www.iaea.org/index.html

Organisation for Security and Cooperation in Europe at: www.osce.org

Non-governmental organisations

Amnesty International at: www.amnesty.org.uk

Greenpeace at: www.greenpeace.org

Oxfam at: www.oxfam.org

Human Rights Watch at: www.hrw.org

Global Witness at: www.globalwitness.org

International Committee of the Red Cross at: www.icrc.org

Women's International League for Peace and Freedom at: www.wilpf.int.ch

International Alert at: www.international-alert.org

World Vision at: www.worldvision.org

Suggestions for further reading

General reading

L. Amoore (ed.), *The Global Resistance Reader* (Routledge, 2005).

C. Archer, *International Organizations*, 3rd edn (Routledge, 2001).

A. F. Cooper, *Celebrity Diplomacy* (Paradigm, 2008).

D. Josselin and W. Wallace (eds), *Non-State Actors in World Politics* (Palgrave, 2001).

M. E. Keck and K. Sikkink, *Activists Beyond Borders: Advocacy Networks in International Politics* (Cornell University Press, 1998).

T. Risse-Kappen (ed.), *Bringing Transnational Relations Back In. Non-State Actors, Domestic Structures and International Institutions* (Cambridge University Press, 1995).

V. Rittberger, B. Zangl and M. Staisch, *International Organization: Polity, Politics and Policies* (Routledge, 2006).

J. N. Rosenau, *People Count: Networked Individuals in Global Politics* (Paradigm, 2008).

P. Willetts, 'Transnational actors and international organisations in global politics', in J. Baylis, S. Smith and P. Owens (eds), *The Globalization of World Politics: An Introduction to International Relations*, 4th edn (Oxford University Press, 2008).

P. Willetts, *Non-Governmental Organizations in World Politics* (Routledge, 2009).

A Globalising World

Contents

Overview

Throughout this book we have highlighted the way in which international relations (IR) is increasingly viewed through the lens of an interconnected world. This is a point that we have explored in Chapters 7 and 8 through our analysis of state and non-state actors. In Chapter 11 we will look at the case of European integration as an example of this interconnection. A common theme in these chapters is one of change. Many of the changes that have impacted on nation-states, non-state actors, regional organisations and individuals have been presented in the context of globalisation. This initially suggests that globalisation is an all-encompassing term that can be used to describe a whole range of developments, such as the retreat of the state, the end of distinct national cultures and the manifestation of an information-based society. However, while globalisation is a term to which many people can relate, it is none the less unlikely that everyone could give a precise definition of what it actually means. This is due in part to the fact that while some individuals view globalisation in a positive light, others view it in a negative way. In this chapter we look at these issues in more detail to find out what is meant by globalisation and to ask the question whether we live in a globalising world?

Key issues to be covered in this chapter

- An appreciation of how globalisation relates to different issues and debates
- An awareness of the way in which globalisation can be positioned as part of an historical process
- Understanding of the issues that are central to debates on globalisation
- The way in which globalisation impacts on economic activity and an understanding of the differences of impact between countries
- The extent to which globalisation challenges the role of nation-states
- Theories that can be used to analyse globalisation

Understanding globalisation

Globalisation has rapidly become a standard reference term in the vocabulary of a majority of individuals. But what exactly does it mean? For many, it refers to the fact that the world has become a smaller and ever more interconnected place: products are sourced from far-flung corners of the globe; capital is electronically exchanged between countries; time and distance have been eroded by the advent of jet air travel; messages can be sent to a friend in another country as easily and quickly as they can to a friend in an adjacent room; companies focus on global rather than national markets; and individual nation-states respond to developments that occur in distant countries.

This suggests that we live in an interconnected world that is blending individual national differences together so that it is hard to identify distinct economic, political and cultural activity (Box 9.1). It also suggests a situation in which our lives are being shaped by events and decisions over which we have little control. Such a view raises important questions about the particular impact of globalisation on nation-states, as well as on individuals, and whether globalisation impacts on all countries in an equal way. In other words, does globalisation lead to a situation whereby there are so-called winners and losers?

Many authors view globalisation in economic terms by highlighting the way in which the world's economies have become interlinked, as evidenced by products being bought and sold across all corners of

---

Box 9.1 What is globalisation?

- An interconnected world.
- Local events are shaped by decisions on the other side of the world.
- Dominance of large companies.
- Technology plays an important role in bringing countries and cultures together.
- Applied to many different issues, such as cultural, economic and political ties.
- Can be viewed in a positive and a negative light.

the globe. For others, it is a story that is understood through the way in which society and culture have become globalised, often revolving around an Americanised point of view. This might, for instance, result in concern being voiced about the way in which the expansion in the use of the English language erodes distinct national languages. At the same time, the spread of Western viewpoints has led some commentators to suggest that for Third World countries contemporary globalisation actually reflects a form of colonisation as Western standards and approaches are imposed upon them. In this sense, globalisation is a new form of imperialism that was previously typical of the nineteenth century (see Chapter 2).[1]

Some academics consider that the best way to understand globalisation is through attempting to predict where it might end. Malcolm Waters has suggested that 'In a globalized world there will be a single society and culture occupying the planet.'[2] This picture of a dramatically changing world was reinforced by the sociologist, Anthony Giddens, when he gave the theme of his 1999 BBC Reith Lectures on globalisation the title 'Runaway World'. For Giddens, this meant that globalisation was not 'just a matter of people adding modern paraphernalia – videos, TVs, personal computers and so forth – to their traditional ways of life'. Instead, he noted that 'We live in a world of transformations, affecting almost every aspect of what we do. For better or worse, we are being propelled into a global order that no one fully understands, but which is making its effects felt upon all of us.'[3] Thus, globalisation refers to a story of global change, with this not just being about the goods that we put into our shopping basket or the way in which companies such as McDonald's restaurants operate in global markets. To this end, globalisation refers to a change in society and the interconnectedness of nations and issues that was not apparent in earlier generations when the world was not treated as a single place, but rather contained distinct arenas of activity.

At first glance a student could, therefore, conclude that globalisation basically means that the world has become a smaller place, that nation-states do not have complete control of their economies and that individual national cultures are increasingly being eroded by external pressures. One assumption that could be drawn from this information is that globalisation is reflective of a giant melting pot whereby national identities, practices and cultures are diluted in a vast bubbling cauldron that produces a homogeneous stew which does not reflect any particular identity.

Such a view would suggest an outcome that did not reflect the dominance of a particular country or group of countries. Yet, the fact of the matter is that globalisation does not affect all countries equally. Indeed, while there has been a significant increase in global GDP in both the developed and developing world, it is none the less evident that not all countries have benefited equally. For instance, at the tenth UNCTAD conference in 2000 the High-level Round Table on Trade and Development was able to conclude that:

> development has been very uneven between countries and within countries. The pattern of development has been such that it has widened the economic gap between the industrialized world and much of the developing world. It has also increased the economic distance between the newly industrializing countries, and the least developed nations. At the same time, economic disparities between regions and between people within countries have registered an increase. In other words, many parts of the world and a significant proportion of its people, have been largely excluded from development.[4]

In Table 9.1 we look at this picture in more detail, and what emerges is a situation of considerable regional disparity between the world's developing economies. For instance, although in an overall context developing countries do not have a significant impact in terms of market share of high-value-added production, such as electronics and manufacturing, it is evident that there is considerable variation between regions: for example, technology accounts for a third of the manufactured exports of East Asia and the Pacific. There are more salient indicators about the way in which life has been changed (or not) by globalisation, with life expectancy being lowest in Sub-Saharan Africa, where a child born in 2006 is only expected to live until the age of fifty, whereas a child in Latin America and the Caribbean could expect to live until seventy-three. Low life expectancy in Sub-Saharan Africa has been particularly influenced by the presence of high HIV/AIDS infection rates, but in overall terms we can see that this is a region that faces particular challenges in terms of having, relatively speaking, the lowest income levels and the highest dependency on aid and consequently means that its ability to meet the Millennium Development Goals that we

Region	Population (millions)	Life expectancy at birth	Gross national income (US$ billions)	Total net aid received (US$ billions)	Paved roads (% of total)	PCs per 100 people	High-tech exports (% of manufactured exports)
East Asia and Pacific	1,899	71	3,525	7.9	11.4	4.1	33
Europe and Central Asia	461	69	2,217	6.2	–	10.2	9
Latin America and Caribbean	556	73	2,261	6.9	24.3	11.3	12
Middle East and North Africa	311	70	779	16.8	70.2	5.6	5
South Asia	1,499	64	1,151	9.3	56.9	1.4	4
Sub-Saharan Africa	782	50	648	40.5	11.9	1.8	–

Table 9.1 Key world development indicators of globalisation, 2006[5]

noted in Chapter 8 are more difficult. We have already discussed in Chapter 3 some of the reasons for the poor levels of development in this region, many of which can be traced back to the effects of colonisation, but it is also evident that this is a region that is in many senses at the mercy of the policies taken by developed nations who have considerable influence over the granting of loans and investment decisions. It is a point which gives further weight to Marxist critiques which stress the way in which the poverty encountered by many countries can be traced back to the policies pursued by rich countries. Indeed, such is the plight of many of these countries that day to day survival for many individuals is increasingly dependent on the money that is sent back home by workers who are employed in foreign countries, thereby demonstrating the relative fragility of their economic base.

It is also evident that some countries are able to exercise a greater influence in a globalised world than others. This particularly applies to the United States, whereby the hard power of American capitalism and the soft power of American culture means that it has a significant impact in shaping a globalising world around its views. So, while the significance of American influence can be traced back to such examples as the post-war settlement whereby the **Marshall Plan** provided financial support to European countries that critics would argue enabled them to purchase American products (see Chapter 3), some authors, such as Peter Gowan, have argued that in the post-Cold War era the United States has deliberately pursued a policy of constructing a global empire.[6]

Inevitably, debates about globalisation are broadly rooted in supportive and opposing camps, whereby some authors consider that globalisation has reduced inequality between nations, while others believe that the gap between nations has widened (Box 9.2).[7] At one end of the spectrum stand the 'globalists', who consider globalisation to be an inevitable process which reduces individual national cultures, politics and economies into an overall global

Box 9.2 Different views of globalisation

- Globalists regard globalisation to be an inevitable process.
- Positive globalists consider that globalisation brings considerable benefits by opening trading links which will improve living standards.
- Pessimistic globalists criticise the disproportionate impact of large companies and question the extent to which globalisation brings equal benefits.
- Sceptics believe that the case for globalisation has been overstated and argue that nation-states are the main forces that shape the global agenda.

network that cannot be controlled through nation-states. Within this 'globalist' camp there is a clear divide between those who regard globalisation as a positive development and those who view it in a negative way. Positive globalists consider globalisation to be a process that is to be welcomed and one which brings benefits in terms of improving living standards and reducing the opportunity for misunderstanding in the world by bringing people together. Advocates of this view have often come from the world of business and stress a neoliberal agenda of free trade and open markets.[8] This positive outlook is not, however, shared by pessimistic globalists. As their name suggests, they are sceptical about the benefits of having a more homogeneous world that limits the chance of diversity and criticise the disproportionate impact that global companies have on the global economy.[9] They also question the extent to which globalisation actually brings real benefits to all. This is because, although globalisation may create benefits for some, this is often in a limited number of countries such as the United States, Japan and Western Europe.

At the opposite end of the spectrum to the globalist position stand the 'sceptics', who doubt the very existence of globalisation.[10] Authors in this camp tend to stress that the increased economic interaction between countries is part of a continuing process of trading that has taken place since previous generations. Advocates of this view, therefore, stress that internationalisation is a more appropriate term than globalisation. This is because much of the increased activity that takes place between countries happens at a regional rather than a global level. Moreover, the MNCs that are supposed to form the bedrock of the global economy often have a tendency to establish policies and procedures that are reflective of their national base rather than a global outlook. The upshot of these points is that a number of authors conclude that nation-states continue to be the dominant actors as they play a key role in taking decisions about the strategic direction of countries, including attempting to improve the competitiveness of their economies. For instance, it has been highlighted that many states have redefined their role by setting out programmes that 'stress investment in human capital and technical skills – to make national economies more competitive – as against the provision of "passive" welfare benefits'.[11]

A recent development?

One of the difficulties of examining globalisation is trying to ascertain the extent to which it is a new development or whether it is an extension of activities that have taken place for centuries. Along with other authors, Jan Aart Scholte has raised the question as to whether globalisation is an 'old or new' process.[12] The 1700s and 1800s were, for instance, years of great exploration and expansion for many countries, symbolised by the creation of the British Empire. Although trade was a particular feature of this period, the settlement of the Americas resulted in the significant migration of populations. The development of interstate relations in this period led Jeremy Benthan to coin the term 'international' in the 1780s to refer to the relations between states.[13] Trade and links between countries did, of course, happen before this period; the East India Company was founded in 1600, while before this time there is plenty of evidence of trading taking place between cultures over a period of hundreds of years.

This state of affairs has led many authors to argue that there is nothing particularly new about globalisation. In this context, they are often able to point out that twenty-first century examples of investment between countries and the migration of people is not really any different to what went on in previous centuries.[14] Indeed, some commentators would go so far as to argue that in relative terms the impact of events in previous years was even greater than that of today. It is certainly the case that from the 1800s onwards there were significant developments that linked countries and peoples together in a way that was different from earlier years. The first global regulatory agency, the International Telegraph Union, was established in 1865, while nearly twenty years later in 1884 the worldwide co-ordination of clocks commenced. Advancements in technology resulted in the first global radio broadcast being made by King George V when he opened the London Naval Conference in 1930, with the speech being relayed to some 242 radio stations in six continents.

Despite these dramatic developments, it was not until the years after 1945 that technological changes brought about profound social transformations. These included the construction of the first digital computer in 1946, the first transoceanic telephone cable link in 1956, the first ICBMs in 1957, the first communications satellite in 1962, the first direct broadcast satellite in 1976 (permitting transmission to rooftop receivers), the creation of the World Wide Web in 1991 and the completion of a fibre-optic cable that stretches around world in 1997. While these developments signify technological advancements, to which globalisation is directly related, technology has also enabled the charting of issues that equally highlight our own vulnerability and point to shared interests that transcend national boundaries.

What we can, therefore, deduce from these points is that although it is possible to adopt a historical approach to trace globalisation prior to 1900, it is nevertheless the case that the changes which have taken place since 1945 have had a direct impact on everyday life in a manner that is not true of previous centuries.

Global issues

In looking at the issues that are of particular relevance to globalisation, it is evident that this is a process that has resulted in a range of issues that transcend borders, such as the linking of culture, politics, economics and the environment. It is a point that is particularly apparent with regard to environmental change, where **global warming** affects all people. This level of interconnectedness was made strikingly apparent by the photograph of the Earth with the moon's surface in the foreground taken by the crew of the Apollo 8 space mission on Christmas Eve 1968 – the iconic picture, named *Earthrise*, demonstrated how vulnerable the biosphere appears from space – while nearly twenty years later in 1987 it became apparent that there was a hole in the ozone layer over Antarctica. This development had a particularly important effect in advancing global awareness of ecological issues, with our awareness of environmental disasters or regional troubles, including famine, being fed instantaneously by a global media. It is also evident that environmental concerns have spurred **pressure groups** like Greenpeace to campaign across the planet irrespective of national boundaries, which has in many instances resulted in conflicts with nation-states. One of the most public examples occurred on 10 July 1985 when a French secret service agent – Jean Michel Bartelo – deliberately sank the

Greenpeace ship, *Rainbow Warrior*, in Auckland, New Zealand to prevent the ship from campaigning against French nuclear testing in the Pacific.

Although environmental concerns have emerged as a common concern for all nations, it is none the less the case that the impact of environmental problems is often more keenly felt in some countries rather than in others. As we noted in Chapter 1, the President of the Maldives took the decision in 2008 to divert a share of the country's tourist revenues to provide the country with the means of buying a new homeland in the future, because the impact of rising sea levels is likely to have a devastating affect on the islands given that most parts of the Maldives are only 1.5 metres above sea level and UN forecasts indicate that sea levels are likely to rise by 59 cm by 2100.[15]

In the case of the environment it is also evident that the desire and capacity to tackle environmental concerns is directly linked to the operation of the global economy. This is because at times of high economic growth there is an inevitably high demand for raw materials, such as oil and copper, to make the goods that consumers demands. In a competitive marketplace the interaction between demand and supply often means that there is not sufficient primary raw materials to go round and as such manufacturers are keen to gain hold of supplies of recycled materials from which they can make their goods, thereby increasing the price that they are willing to pay for recycled materials. However, when the global economy is in recession there is often enough raw materials to go round and this can lead to a collapse in the price that companies are willing to pay for recycled goods. This can, therefore, mean that at times of low economic growth the potential to recycle goods can be lessened.

However, while our example of the environment highlights the existence of common concerns, it is none the less the case that globalisation has not eliminated disputes over trade and the access of products to markets, nor has it rendered obsolete issues of national identity. If anything, **nationalism** has increased in certain areas of the world. During the 1990s this was most evident in the case of the former Yugoslavia where **civil war** resulted in its break up and the subsequent creation of the new countries of Slovenia, Croatia, Serbia, Macedonia, Montenegro and Bosnia-Herzegovina, while Kosovo was recognised as an autonomous province. This notion of national **self-determination** has been particularly evident since the end of the **Cold War**, with the demise of communism which acted as the glue keeping many countries together. In practical terms this has also meant that the removal of Cold War divisions has created the potential for significant population movements which is a feature of a globalised world. An example of this is the way in which the enlargement of the EU in 2004 to include the countries of Central and Eastern Europe resulted in significant numbers of people seeking employment in EU countries such as France, Germany and Britain. For these countries, it has been argued, immigration has created certain economic benefits through having access to cheaper skilled labour, which has also helped to keep domestic inflation under control. At the same time, however, immigration has also created resentment among certain sectors of the 'domestic' population because of concerns about the erosion of national identity and the lack of jobs for local workers.

It is also worth pointing out that not everyone is affected by globalisation in the same way. Issues of race, religion, sex, class and nationality affect the manner in which people live their life and often create a barrier to the other influences that may affect them. There is also evidence that far from creating a homogeneous world, the process of globalisation is increasingly being challenged. Thus, while some may view globalisation in a positive light, others may view it pessimistically as globalisation threatens cultures at a local level. A good example of this is the way in which the spread of Islam can be viewed as a direct response to the way in which globalisation has been viewed as a threat to the erosion of traditional cultures. Other examples include the way in which protest movements and organisations have come together to form what has been termed a global civil society. In this context, groups such Greenpeace, Amnesty International and Oxfam are increasingly viewed as important voices in campaigning against what is often viewed as the neoliberal agenda.

Globalisation of economic activity

One of the most striking developments since 1945 has been the development of a globalised economy. This is a story that relates to the increase in the volume of transactions that take place across national boundaries and the extent to which economic activity in one country is linked to activities in another. As Grieco and Ikenberry have commented:

> Economic globalization refers to the growing integration since World War II of the national economies of most of the advanced industrialized countries of the world and of an increasing number of developing nations, to the degree that we may be witnessing the emergence and operation of a single, worldwide economy.[16]

Such developments have been shaped by the profound technological changes noted above, especially the revolution in information and communications technology. And while these developments signify technological advancements, which globalisation is directly related to, technology has also enabled the charting of issues that equally highlight our own vulnerability and point to shared interests that transcend national boundaries.

On a day to day level globalisation is illustrated by the clothes we wear and the food we eat. In many countries, particularly those in the developing world, these products are primarily sourced and produced at a local and national level. For others, especially in the developed world, these products are increasingly sourced from **developing countries** where the cost of labour is significantly lower. For companies selling products in developed countries the competitive nature of the marketplace means that by producing products in countries where wages are lower ensures that the price of products is kept down.

The context here is that the ability to produce lower cost goods ensures that the consumer is presented with a range of choices, and as consumers tend to choose the lowest price this forces manufacturers to respond to price competition. This interaction between demand and supply is known as the price mechanism and in 1776 the Scottish economist, Adam Smith, referred to the way in which prices are set as a result of this interaction as the 'invisible hand'. For Smith, this interaction took place in a free market, but it is also evident that there are considerable implications from the operation of a free market. In the United Kingdom, for instance, a survey conducted by *The Independent* newspaper in 1999 concluded that half of all the clothes sold in Britain's high street stores were produced in developing countries.[17] Today, the figure is no doubt higher.

Although many of the products we buy are sourced from global markets, we rarely fully consider the consequences of these choices in terms of how they arrive in our shopping basket. A good example here is that buying organic fruit and vegetables is not always the most environmentally friendly option. This is because many organic products are produced in foreign countries, which may mean that local non-organic products are better for the environment than imported organic products. In other words, the process of transportation can in itself directly damage the environment through carbon emissions from planes, ships and trucks.

In looking at the economic issues associated with globalisation, one of the most striking factors is the dominance of large companies. This is an issue that we have already explored in Chapter 8 in relation to the role of MNCs as **non-state actors**, with one of the most striking features being the fact only twenty-six of the 192 member states of the UN have a **gross domestic product (GDP)** greater than the annual revenue of Wal-Mart. Companies such as Wal-Mart, therefore, have immense influence in the global economy and the decisions that they take on where to source and manufacture products have a significant impact on the economies in which they operate. As MNCs are fundamentally concerned with economic competitiveness, investment decisions are inevitably shaped by such issues as labour costs which in practical terms often result in the movement of production to developing countries.

A competitive environment also means that arguments can be made about the benefits to be achieved from economies of scale, and this has resulted in a situation where a relatively few companies can dominate an industry. For Britain, this is highlighted by the importance of such companies as BP and Royal-Dutch Shell in the global petroleum industry despite the fact that Britain's domestic petroleum reserves are relatively small. Moreover, as we saw in Chapter 8, the British mobile telephone company, Vodafone, was by 2005 the second-largest non-financial company in the world. But just as these companies can be viewed as national champions benefiting from globalisation, what is equally striking is the way in which the last thirty years have witnessed the evaporation of a British-owned car manufacturing industry. That is not to say that cars are not manufactured in Britain, it is just that they are manufactured by Ford, Nissan, General Motors, BMW and Toyota.

Some observers would not be overly worried about this situation and, indeed, the foreign-owned companies often bring resources and investment that nationally-based companies cannot provide. This state of affairs does, however, provide us with three lessons that relate to globalisation. The first of these relates to the fact that companies are free to invest in a whole range of countries around the world. Why then should they choose to invest in Britain, for example? The answer partly relates to Britain having a trained and educated labour force, as well as the presence of good infrastructure networks such as roads and railways. But a more telling reason is the incentives that governments often provide to companies to establish bases in their country. Our second point is that in times of economic crisis foreign-owned MNCs are often more willing to protect employment in their home country of operation than their operations in foreign countries. In this sense, they tend to contract their base of operation so as to reduce costs. The third point is that globalisation encourages specialisation because global capital markets basically allocate resources on the most cost-effective basis, which can result in countries often becoming overly reliant on specific industries.

Apart from an ability to determine the distribution of resources, MNCs are also able to exercise significant impact on working practices at a global level, often resulting in the homogenisation of work experiences. This can be a negative process which results in lower wage levels and a move towards short-term contracts that are often wrapped up in arguments over the need for a flexible labour market in developed countries. Such strategies can create gaps between rich and poor in developed countries as established working conditions are eroded. At the same time the wealth accrued from MNC activity tends to go back into the host country which is often another developed nation.

For developed countries with relatively high labour costs this has tended to lead to a restructuring of the labour market. In Britain, one of the most notable features of recent times has been the decline in the importance of the manufacturing sector and the increase in the importance of the service sector, such as banking and insurance.

In broader terms this has resulted in successive governments trying to re-position Britain around the theme of having a 'knowledge economy' because of a belief that the country cannot be competitive in producing products that can be made more cheaply elsewhere. This has manifested itself in the view that Britain's competitive advantage rests in having a highly trained labour force, of which one feature has been the attempt to increase the proportion of school leavers who undertake university-level education.

The practical reality of these changes has been most starkly felt in those communities that had a greater reliance on producing products that could easily be duplicated in other countries with lower wage rates. Relevant examples include the clothing and shoe industry, with the manufacture of these products having largely been relocated from Britain to such countries as China and Vietnam. Although such changes have brought considerable pain to the communities concerned because of the inevitable economic consequences of job losses, some commentators would argue that the outcome is an inevitable one given the ability of firms to produce goods in a global economy that is no longer bound by the ideological divides that were apparent during the Cold War. Developing countries do, of course, welcome the opportunities that are brought about by the relocation of manufacturing production. Yet, this focus on the purely economic aspects of production often overlooks the social and human issues that are bound up in the notion of ethical standards. This is because working conditions in developing countries tend to be less regulated than in developed countries, and as such it is not uncommon to find employees working long hours for low wages and in poor conditions. Such issues led the International Labour Organisation to organise a 'Forum on Decent Work for a Fair Globalisation' in Lisbon from 31 October to 2 November 2007 to address these very points.[18] But while these 'sweatshop' environments can rightly be regarded as the unacceptable face of globalisation, it is also the case that the jobs that the workers have – albeit often with poor employment conditions – can provide important income to families in developing countries and there are often plenty of people willing to do the work.

The reality of sweatshop production environments has in recent times resulted in significant campaigns against companies using such manufacturing facilities. This is part of a broader trend towards ethical standards and fair trade production. In some developed countries, concern about the relocation of manufacturing to developing countries has led to campaigns to purchase domestically produced goods. One of the most prominent examples of this has been the case of American Apparel, which has taken the deliberate decision to manufacture all of its products in the United States, thereby going against the general trend of outsourcing production to foreign countries.

Although the example of American Apparel is a useful one in terms of highlighting domestic concerns about the impact of globalisation, it also raises broader issues about whether it smacks of a return to economic nationalism. This is an issue that has emerged at the top of the political agenda in recent years as a result of the global credit crisis that has arisen because of significant problems in the banking sector, and which resulted in many banks having to either be nationalised or taken over by other banks – albeit with government help – to stop them collapsing under the weight of bad debt. The tightening of credit markets has had a knock-on effect in restricting and in some cases taking away normal lines of credit for businesses that require open credit lines with banks to operate on a day to day basis. With the removal of these credit lines businesses have either ceased to operate or have gone cap in hand to government to secure vital finance. However, to remedy these global problems – which are felt at a domestic level – politicians have been keen to protect domestic jobs by, for instance, trying to instruct banks to lend to domestic rather than to foreign companies.

The problem with strategies that are aimed at protecting domestic industries is that past experience has shown that they have a tendency to lead to a situation of **protectionism**, which in its most stark form is highlighted by the raising of import taxes so as to protect domestically-produced goods from foreign competition. Such a strategy goes against the grain of international economic co-operation and, as countries engage in both imports and exports, the restricting of this activity to appease domestic constituencies rarely helps to ease the economic problems typified by recession and high unemployment. The most pertinent example of this is the fact that the Smoot–Hawley tariff that was passed by the US Congress in 1930 to protect domestic jobs by raising American tariffs actually had the opposite effect, because rather than curing the **Great Depression** it exacerbated it because it did nothing to foster co-operation between nations. We can, therefore, see from this discussion of economic globalisation that we live in an interconnected economy and that the actions of one state have a direct impact on another.

Globalisation and the state

In tandem with the growth of globalisation has been the question over the role of the state. Although the twentieth century was witness to a significant expansion in the activities undertaken by the state with the emergence of the national welfare state, globalisation has had a significant impact in redefining the role of the state. One aspect of these developments is that some scholars argue that individual nation-states are less able to fully determine their own domestic economic policies in the face of external economic and political forces. One of the most prominent academics who have argued that globalisation has resulted in new developments that have challenged the **sovereignty** of the nation-state is Kenichi Ohmae. Writing in *The End of the Nation State*[19] and *The Borderless World*[20] Ohmae has argued that nation-states are less relevant because of the economic and technological changes that have taken place. In *The End of the Nation State* Ohmae has argued that 'On the political map, the boundaries between countries are as clear as ever. But on the competitive map, a map showing the real flows of financial and industrial activity, those boundaries have largely disappeared'.[21] In *The Borderless World* he has written that 'the modern nation-state itself – the architect of the eighteenth and nineteenth centuries – has begun to crumble'.[22]

Despite the relevancy and significance of Ohmae's views in helping us to understand the impact of globalisation, we do not share his view that the nation-state has somehow lost its relevancy. Indeed, as we have argued elsewhere in this book, the nation-state continues to be the key actor in the international system, and, as the global credit crisis has shown, it is the only actor that is fully capable of responding to it. Nevertheless, what is evident is that there has been a marked change in the environment in which states operate as governmental authority has been challenged by, for instance, MNCs. In basic terms, the concept of a state having control over all affairs within a nation no longer holds true. The creation of the EU has meant those member states of that body have further reference to a superior authority; European law has precedence over domestic law, while there has in many instances been a transfer of power from national government to a devolved or local level. This has resulted in the emergence of the term 'local foreign policy' and the use of the term 'glocalisation' to highlight the interaction between the global level and local policy.

It is also evident that globalisation has created particular problems for states that generally based their activities around borders. This is because the contemporary state is not able to control global economic trading, strategic intelligence via satellites (such as photographs) and environmental problems. Individuals also do not just have a loyalty to their state, but instead have feelings that go beyond traditional concepts of state sovereignty. Bonds are often shared with those who have similar beliefs in other countries, including the disabled and lesbian and gay groups.

Despite these developments, however, the contemporary state has not withered away. Indeed, it plays a crucial role in the organisation of world affairs as the spread of global economic activity and the influence of MNCs has necessitated the need for state intervention to regulate these activities.

To take but one example, the very environment that favours an MNC establishing a base in a particular state is influenced by the prevalent conditions set by that government, including tax rates. At a further level, Chinese authorities have controlled the penetration of global news. Within the state there has, however, been further change with an augmentation in the power of sub-state government. This has meant that sub-state authorities have been able to bypass central government and establish networks with other **subnational** authorities in other countries. For instance, most of the states within the United States have a diplomatic mission to the EU as well as other diplomatic missions abroad. The EU has also fostered a climate of regional governance through the Committee of the Regions, whereby representatives of local and regional authorities deal with subjects relevant to the local citizen.

Interpreting globalisation

From the above points it should be apparent that analytical reflections of globalisation draw on the extent to which increased con-
nectivity between nations has impacted on the distinctiveness of
national economies and cultures. In this context, cultural, economic
and political processes are evermore stretched across nation-states,
while at the same time there has emerged a network of infrastructure
at a global level that has resulted in people referring to 'global governance' (Box 9.3). This includes the WTO, UN, World Bank and the
IMF. Such infrastructure plays an important role in regulating global
trade and co-ordinating economic activity across different national
financial markets which are linked together by information and communication technologies. These financial markets operate in a global
context, whereby economic activity chases around the world with the
opening and closing of major economic markets in Tokyo, Frankfurt,
London and New York. Good and bad news spreads instantly and
nation-states are often unable to tame the tide of global economic
developments. For some authors, these developments have severely
challenged the power and authority of nation-states, with Ohmae
noting the emergence of a 'borderless world' where the success and
failure of the global economy is dependent on the rise and fall of
stock markets.[23]

A conclusion that could be drawn from this point is that nation-
states have been usurped as sources of power by a small number
of cities forming the key nodes in global financial networks. At first
glance this might seem a fanciful suggestion, but on closer investigation it is evident that there is actually a degree of truth to this

---

Box 9.3 Actors involved in globalisation

- Nation-states
- IGOs
- NGOs
- MNCs
- Social movements

statement. Our previous discussion on nation-states in Chapter 7 noted the importance of military power, and it is certainly the case that nobody would deny the military might of the world's five recognised nuclear powers, namely the United States, Russia, China, France and Britain. Some observers might conclude that the military strength of these countries means that they are the main powers of the world. Yet the leaders of these same countries often have less control on the economic events that happen within their own countries, albeit with China being a possible exception because of the nature of Communist government. For the other countries it is as if the leaders have two levers of power that they can control: military and economic. For the military lever they are able to issue a command and a direct action follows, whether that be dispatching a ship to patrol the world's oceans or sending humanitarian aid to assist in a natural disaster. In the case of the economic lever their ability to control events is less sure. This is because economic activity within a country is not controlled by government in the same way that military activity is, as national economies are influenced by market traders who make judgments on the value of the wealth of companies as well as the economic policies of a government, with these judgments being reflected in a country's stock market. For instance, a government may cut interest rates to increase economic spending because of a fear of recession, but the stock market may not react positively to this decision because of a belief that a greater interest rate cut is needed – in essence, market traders have judged (or bet) against the government. But while this state of affairs presents us with a view that nation-states are economically impotent, it is often the case that they are the only actors that are able to intervene to make these changes.

Apart from these analytical viewpoints, it is also possible to offer discrete theoretical interpretations of globalisation. Drawing on the theories that we examined in Chapter 6, it is evident that the Realist perspective emphasises that the state is the dominant actor. The importance that **Realism** attaches to state sovereignty means that Realists regard globalisation to be an ambiguous term which does not reflect the reality that the deepening of relations between countries is in reality a process of internationalisation. Realists would, for instance, stress the fact that the main structures that govern developments at an international level are of an intergovernmental nature. Although in recent years this Realist view of the world has gained strength from the fact that states have taken the major role in responding to the global credit crunch, it is none the less the case that it is a view which is challenged by the actuality of globalisation. Thus, while the state might have been the only actor able to intervene in the global credit crunch, the capacity and ability of the state to intervene has often been found to be wanting. Moreover, in the post-1945 era a whole range of institutions have emerged that operate at a global level and which challenge the notion of state sovereignty. The most prominent example of this is the EU. At the same time there is also sign of the emergence of a global civil society that is less rooted in national concerns and which is shaped by issues, such as global warming and **human rights**. As a result it is possible to conclude that despite its value as an analytical tool, the Realist assumption presents an inadequate account of the world in which we live. In essence, the world is more complex than the Realist view considers.

In contrast to the Realist account, **Liberalism** stresses that we live in an interdependent world resulting in the need for the creation of common policies. Thus, whereas the Realist account stresses the importance of securing national interests in an anarchic international system, Liberals emphasise that the growing interdependence of the world economy necessitates the need for states to enter into co-operation with each other and for general policies to be established. In other words, common pressures require common policies. This is a view that gained prominence from the 1970s onwards, being influenced by the writings of such academics as Robert Keohane and Joseph Nye. In their publication, *Power and Interdependence*, they noted that the establishment of common policies went beyond just the influence of nation-states and instead took in a whole range of actors, including MNCs and NGOs. In practical terms this means that for Liberals the state is one actor among others.[24] Moreover, by engaging in agreements with other actors, individual nation-states have to relinquish some of their national sovereignty.

Whereas Realist and Liberal interpretations of globalisation pay attention to the role of state and non-state actors, Marxist analysis focuses on the nature of the global economy and the way in which power is exercised. Marxists are particularly concerned about the

Table 9.2 Current distribution of IMF quota shares[26]

Country/Region	Actual quota share (%)	Nominal quotas
United States	17.1	37,149
EU	32.4	70,404
Asia	11.5	25,010
China	3.7	8,090
India	1.9	4,158
Korea	1.3	2,927
Middle East and Turkey	7.6	16,426
Turkey	0.5	1,191
Latin America	7.6	16,501
Mexico	1.5	3,153
Brazil	1.4	3,036
Africa	5.3	11,498
Canada	2.9	6,369
Russian Federation	2.7	5,945
Switzerland	1.6	3,459
Australia	1.5	3,236
All other countries	9.8	21,317

impact that global competition has on the spread of wealth throughout the world and the way in which power continues to rest in the hands of a small number of states. A particularly good example of this is the distributing of voting rights in the IMF. As we show in Table 9.2, even after the most recent initiatives to even out the distribution of IMF voting rights, it is still the case that the rights favour developed countries of the world over developing countries. Increases in the quotas of developing countries are particularly important because they ensure that these countries have more voting power and, therefore, have a greater voice within the organisation.

This applies just as much to increasing the influence of the PRC, which has only 3.7 per cent of the quota share and yet is the world's most populous country.

The reason for the disproportionate influence of developed countries is that voting rights are broadly reflective of the economic wealth of the country despite reforms to even out the process. This inevitably means that poor countries which have the greatest involvement from the IMF for their social and economic needs have in reality little influence in the IMF decision-making process. For example, Bangladesh, with 153 million people and its position as the world's sixth most populated country, has 0.25 per cent of IMF votes, which is fewer than Ireland which has 0.39 per cent of votes and yet has just four million people. In Africa, Mozambique has a population of just under seventeen million people and has only 0.06 per cent of the votes, while Luxembourg with a population of 400,000 has 0.14 per cent of the votes.[25]

From this information we can see that **Marxism** continues to be of value to IR theorists beyond the end of the Cold War because it is a theoretical tool of analysis which can be used to explain the North–South division that continues to exist in the global economy. Analysis of the economic underdevelopment of Africa can, therefore, be taken from a Marxist viewpoint.

Summary

Globalisation has led to a network of relationships involving companies, states and individuals that has spread beyond traditional state boundaries. A globalised world faces common concerns, including the environment and AIDS. Many of these issues are tackled by such groups as Greenpeace, Amnesty International and Christian Aid. These organisations perceive themselves to be global and not bound by state borders, and have helped to promote an awareness of issues throughout the world. While these points and the growth in power of media organisations challenge the power of the state, that does not mean that the state has withered away. It is true that individuals, like Bill Gates who owns Microsoft, exercise a great deal of influence throughout the world, but they still operate within parameters established by states and institutions set up by states. Nevertheless, there has been a dramatic acceleration in the speed with which issues affect individuals throughout the world. This, in conjunction with the withering of traditional definitions of society relations, such as borders, time and distances, which have been essentially caused by revolutions in technology, have led to an interconnected world where it is not possible to distinguish distinct influences that shape the world in which we live.

Although a whole range of actors are involved in the process of globalisation, including nation-states, international organisations, MNCs, regional organisations and individuals, it is nevertheless the case that the key actors tend to come from the developed countries of the West. In this sense, studies of globalisation need to take into consideration the extent to which it is a process that is driven by the spread of Western values and the fact that it is not an equal process. Thus, while some commentators may argue that globalisation will lead to a more interconnected world and that this will bring about economic transformation, this view does not reflect the fact that there remains considerable disparity of wealth throughout the world. Indeed, the growth in the number of links between nations and the level of issues that transcend boundaries has been a feature primarily applicable to Europe, North America and the Pacific Rim. By contrast, central Asia and Sub-Saharan Africa have been less affected by technological communication, such as electronic mail, and companies that operate in a global environment. In addition to this distinction, globalisation has also tended to affect those who live within cities to a greater extent than rural dwellers. At a basic level, it is easier and cheaper to supply the products (and be supplied by the producers) that go in tandem with globalisation to those who live in a city. The very ability to access the global media requires certain infrastructure, including satellite dishes and cable networks. Thus, while globalisation suggests an interconnected world, in reality it affects some more than others.

. . . .

✔ What you should have learnt from reading this chapter

- Globalisation is a recent phenomenon and impacts all aspects of life, including culture, economics and politics.

- Although globalisation impacts on all countries, some countries are more involved than others.

- Despite the fact that globalisation raises important questions about the nature of state sovereignty, it is nevertheless the case that nation-states remain important.

- Technological advances, such as instantaneous communication, have brought countries and cultures closer together and are directly linked to the globalisation thesis.

- Globalisation can be interpreted from both a positive and pessimistic viewpoint.

Likely examination questions

What are the key aspects of globalisation?

Has state sovereignty been eroded by globalisation?

Is globalisation an unstoppable process?

In what ways can globalisation be viewed differently in a developing country than in a developed country?

To what extent are claims that we live in a globalised world exaggerated?

Is the gap between rich and poor countries the most dangerous issue in contemporary international relations?

In what ways is the global economy structured by developing countries?

To what extent is colonialism responsible for the poverty in developing countries?

What is the significance of the Marxist critique of globalisation?

Is it correct for developing countries to give more priority to economic development than environmental concerns?

Helpful websites

World Trade Organisation at: www.wto.org

International Monetary Fund at: www.imf.org

World Bank at: www.worldbank.org

Third World Network at: www.twnside.org.sg/index.htm

International Labour Organisation at: www.ilo.org

Oxfam at: www.oxfam.org

UNICEF at: www.unicef.org

Fantasy World Order at: www.fantasyworldorder.com

 Suggestions for further reading

J. Bhagwati, *In Defense of Globalization* (Oxford University Press, 2004).

J. Glenn, *Globalization: North–South Perspectives* (Routledge, 2007).

D. Held, A. McGrew, D. Goldblatt and J. Perraton, *Global Transformations* (Polity, 1999).

D. Held and A. McGrew (eds), *Governing Globalization: Power, Authority and Global Governance* (Polity, 2002).

F. J. Lechner and J. Boli (eds), *The Globalization Reader*, 2nd edn (Blackwell, 2004).

J. Ravenhill (ed.), *Global Political Economy* (Oxford University Press, 2004).

J. A. Scholte, *Globalization: A Critical Introduction*, 2nd edn (Palgrave, 2005).

R. Stubbs and G. R. D. Underhill (eds), *Political Economy and the Changing Global Order*, 3rd edn (Oxford University Press, 2005).

R. Wilkinson (ed.), *The Global Governance Reader* (Routledge, 2005).

CHAPTER 10

Order, Justice and Security

Contents

Overview

This chapter explores the related concepts of order, justice and security. In the discipline of IR, as well as in the real world of international politics, each concept is the subject of heated contestation over its scope and definition, and there is also much debate about which concept, or even which interpretation of each concept, should take priority – for example, is security of the state more important than the freedom and security of the individual, and should matters of justice take priority over the stability and orderly functioning of the international system? To complicate matters further, each of the theories we explored in Chapter 6 takes a different approach to these issues. We do not have space to examine each of these approaches, so we will concentrate mainly on how the debate between Realism and Liberalism plays out concerning questions of security, international order and justice. This chapter examines the connections and tensions between these concepts, as well as how the nature of these issues has changed over time.

Key issues to be covered in this chapter

- Theoretical approaches to the study of international security
- The UN and peace and security
- Human rights and international law
- The diversity of security threats that states face
- The maintenance of international order

National security and collective security

As we saw in Chapter 6, of all the theoretical approaches to the study of international politics, the Realist approach is the one most concerned with matters of national security, generally defined as the protection of a state's physical integrity (that is, the absence of major military threats). Due to the condition of international **anarchy** (the absence of a world state), Realists and Neorealists such as Kenneth Waltz have emphasised the 'self-help' nature of the **international system** – with no world government armed with a world military force able to police international politics, each state can rely only on itself to provide for its own defence. John Mearsheimer has described this as 'the 911 problem' (in the United Kingdom this would be rendered as 'the 999 problem'): when your state is under attack, who can you call? There is no entity in the international system analogous to domestic police forces which have the function of arresting wrongdoers and maintaining order. States often form alliances against states which threaten them, but as there is no institution with authority over the members of an alliance, if war breaks out it is possible that some members of an alliance may adopt a 'buck-passing' strategy, keeping out of the conflict while allowing other members of the alliance to risk their soldiers' lives. Even within NATO, the world's most powerful and successful military alliance, the apparent unwillingness of certain states to risk the lives of their military personnel in combating the Taliban insurgency in Afghanistan is a source of some tension between the alliance's member states. Realists stress that each state's guiding star is its **national interest** and a state cannot and should not count on others to come to its rescue when it is not in their national interests to do so.

With each state pursuing its national interest, Realists are very sceptical of the possibility of collective security, which has historically been the aim of many Liberal theorists. Models of collective security seek to modify or replace the anarchical nature of the international system with a form of world government backed with military forces capable of policing the world. Liberals are dissatisfied with the Realists' emphasis on national security, which, as we saw in Chapter 6, frequently results in the **security dilemma**, **arms races** and international instability and war. A collective security organisation providing protection for all states in the international system would solve the problem of international anarchy. As we saw in Chapters 1 and 2, the inter-war period witnessed a failed attempt to establish a collective security system through the League of Nations. The UN Security Council is charged with a similar task, with its main function being to maintain international peace and security according to its charter. In its pursuit of this objective, it is armed with the authority to impose binding economic **sanctions** and to authorise the use of military force. While the UN has not suffered from some of the problems that afflicted the League of Nations, such as powerful states withdrawing from the organisation, its success has none the less been limited due to a number of factors.

The problems with collective security in practice

During the **Cold War**, the **East–West** division of the globe was reproduced in the Security Council, which made agreement between the superpowers and their allies almost impossible to achieve. The five permanent members, but especially the superpowers, used or threatened to use their veto power to kill off any resolution that did not favour their interests or those of their allies with such frequency that the Security Council rarely met (for example, in 1959 the council met only five times). Sir David Hannay, Britain's former Permanent Representative to the UN, has noted for instance that 'For most of the Cold War the permanent members were not a group at all, but were at daggers drawn.'[1] During the Cold War, the veto was used on 240 occasions and the council passed on average less than fifteen resolutions a year: between 1945 and the end of 1989 there were 646 resolutions (see Figure 10.1). Very few of these dealt with problems in a meaningful and authoritative way. Only on the issue of racial discrimination were the communist and liberal-capitalist worlds able to reach agreement – binding sanctions were imposed on the white minority government of Southern Rhodesia which illegally declared independence unilaterally in 1965 and on the apartheid regime in South Africa. Without the ability to resolve any of the other major conflicts in the world during this period, the Security Council instead developed a means of freezing them through the deployment of **peacekeeping** forces.

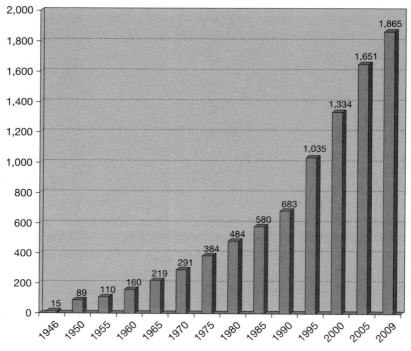

Figure 10.1 UN Security Council resolutions, 1945–2009

Although the first UN peacekeeping mission took place in 1948, when the Security Council instructed UN military observers to be deployed to the Middle East so as to monitor the Armistice Agreement between Israel and its Arab neighbours, the first fully-developed peacekeeping operation took place during the 1956 Suez Crisis. This operation was in response to the Egyptian nationalisation of the Suez Canal (owned by Britain and France), which led the governments in London and Paris to concoct a plan whereby Israel would invade Egypt and in response British and French forces would invade to protect the canal. In response to these developments the UN General Assembly called for a ceasefire and established a UN Emergency Force (UNEF) in November 1956 comprising some 6,000 soldiers from ten countries that was deployed to the Suez Canal to stabilise the region.

Interestingly, the word 'peacekeeping', which has come to be seen as one of the UN's main activities, does not appear in the UN Charter. This led the second UN Secretary-General, Dag Hammarskjöld, to quip that peacekeeping belonged to 'Chapter Six and a Half' of the UN Charter. By this he meant that peacekeeping lay between the traditional approaches to dispute resolution, such as negotiation and mediation provided for in Chapter 6 of the Charter, and the more forceful action listed under Chapter 7 of the Charter. In this context, it is evident that peacekeeping missions comprising lightly-armed military forces, from nations that were almost always neutral with regard to the Cold War, was an improvisation in response to the needs of the time. It is also evident that it was an improvisation that was used only occasionally. As we show in Table 10.1, between 1948 and the end of the Cold War in 1989 there were only eighteen peacekeeping missions out of a total of sixty-three UN peacekeeping operations that had been deployed as of 2008.

The end of the Cold War removed the division in the Security Council and this resulted in a significant expansion in the number of resolutions that were passed. Whereas the first forty-four years of the UN's existence produced 646 resolutions (1945–89), by the end of 1995 the list of resolutions had reached 1,035 (Security Council resolutions are numbered in a sequential order from the establishment of the UN). Thus, in those five years the Security Council adopted over half the number of resolutions (389) it had in the previous forty-five. By 2009 the list of resolutions had reached 1,865.

In the early post-Cold War years it appeared that the UN would function as was originally intended. In response to Saddam Hussein's invasion of Kuwait in August 1990 the Council passed a series of resolutions initially condemning the invasion and then imposing binding economic sanctions on Iraq, culminating in Resolution No. 678, which authorised the use of military force to liberate Kuwait. Following 'Operation Desert Storm' (the American-led coalition's rapid and successful ejection of Iraqi forces from Kuwait), Resolution No. 687 demonstrated that the Security Council could act as a world government when there is agreement – or at least not major disagreement – among the permanent members. This resolution established the terms of the peace and imposed significant restrictions and obligations on the state of Iraq, including the requirement to destroy all chemical, biological and nuclear weapons programmes, to be policed

Table 10.1 List of UN peacekeeping operations[2]

Abbreviation	Full name	Start date	End date
UNTSO	United Nations Truce Supervision Organisation	May 1948	Present
UNMOGIP	United Nations Military Observer Group in India and Pakistan	January 1949	Present
UNEF I	First United Nations Emergency Force	November 1956	June 1967
UNOGIL	United Nations Observation Group in Lebanon	June 1958	December 1958
UNOC	United Nations Operation in the Congo	July 1960	June 1964
UNSF	United Nations Security Force in West New Guinea	October 1962	April 1963
UNYOM	United Nations Yemen Observation Mission	July 1963	September 1964
UNFICYP	United Nations Peacekeeping Force in Cyprus	March 1964	Present
DOMREP	Mission of the Representative of the SG in the Dominican Republic	May 1965	October 1966
UNIPOM	United Nations India–Pakistan Observation Force	October 1973	July 1979
UNDOF	United Nations Disengagement Force	June 1974	Present
UNIFIL	United Nations Interim Force in Lebanon	March 1978	Present

Table 10.1 (*cont.*)

Abbreviation	Full name	Start date	End date
UNGOMAP	United Nations Good Offices Mission in Afghanistan and Pakistan	May 1988	March 1990
UNIIMOG	United Nations Iran–Iraq Military Observer Group	August 1988	February 1991
UNAVEM I	United Nations Angola Verification Mission I	January 1989	June 1991
UNTAG	United Nations Transition Assistance Group	April 1989	March 1990
ONUCA	United Nations Observer Group in Central America	November 1989	January 1992
UNIKOM	United Nations Iraq–Kuwait Observation Mission	April 1991	October 2003
MINURSO	United Nations Mission for the Referendum in Western Sahara	April 1991	Present
UNAVEM II	United Nations Angola Verification Mission II	June 1991	February 1995
ONUSAL	United Nations Observer Mission in El Salvador	July 1991	April 1995
UNAMIC	United Nations Advance Mission in Cambodia	October 1991	March 1992
UNPROFOR	United Nations Protection Force	February 1992	March 1995
UNTAC	United Nations Transitional Authority in Cambodia	March 1992	September 1993

Table 10.1 (*cont.*)

Abbreviation	Full name	Start date	End date
UNOSOM I	United Nations Operation in Somalia I	April 1992	March 1993
ONUMOZ	United Nations Operation in Mozambique	December 1992	December 1994
UNOSOM II	United Nations Operation in Somalia II	March 1993	March 1995
UNOMUR	United Nations Observer Mission Uganda–Rwanda	June 1993	September 1994
UNOMIG	United Nations Observer Mission in Georgia	August 1993	Present
UNOMIL	United Nations Observer Mission in Liberia	September 1993	September 1997
UNMIH	United Nations Mission in Haiti	September 1993	June 1996
UNAMIR	United Nations Assistance Mission for Rwanda	October 1993	March 1996
UNASOG	United Nations Aouzou Strip Observer Group	May 1994	June 1994
UNMOT	United Nations Mission of Observers in Tajikstan	December 1994	May 2000
UNAVEM III	United Nations Angola Verification Mission III	February 1995	June 1997
UNCRO	United Nations Confidence Restoration Operation in Croatia	May 1995	January 1996

Table 10.1 (cont.)

Abbreviation	Full name	Start date	End date
UNPREDEP	United Nations Preventive Deployment Force	March 1995	February 1999
UNMIBH	United Nations Mission in Bosnia and Herzegovina	December 1995	December 2002
UNTAES	United Nations Transitional Administration for Eastern Slavonia, Baranja and Western Sirmium	January 1996	January 1998
UNMOP	United Nations Mission of Observers in Prevlaka	January 1996	December 2002
UNSMIH	United Nations Support Mission in Haiti	July 1996	July 1997
MINUGUA	United Nations Verification Mission in Guatemala	January 1997	May 1997
MONUA	United Nations Observer Mission in Angola	June 1997	February 1999
UNTMIH	United Nations Observer Mission in Haiti	August 1997	November 1997
MINOPUH	UN Civilian Peace Mission in Haiti	December 1997	March 2000
UN Civilian Police Support Group		January 1998	October 1998
MINURCA	United Nations Mission in the Central African Republic	April 1998	February 2000

Table 10.1 (*cont.*)

Abbreviation	Full name	Start date	End date
UNOMSIL	United Nations Observer Mission in Sierra Leone	July 1998	October 1999
UNMIK	United Nations Administration Mission in Kosovo	June 1999	Present
UNAMSIL	United Nations Mission in Sierra Leone	October 1999	December 2005
UNTAET	United Nations Transitional Administration in East Timor	October 1999	May 2002
MONUC	UN Organisation in the Democratic Republic of the Congo	November 1999	Present
UNMEE	United Nations Mission in Ethiopia and Eritrea	July 2000	July 2008
UNMISET	United Nations Mission of Support in East Timor	May 2002	May 2005
UNMIL	United Nations in Liberia	September 2003	Present
UNOCI	United Nations Operation in Cote d'Ivoire	April 2004	Present
MINUSTAH	United Nations Stabilisation Mission in Haiti	June 2004	Present
ONUB	United Nations Operation in Burundi	June 2004	December 2006
UNMIS	United Nations in the Sudan	March 2005	Present

Table 10.1 (cont.)			
Abbreviation	**Full name**	**Start date**	**End date**
UNMIT	United Nations Integrated Mission in the Timor–Leste	August 2006	Present
UNAMID	African Union/United Nations Hybrid Operation in Darfur	July 2007	Present
MINURCAT	United Nations Mission in the Central African Republic and Chad	September 2007	Present

by the UN Special Commission (UNSCOM), missiles with a range of over 150 km were dismantled, the UN Iraq–Kuwait Observation Mission was created to secure the border between the two states and the UN Compensation Commission was set up to hear the claims of over 2.5 million individuals and companies who suffered following Iraq's invasion. One-third of Iraq's oil revenue was paid into a compensation fund to cover these claims. The key point is that all these conditions were imposed on Iraq by the Security Council without Iraq's consent.

The 1990s saw the Security Council assert its authority in a number of other ways. Binding economic sanctions were employed much more frequently (for example, on Libya for not co-operating in the investigation of the blowing up of an American airliner over the Scottish town of Lockerbie in 1988 and on the Taliban regime in Afghanistan for not handing over Osama bin Laden (the leader of **al-Qaeda**) following the terrorist attacks on US embassies in Kenya and Tanzania in 1998). Peacekeeping operations were also deployed much more frequently (between 1990 and 2000 the Security Council authorised over three times as many peacekeeping missions as during the preceding forty-five years), and were substantially beefed up in an attempt to create peace in situations of ongoing conflict ('peace enforcement' rather than peacekeeping). Following

'Operation Provide Comfort', which created 'safe havens' in northern Iraq to protect the Kurds from the vengeance of Saddam Hussein's Republican Guard, the UN authorised the sending of armed forces into a number of other conflict zones including Somalia, Bosnia, Sierra Leone and East Timor. The 1990s also saw the UN establish war crimes tribunals for the former Yugoslavia and Rwanda. With regard to the latter this resulted in the former prime minister and head of the Rwandan government, Jean Kambanda, being sentenced to life imprisonment for crimes against humanity (see Box 10.1).

As Mary Kaldor put it, the 1990s were the decade of 'humanitarian intervention', as military force was used to protect civilian populations from oppressive states, warlords or the ravages of civil war (see Box 10.2).[5] However, following NATO's bombing of Serbia in 1999 to protect the ethnic Albanian population of Kosovo, which was undertaken without a UN mandate, and especially since the American-led invasion of Iraq in 2003, divisions between the permanent members of the Security Council have re-opened and the consensual period of the early 1990s, when there was no use of the veto in a two-and-a-half-year period, seems unlikely to return.

The UN's ability to maintain international peace and security is limited in other ways. Despite a provision in the UN Charter, the UN lacks its own armed forces. When the Security Council authorises a military operation, the UN is dependent on member states providing the military personnel and equipment. As former Secretary General, Kofi Annan, put it, drawing on the analogy at the heart of 'the 911 problem': 'The UN is the only fire brigade in the world which, when the alarm sounds, must first procure a fire engine.' While some of the major powers were willing to provide military personnel and equipment in the above instances, there were also occasions when they were not willing to shoulder this burden, especially when their national interests were not at stake. Most notoriously, in 1994 the Security Council failed to respond adequately to the genocide in Rwanda where 800,000 Tutsi and moderate Hutus were massacred by Hutu militias. Even when UN peacekeepers were deployed there have been problems: they failed to protect civilians (Srebrenica in Bosnia); or they were pulled out after a small number of casualties (Somalia); or they came too late to prevent the worst atrocities (East Timor).

Box 10.1 Rwandan genocide

The case study of Rwanda provides an example of how the world stood by in 1994 and witnessed an act of genocide as some 800,000 people were killed in just 100 days. A student of IR should rightly ask what were the factors that influenced this situation and why nothing was done to stop the killing. Prior to 1994 there had been considerable unrest in Rwanda and neighbouring countries and in October 1993 the UN Security Council deployed a small peacekeeping force of 2,500 soldiers from Belgium, Ghana and Pakistan. The peacekeeping force was called the UN Assistance Mission for Rwanda (UNAMIR) and had the task of implementing a ceasefire between the Hutu Government and Tutsi rebels. However, when the aeroplane carrying the Rwandan Hutu President Juvenal Habyarimana and Burundi President Cyprien Ntaryamira was shot down by a rocket in Tanzania on 6 April 1994 a crisis emerged in Rwanda. In response to the attack the Rwandan presidential guard started hunting down the Hutu and Tutsi opponents of President Habyarimana. This included the Prime Minister, Agathe Uwilingiyimana who was killed on 7 April along with the Belgian peacekeeping troops who had been sent to protect her.

In response to this development and the news that the Hutu Government sought to kill Tutsis, the UNAMIR commander sought approval from the then head of UN peacekeeping, Kofi Annan (and future UN Secretary General), to seize weapons. However, this approval was not provided and UNAMIR troops were instructed not to take any other action without prior authorisation. The net effect of this was that UN peacekeepers basically did nothing as Hutu's went on a rampage killing and raping the minority Tutsi population. Those Tutsis who were able sought refuge in UN camps.

To challenge the Hutu onslaught the Tutsi rebel force of the Rwandan Patriotic Front (RPF) commenced a counter-attack which resulted in mass population movements as the predominant Hutu population left the capital city of Kigali. Faced with the impending crisis the UN Secretary General recommended on 22 April that the Security Council either provide more heavily armed peacekeepers or withdraw all the peacekeepers from Rwanda. The Security Council took the latter decision and left a mere 270 peacekeepers in the country.

With the UN forces withdrawing there was no longer anyone to protect the Tutsis who had been in the UN camps which led to the Hutus killing the thousands in the camps. In July 1994 the capital of

Rwanda had fallen to the Tutsi-backed RPF, resulting in the establishment of a new government being formed by the Tutsi minority. By that stage some 800,000 people had been killed in the genocide, and over one million Hutus had sought refuge in neighbouring countries.

It is evident that the UNAMIR mission (October 1993–March 1996) spectacularly failed to protect against one of the largest acts of genocide since the Second World War. One of the reasons for this outcome was that the disastrous UN intervention in Somalia in 1993 resulted in an unwillingness on the part of the UN and the United States to undertake further inventions. The British Permanent Representative to the UN at the time of the crisis, Sir David Hannay, has written that the Somalia 'disaster instilled a general sense of risk aversion in the Security Council and among the potential pool of troop providers'.[3] Reflecting on the Rwandan crisis, Hannay further commented that 'it does seem to me that what occurred was in fact a massive collective act of failure by the international community and by the policies and institutions which it had established under the Charter of the UN and the Genocide Convention of 1948'.[4]

The UN also confronts a world its founders had not envisaged. The framers of the UN Charter, meeting in San Francisco in 1945, had in the front of their minds the aggression of Germany and Japan that plunged the world into the Second World War. Hence, the Security Council was created to deal with similar states in the future. However, most conflicts in the post-Cold War era have been much more complicated and far messier than clear-cut cases of aggression by one state on another. Of the eighty-two major conflicts in the world between 1989 and 1999, only three were conflicts between states. Therefore, the UN tries to maintain order in a world afflicted by many civil wars. In such cases, it is generally very difficult to attribute blame, as all sides are usually guilty to some extent, and military interventions will be fraught with risks and thus appear unattractive to the major powers.

Behind these specific problems with attempts at collective security, Realists discern a more general cause: the primacy of national over collective interests in the calculations of most states. Although the

Box 10.2   Humanitarian intervention in the 1990s

Humanitarian intervention refers to the use of force by a state, coalition of states or states working under the auspices of an international organisation, in an attempt to prevent systematic and serious abuses of human rights without the consent of the target state (because either it has dissolved or is the main perpetrator of human rights violations). There were instances of humanitarian intervention before the 1990s. During the 1970s, India invaded East Pakistan (which subsequently became Bangladesh) to halt the Pakistani army's attacks on the Bengali population, Vietnam invaded Cambodia to remove the murderous Pol Pot from power and Tanzania invaded Uganda to force the barbarous Idi Amin into exile. However, all of these actions were also motivated by national interests and were almost universally condemned at the time. Humanitarian intervention during the 1990s was a different animal: states usually acted together, often with UN authorisation and the approval of most of the international community, and were guided almost solely by a concern to alleviate human suffering. During the 1990s the following actions were undertaken:

1991	Iraq	Operation Provide Comfort to provide safe havens for the Kurds.
1992	Bosnia	Safe havens and protection for humanitarian aid convoys.
1992	Somalia	Protection for humanitarian convoys.
1994	Rwanda	French-led mission to protect refugees after worst of violence had ended.
1994	Haiti	Elected government restored to power.
1999	Serbia	Bombing by NATO forces to end violence against ethnic Albanians in Kosovo.
1999	East Timor	Intervention to halt violence following referendum on independence.
2000	Sierra Leone	Intervention to combat rebels guilty of crimes against humanity.

Although efforts were made by Prime Minister Tony Blair to present the 2003 invasion of Iraq as a case of humanitarian intervention, it lacked many of the legitimating features of the above operations (that is, UN authorisation or support from most liberal democratic states).

early 1990s was a period of relative consensus – or at least acqui-escence, as China sometimes abstained – among the permanent members of the Security Council, when their national interests collided, agreement proved impossible to achieve. Some hard-line Realists even go so far as to suggest that the UN has made no contri-bution to international security whatsoever, arguing that, for example, the American-led mission to liberate Kuwait would still have taken place without a UN resolution to authorise it. The major powers will act when it is in their interests to do so, with or without the UN (the Iraq War in 2003 and Russia's invasion of Georgia in 2008 are cases in point). For Realists, international organisations are little more than arenas in which power rivalries are played out, but which make little difference to outcomes in international politics other than providing a stage for grandstanding by state leaders. The Realists clearly see the joke in Principal Skinner's chiding remark in the episode of *The Simpsons* in which Bart and Lisa participate in a model UN: 'Do you kids want to be like the real United Nations, or do you just want to squabble and waste time?'

Regional and expanded notions of security

Critics of the Realist approach to security object that it is too narrow. They argue that the range of threats facing states and indi-viduals today is much wider and is often more serious than military threats posed by other states. To some extent this is recognition of regional variations. Attempts to analyse security at the global level inevitably paper over major differences between regions of the world, which have their own unique histories and sources of animosity or friendship between states. For example, Europe has been the most peaceful region in the world since 1945 and the Middle East the most conflict prone region, while in South America interstate war has been infrequent compared with state repression of domestic populations. Barry Buzan devised the concept of a 'regional security complex' in order to capture and analyse these regional differences.[6]

Buzan was also an early advocate of expanding the notion of security to take into account political, economic and social threats that communities might face. Other writers have pushed the expansion of the concept even further, to incorporate health and environmental problems, such as the spread of HIV/AIDS and the increased incidence of skin cancer due to the depletion of the ozone layer. In 1995 the UN Commission on Global Governance published its report *Our Global Neighbourhood*, which stressed that policy-making should be increasingly focused on international concerns, such as the rights of children, women and minorities, the environment and poverty.[7] Shortly after 9/11 former President Bill Clinton went so far as to declare AIDS a greater threat to international peace than **terrorism** and called for a collective response.[8] In the 1950s the Realist John Herz predicted the eclipse of the nation-state in an era of ICBMs armed with nuclear warheads, arguing that states could no longer defend their borders against attacks using such weapons.[9] Herz turned out to be wrong – by acquiring their own nuclear weapons states were able to defend their populations by deterring such attacks – but his argument is stronger when applied to ecological problems. States are not able to defend their borders against airborne pollution or many of the consequences of **global warming**. These broader approaches to security also recognise that far from providing protection from threats, many states are themselves often the greatest threat faced by their domestic populations.

The conceptualisation of security is at its widest by advocates of the **human security** approach – a more recent concept that was first introduced in the United Nations Human Development Report 1994. For these analysts security should refer not to states or communities but to individuals, and should catalogue all of the threats they face, from military forces, whether of their own state or another, to threats to their health, home, culture and economic wellbeing (see Box 10.3). Hence, a human security approach is more concerned with questions of economic development and distribution than military affairs. However, this approach is not without its critics, who question the usefulness of compiling a list of threats and for including factors where there is the absence of any intention to do harm or even an actor from whom the threat issues. The analyses of narrowly conceived security problems achieved by Realist and even Liberal approaches are lost in favour of the description of the myriad threats that individuals might face.

Box 10.3 Human security

The idea of human security emerged from the report of the United Nations Development Programme in 1994. It catalogued seven dimensions of human security:

  economic security
  food security
  health security
  environmental security
  personal security
  community security
  political security

Source: United Nations Human Development Report 1994, at: http://hdr. undp.org/en/reports/global/hdr1994/.

The sources of international order

Traditional notions of security are closely related to those of international order, although there are differences. At the level of definitions, security usually refers to states or communities, whereas international order applies to regional or global levels. The concepts can be mutually reinforcing (for example, a situation in which all states feel secure is conducive to international order), although it is possible to achieve order in situations where states feel insecure, such as the Cold War division of the world which was fairly orderly. In this section, we will examine the main mechanisms through which international order has been achieved.

In Chapter 6 we noted that according to the Realist approach, order is maintained through the **balance of power**, whether this is conceived as a mechanism that works automatically or depends on the art and skill of diplomats. Given the scepticism that Realists harbour towards collective security proposals, the most effective means of maintaining international order is through the creation of alliances that prevent threatening states from dominating the international system. However, some Realists have identified another source of international order in the form of **hegemony**, by which they mean the leadership or dominance of the most powerful state which polices the world on behalf of the other states and thus maintains order. The balance of power and hegemony approaches are quite different: the former is driven by the goal of preventing one state from dominating the international system, whereas the latter is premised on the assumption that such a dominant state exists. This apparent tension is resolved when we apply the concepts to particular historical periods. For example, following the defeat of Carthage, ancient Rome was able to dominate its region without a major rival or alliance attempting to constrain it. Alternatively, during the nineteenth century Britain was able to act as a global hegemon, with the Royal Navy policing the oceans, largely because of its deft management of the balance of power in continental Europe which prevented the emergence of a rival coalition of states. Similarly within the Cold War balance of power the United States was often thought of as the leader of the free world. Indeed, given the problems that the United States has had in creating or maintaining order in the early twenty-first century, it seems that world order may be easier to achieve when hegemony and the balance of power work in tandem.

Although it is often derided as not worth the paper is it written on, **international law** is an increasingly important source of international order. International law has a number of sources, including international customary law (that is, regular practices that states recognise as legally binding) and treaties (whether bilateral or conventions, protocols and treaties produced by international conferences and organisations). The negative opinion of international law stems from the fact that there is no world government to enforce it, meaning that states have to enforce it and they will do this only when they are willing and able (that is, powerful enough) to do so. There are many instances in which international laws have been violated and no states have responded. However, this raises the question as to why state officials and diplomats increasingly spend so much time negotiating and drafting international laws. The fact of the matter is that most states obey international law most of the time, and when they do break it they give reasons for doing so. In short, international law means something to most actors in the international system. As the international system becomes increasingly complex, through the processes of globalisation examined in Chapters 1 and 9, international law is seen as more important than ever in order to clearly define and regulate relations between states across a wide variety of issue areas. Indeed, since the 1960s treaty-based international law has displaced customary forms as the most important source of international law largely as a result of the complexity of the contemporary international system.

As we saw above, Liberal theorists place most importance on the role of international organisations in the maintenance of world order, whether through attempts at collective security or through multilateral **diplomacy** more generally. Forums for negotiations and the rules for state interaction that are embodied in such institutions help to regulate the anarchical international system. Recently the concept of global governance has come into fashion, referring to the networks of states, international organisations, NGOs and MNCs that form around certain issues in contemporary international politics and create and sustain a form of international order in an increasingly complex, globalising, but still formally anarchical world.

Human rights in international politics

Over the last sixty years we have seen an explosion in the number of global and regional treaties and declarations concerning **human rights**. This has gone hand-in-hand with the emergence of NGOs such as Amnesty International which champion human rights. Other bodies, such as Human Rights Watch, have also been established

Respect for human rights is grounded in the UN Charter and the 1948 Universal Declaration of Human Rights which sought to establish the principle of justice in international order. The declaration was drawn up by the Human Rights Commission established after the Second World War and which was chaired by Eleanor Roosevelt, wife of former US President Franklin D. Roosevelt. The appetite for establishing a common declaration on human rights was inevitably shaped by the events of the Second World War, most notably the Nazi holocaust, although it is worth noting that the promotion of a rights agenda also built upon earlier developments. The English Bill of Rights of 1689 included a prohibition on 'cruel and unusual punishment', and a hundred years later in 1789 the people of France overthrew their monarchy and established the first French Republic. Out of the revolution came the 'Declaration of the Rights of Man' which stated that 'men are born free and remain equal in rights'. In 1791 the American 'Bill of Rights' was established. The 1815 Congress of Vienna, while being principally concerned with the establishment of a balance of power in Europe after the defeat of Napoleon, also obliged states to abolish the slave trade. However, despite these earlier developments, the significance of the 1948 Universal Declaration lay in the fact that it was the first time that human rights had been specifically mentioned by name in a declaration.

The thirty articles contained in the Universal Declaration cover a broad range of rights, of which the first two set out the core principles that 'all are born free and equal in dignity and rights' and that 'everyone is entitled to all the rights and freedoms set out'. Much of the content of the declaration focuses on political freedom and in this sense was reflective of the Western dominance of the UN at the time. The voting for the declaration was forty-eight for, none against and eight abstentions. It was not surprising that the abstentions included South Africa where the minority white government denied political rights to the majority black population. The Soviet Union and five Soviet bloc countries abstained on the grounds that they wanted the declaration to be shaped according to the economic, national and social conditions of each country, although in reality at a time of emerging Cold War conflict the Soviet view was inevitably influenced by the declaration being reflective of Western thinking. Finally, Saudi Arabia abstained because it objected to the content of Article 18 which provided for individuals to have the freedom to change and practise the religion of their own choice.

Over the years there has been a deepening and broadening of the notion of rights that has built on the declaration, which was itself not enforceable. In 1948 the Convention on the Prevention and Punishment of the Crime of Genocide was signed and in 1965 agreement was reached on the International Convention on the Elimination of All Forms of Racial Discrimination. In 1966 members of the UN signed the International Covenant on Civil and Political Rights, and the International Covenant on Economic, Social and Cultural Rights. The International Convention on the Elimination of Discrimination Against Women was signed in 1979.

In addition to the global UN agreements, the last sixty years have also seen much activity at a regional level. In 1950 the Council of Europe set out the European Convention on Human Rights and also established the European Court of Human Rights as an enforcing mechanism. These agreements are outside the EU, which negotiated a Charter on Fundamental Rights in the 2000 Treaty of Nice. Countries in Africa have similarly sought to develop the notion of human rights, and in 1981 the Organisation of African Unity (OAU) – subsequently becoming the African Union (AU) – adopted the African Charter on Human and Peoples' Rights (otherwise known as the Banjul Charter).

Throughout the Cold War the West found it convenient to criticise the Soviet Union and Soviet bloc countries on their human rights records. This was a task that was made easier after the signing of the 1975 Helsinki Final Act which established the **Conference on Security and Cooperation in Europe (CSCE)** which attached specific importance to human rights. Yet the West rarely acted on these statements, partly because the power of the Soviet Union made it imprudent to intervene and the fact that the West and countries associated with it were not without blame themselves. For instance, in 1971 the British government removed the indigenous population of the Chagos Islands in the Indian Ocean so as to allow the United States to build a military base on Diego Garcia. In recent years many of the former islanders have fought a legal battle to return to the Chagos Islands, with the UK Labour Government arguing in 2008 that returning the islanders would be a costly operation and that any return would create an unacceptable risk to the US base, the importance of which has increased because of the American intervention in Afghanistan and Iraq as part of the war on terror.

The lesson that can be drawn from the example of the Chagos Islands is that where human rights issues clash with national foreign policy agendas, it is often the case that the latter wins. Indeed, even though the same UK Labour Government noted in 1997 that it would establish an ethical foreign policy and that human rights would be at the heart of its foreign policy, it has been somewhat predictable as well as unfortunate that politics have impacted on the creation of an ethical foreign policy. As has been indicated above, many of these decisions have in recent years been shaped by the so-called war on terror, which has seen many countries in the West undertake policies that violate human rights because such policies are supposedly in the national interest. The United States has, for example, engaged in secret rendition missions where alleged terrorists have been flown, without the permission of the courts, to countries where human rights laws have no force to be interrogated. Many of these suspected terrorists have ended up being detained at the American base on Guantanamo Bay, Cuba which America has used as a detention camp since 2002. This policy has, however, been subject to severe international criticism and eroded the credibility of the foreign policy pursued by US President George W. Bush. It is, therefore, not surprising that in the face of international criticism, that one of the first acts of the new Democrat President, Barack Obama, after being sworn into office on 20 January 2009 was to sign an executive order to close Guantanamo Bay detention camp within a year. For President Obama such a course of action was influenced by a desire to restore credibility to US foreign policy.

Another aspect of human rights abuses is the way in which slavery continues to be practiced some sixty years after the Universal Declaration and nearly 200 years after the Congress of Vienna. While the number of slaves is difficult to quantify exactly, it is estimated that there are in the region of thirty million slaves in the world, of which ten million are estimated to be children. The modern reality of slavery is quite different from the historic image and reflects the fact that the definition of slavery is a situation where an individual is controlled for economic gain. Slavery does, in fact, range from the sale of children and adults to work in the sex industry to the sale of children and adults to undertake other economic work such as domestic servants. It is, in fact, common practice for poor families in the **less developed countries (LDCs)** to sell children for financial reward. Although much slavery takes place at a local level, it is also the case that the modern slave trade has an international dimension with people being trafficked between countries. This form of human trafficking tends to take the form of the movement of people with little education from poor countries to work in developed countries. Some victims leave their own country under false pretences through adverts to undertake work in developed countries, such as the United Kingdom, where they hope to build a better life, but they often end up working in the sex industry as slaves. Since the end of the Cold War and the collapse of East–West divisions there have been significant numbers of trafficked victims coming from former Soviet bloc countries ranging from Latvia to Romania.

The tension between order and justice in international politics

Traditionally the relationship between order and justice in world politics has been fraught with tension. The two objectives are often presented as being mutually exclusive, or at least gains in one cannot be made without a marked deterioration in the other. Traditionally the question of international order has been given priority, because disorder at the international level is often terrible and occasionally is the very worst thing that can happen. The major conflagrations of the two world wars, with all the death and destruction they entailed, are obvious cases in point. From a concern to protect the orderly conduct of international politics, in terms of the absence of system-wide conflict, stable diplomatic relations and the unhindered formation of alliances and balances of power, issues of global justice seem to pose a threat to international order. This tension is neatly encapsulated in the Latin phrase *fiat justitia et pereat mundus*, 'let justice be done and the world perishes', which was first attributed to Cato the Younger but was the favourite motto of Emperor Ferdinand I. This statement is open to two interpretations: moralist, that is, do the morally right thing, even if it results in the destruction of the world; and Realist, that is, highlighting the danger inherent in pursing justice at the international level without at least one eye on the political consequences. The latter approach emphasises the importance of prudence – the careful application of moral principles, paying full attention to the possibility of undermining world order. Hedley Bull, therefore, concluded his renowned study of world order by giving priority to order, because disorder at the international level can be catastrophic and actually undermine all efforts in pursuit of international justice.[10]

To illustrate these arguments, let's take the issue of human rights. Realists frequently emphasise that human rights abuses, by states against their resident populations, are as old as recorded history.

Therefore, it would be naive to believe that human rights can be suddenly and adequately protected by the signing of treaties and attempts to protect such rights. For instance, around seventy states currently practise torture as official state policy. To take on each and every one of these states on this issue through economic sanctions would have a serious impact on international trade, while attempts to coerce these states into changing their ways through threats or actual use of military force would plunge the world into unending war. It took NATO, the most powerful military alliance the world has ever seen, seventy-nine days of bombing to coerce the small state of Serbia into withdrawing its paramilitary forces from the province of Kosovo in 1999, where they were systematically murdering and displacing the majority ethnic Albanian population. To undertake such actions against all states that abuse the human rights of their peoples would result in perpetual global conflict and disorder and would make the situation of most people much worse. Similarly, as we saw in our discussion of Marxist IR theory in Chapter 6, attempts to radically redress the problem of global economic inequality might result in an oppressive world state that would trample on individual freedoms and see widescale persecution – Stalinism at the global level. Realists are, therefore, mindful of the statement that 'the road to hell is paved with good intentions'. To be guided by morality without paying attention to the political consequences is to court global disaster.

There are three elements to this conundrum: state **sovereignty**; political responsibility; and multiculturalism. First, sovereignty, along with the attendant principle of non-intervention in the domestic affairs of states, is the core ordering principle of the international system. Issues of international justice obviously run up against this principle. Since 1945 there have been a number of developments that have undermined the principle of state sovereignty. For instance, the European Court of Human Rights in Strasbourg accepts petitions from individual citizens from the member states of the Council of Europe and has the authority to force states to change their domestic laws and procedures if they are found to violate the human rights of their citizens. However, this court's jurisdiction is limited to members of the Council of Europe, and, while it does much to protect human rights in those countries, these tend to be liberal democratic states which generally observe the letter of human rights resolutions. This powerful protector of human rights would have been much more effective had it been located in Africa, for example. But African leaders jealously guard their sovereignty and are reluctant to even criticise each other over their treatment of their citizens, let alone create a supranational institution with the authority to interfere and compel them to behave. Similarly, those states that have signed an additional protocol to the 1984 Convention Against Torture, which authorises spot checks and investigations by a special rapporteur, are precisely those states that are free from suspicion of such activity. States that commit torture have not signed up to the convention and are, therefore, exempt from its provisions.

Secondly, there is a conflict between the requirements of justice, which on most counts are universal and apply to all human beings, and both the means of protection, armed forces, which are organised along national lines, and the responsibility of state leaders, which is first and foremost to their domestic populations. While individuals have the 'luxury' of sacrificing their economic livelihoods and even their lives in attempts to promote the welfare of people overseas, state leaders have a narrow responsibility to their citizens and the national interest. Such concerns can also stand in the way of effective political action. For example, in the 1990s Belgium introduced legislation permitting the prosecution of war crimes which might have led to the arrest of Ariel Sharon, Prime Minister of Israel, for his role in massacres that took place in southern Lebanon in 1982, had he stepped foot on Belgian soil. Such legislation would have incapacitated the EU in its efforts to mediate in the Israeli–Palestinian dispute. Finally, some analysts have come at this issue from the other direction, turning their critical gaze on the principles of global justice in which they discern a form of imperialism. On this account, the discourse of human rights is a confection of the West and attempts to protect them on a global scale are actually acts of imposition. However, it is interesting to note that despite their origins, Western conceptions of human rights are appealed to the world over by those whose rights are being violated. These often include former oppressors themselves, such as many affiliates of the former Taliban regime in Afghanistan, which publicly executed women in the football stadium in Kabul for violations of its strict 'moral' codes, but who complained of languishing without trial in the cells of Guantanamo Bay.

However, as Bull came to recognise, gross and unaddressed injustices can actually be a source of disorder.[11] For example, growing economic inequality between North and South in world politics can issue in momentous migration flows, which can destabilise countries and even regions. If injustices are allowed to fester, there is even the possibility that the impoverished of the world may turn to violent means to seek an improvement in their condition. Therefore, the priority of order over justice has to be tempered with the recognition that injustices cannot be completely ignored without potentially serious consequences for world order. With regard to human rights, the post-Cold War order has experienced a marked development in the institutions and mechanisms that seek to protect them, including the Treaty of Rome in 1998 which led to the creation of the International Criminal Court in 2003 and the commencement, if not completion, of legal proceedings for human rights violations against former heads of state, Augusto Pinochet in 1998 and Slobodan Milošević in 2001.

Security, order and justice after 9/11

The terrorist attacks of 11 September 2001 and their aftermath threw many of the tensions referred to above into stark relief. The attacks themselves demonstrated the vulnerability of open, complex societies in a globalised world. Benefiting from email, the Internet, satellite television and cheap air travel, al-Qaeda was able to conceive and execute this mission, transforming civilian airliners into hugely destructive weapons. For many analysts, this was the clearest expression of the privatisation of warfare that many commentators on **globalisation** have referred to. Small groups of terrorists in loosely formed networks are now able to wreak international havoc on a scale that was previously the preserve of well armed states. Although some of the nineteen hijackers of 9/11 came from fairly privileged backgrounds and none of them were born in Africa, the poorest continent, for some the attacks were taken as evidence of resistance to American hegemony and revenge for global injustices and inequality. The United States' response was at first multilateral, working through the UN and NATO to freeze the financial assets of terrorist organisations and to overthrow the Taliban regime in Afghanistan which has provided a base for al-Qaeda. However, the persecution of the **war on terror** in a primarily military form, coupled with the expansion of this pursuit of terrorists into the invasion of Iraq has meant that the United States had become increasingly isolated, which has undermined multilateral efforts to tackle the problem of international terrorism. In the terms we explored in Chapter 6, American use of hard power has undermined its soft power.

Summary

It is questionable whether the militarised approach to the war on terror has enhanced international order. The Iraq War in particular seems to have resulted in domestic instability, even approaching civil war between 2005 and 2007; the country seemed to act as a magnet for Islamist insurgents across the Middle East, and reports of the killing of Iraqi civilians by American soldiers helped to recruit further terrorists worldwide. The war on terror has also seen the demotion of concerns with international justice and human rights in particular, as liberal democratic states have tightened up their anti-terrorist legislation to enable them to detain terrorist suspects without trial, and the United States has carried out so-called 'rendition' flights (transporting suspects to allied countries where they can be more vigorously interrogated), has imprisoned hundreds at its naval base in Guantanamo Bay, Cuba and has authorised the selective use of torture techniques, such as 'water boarding' (simulated drowning). Similarities between the Cold War and the war on terror are often overstated, but the privileging of alliances in a global struggle over a concern for human rights is a clear parallel that can be drawn.

. . . .

 What you should have learnt from reading this chapter

- The maintenance of international order is complicated by the fact that states do not always share the same views and are, therefore, often unwilling to collaborate. This happens even in established alliances such as NATO.

- The Realist view of international relations is sceptical of the capacity of states to work together for the benefit of collective security because states seek to maintain their own national interest. By contrast, Liberal theorists highlight the benefit of collective security.

- The capacity of the UN to maintain international order has been limited by the fact that it is dependent on its own members to provide military resources.

- During the Cold War the effectiveness of the UN Security Council was hampered by the East–West division between communism and capitalism. The result was that the superpowers used or threatened to use their veto to stop agreement being reached on any resolutions that did not reflect their national interest.

- The post-Cold War period initially raised hopes that the UN would function in a more harmonious way, with superpowers not using their veto.

- Over the last sixty years there has been a significant shift in the nature of the threats that the world faces. Whereas the founders of the UN were influenced by the aggression between states that led to the Second World War, the twenty-first century is dominated by a different set of security threats, ranging from global warming to HIV/AIDS.

- Although the post-Second World War period has witnessed a growth in the human rights agenda there continues to be widespread human rights abuses throughout the world. This is typified by the modern slave trade of the human trafficking of children and adults into the sex industry and domestic servitude.

- Maintaining international law is complicated by fact that states often ignore it because there is no world government to enforce it. Nevertheless, it is the case the international law is meaningful to the majority of states because they recognise its value in regulating the relations between states.

? Likely examination questions

'Had the Cold War not ended, the Gulf War of 1991 would have been unthinkable.' Do you agree?

'Constrained by the interests of its members.' Is this an appropriate view of the UN?

What problems has the UN encountered in its attempts to maintain peace in the post-Cold War order?

'In the contemporary international system a state's security is best understood at the regional level rather than the global level.' Discuss.

How can international law exist in a world of nation-states?

'In contrast to domestic law, international law is powerless.' Do you agree with this statement?

Is a state justified in intervening in the internal affairs of another state over the issue of human rights?

To what extent is the universal application of human rights hindered by the differing cultural practices of nation-states?

Why is HIV/AIDS a threat to a nation's security?

To what extent is the poverty of the developing world a threat to global security?

 ## Helpful websites

United Nations

United Nations at: www.un.org

UN Charter at: www.un.org/aboutun/charter and www.yale.edu/lawweb/avalon/un/unchart.htm#art39

UN Security Council Resolutions at: www.un.org/documents/scres.htm

General

Carnegie Endowment for International Peace at: www.carnegieendowment.org

Council on Foreign Relations at: www.cfr.org/issue/135

International law

International Court of Justice at: www.icj-cij.org

The Laws of War at: http://avalon.law.yale.edu/subject_menus/lawwar.asp

Human rights

Universal Declaration on Human Rights at: www.un.org/Overview/rights.html

Amnesty International at: www.amnesty.org

Human Rights Watch at: www.hrw.org

United States Holocaust Memorial Museum at: www.ushmm.org

Arms control

Arms Control Association at: www.armscontrol.org

International Campaign to Ban Landmines at: www.icbl.org

Nuclear Threat Initiative at: www.nti.org/index.php

International Action Network on Small Arms at: www.iansa.org

Centre for Nonproliferation Studies at: http://cns.miis.edu

United Nations Institute for Disarmament Research at: www.unidir.org/html/en/human_security.html

BioWeapons Prevention Project at: www.bwpp.org

Norwegian Institute on Small Arms Transfers at: www.prio.no/NISAT

Human security

International HIV/AIDS Alliance at: www.aidsalliance.org/sw1280.asp

Terrorism

Terrorism Research Center at: www.terrorism.com

 ## Suggestions for further reading

General overview

A. J. Bellamy and Nicholas J. Wheeler, 'Humanitarian intervention in world politics', in J. Baylis, S. Smith and P. Owens (eds), *The Globalization of World Politics: An Introduction to International Relations*, 4th edn (Oxford University Press, 2008), pp. 522–41.

C. Brown, 'Human rights', in J. Baylis, S. Smith and P. Owens (eds), *The Globalization of World Politics: An Introduction to International Relations*, 4th edn (Oxford University Press, 2008), pp. 506–21.

P. Taylor and D. Curtis, 'The United Nations', in J. Baylis, S. Smith and P. Owens (eds), *The Globalization of World Politics: An Introduction to International Relations*, 4th edn (Oxford University Press, 2008), pp. 312–29.

Human rights and human security

T. Dunne and N. J. Wheeler (eds), *Human Rights in Global Politics* (Cambridge University Press, 1999).

M. Kaldor, *Human Security* (Polity, 2007).

Contemporary security challenges

J. Baylis, J. K. Wirtz, E. A. Cohen and C. S. Gray (eds), *Strategy in the Contemporary World: An Introduction to Strategic Studies* (Oxford University Press, 2006).

A. J. Bellamy, R. Bleiker, S. E. Davies and R. Devetak (eds), *Security and the War on Terror* (Routledge, 2007).

A. Collins, *Contemporary Security Studies* (Oxford University Press, 2006).

R. Dannreuther, *International Security: The Contemporary Agenda* (Polity, 2007).

P. Hough, *Understanding Global Security*, 2nd edn (Routledge, 2008).

P. Rogers, *Global Security and the War on Terror: Elite Power and the Illusion of Control* (Routledge, 2007).

P. Williams, *Security Studies: An Introduction* (Routledge, 2008).

United Nations, peacekeeping, humanitarian intervention and international law

A. J. Bellamy, P. Williams and S. Griffin, *Understanding Peacekeeping* (Polity, 2004).

B. Cronin and I. Hurd, *The UN Security Council and the Politics of International Authority* (Routledge, 2007).

R. A. Falk, *The Costs of War: International Law, the UN and World Order After Iraq* (Routledge, 2007).

C. Gray, *International Law and the Use of Force*, 2nd edn (Oxford University Press, 2004).

D. Hannay, *New World Disorder: The UN after the Cold War – An Insider's View* (Tauris, 2008).

N. MacQueen, *The United Nations since 1945* (Longman 1999).

D. Malone (ed.), *The UN Security Council: From the Cold War to the 21st Century* (Lynne Rienner, 2004).

R. Thakur, *The United Nations, Peace and Security* (Cambridge University Press, 2006).

T. G. Weiss, *Humanitarian Intervention* (Polity, 2007).

Diplomacy

G. R. Berridge, *Diplomacy: Theory and Practice*, 3rd edn (Palgrave, 2005).

S. Riordan, *The New Diplomacy* (Polity, 2003).

European Integration

Contents

Overview

The previous chapters have examined key topics in the study of IR, such as the role of the state, the impact of non-state actors and the relevance of theory. In this chapter we look at all these issues through the case study of the European Union (EU). Through an analysis of the history, policy-making scope and institutional dynamics of the EU, we highlight the way in which the EU has impacted on its member states, non-member states and non-state actors. At the same time, our study of the EU provides a useful example of the way in which the post-Second World War world has changed, moving from a Cold War to post-Cold War environment.

Key issues to be covered in this chapter

- The reason for European integration
- The origins, development and transformation of the EU
- The major institutions of the EU
- The main decision-making mechanisms of the EU
- The key policies of the EU
- The relationship between the EU and its member states

The context of European integration

Barely a day goes by without some reference in the media to European integration, with stories portraying both positive and negative attitudes. One of the complexities of analysing the EU is that many individuals are unclear about what the EU stands for, what the governing institutions do and how many member states there are in the EU. In essence this raises a question about how we define the EU. In Britain, for instance, it is common for people to refer to the EU as being a distinct level of activity that is separated from everyday national life despite the fact that Britain is a member of the EU. It is, therefore, common for people to refer to 'Britain and Europe' as if they were somehow separated from each other. While this is, of course, influenced by Britain being an island nation, it is nevertheless the case that the same level of distinctiveness tends not to happen among other EU member states.

Just as geographical location can have an impact on how attitudes toward the EU differ among member states, it is also evident that there are different views about the implications of the borders that geographically define Europe and how they relate to European integration. On the one hand, it is common to regard Europe as extending as far east as the Ural Mountains, and thereby to include such countries as Russia, Belarus, Ukraine, Moldova, Georgia, Armenia, Azerbaijan and Turkey. During the Cold War it was accepted that the geographical dividing line of European integration was marked by the Iron Curtain that separated East and West Germany, and which ensured that such countries as the former Czechoslovakia, Hungary and Romania lay outside of the orbit of European integration. Yet the end of the Cold War extended the EU's geographical map eastwards as former Eastern Bloc countries sought EU membership (Figure 11.1). For many of these countries, becoming an EU member state was an important means of demonstrating their new-found independence, while for existing EU member states the enlargement of the EU was an important means of imparting stability on the European continent.

This enlargement of membership meant that by 2009 there were twenty-seven EU member states. This expansion in membership has resulted in serious debates about the nature of EU membership. Having started off with just six member states in 1958, the expansion in membership has meant that some states have been concerned

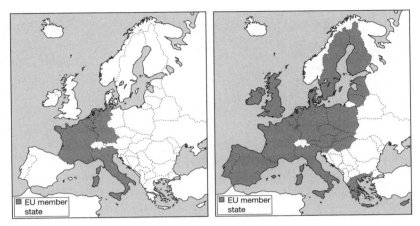

Figure 11.1 Comparing EU membership in 1957 and 2009

about the impact that this widening has had on the overall deepening of the European project. In other words, the more members the EU has, the more difficult it is for all the members to proceed at the same pace of European integration. For some countries, such as Britain, the expansion of EU membership has been viewed as a means of lessening the desires of more integrationist member states and thereby creating an EU that primarily focuses on economic integration. The problem with this view is that the very expansion of EU membership has increased the EU's influence on global affairs, with the EU increasingly viewed as having an important role in securing peace and stability outside its own borders. This obviously necessitates the development of policies and competencies at an EU level which require member states to pass authority from national decision-makers to EU decision-makers. A key question that we, therefore, need to ask is why countries would want to give up part of their national sovereignty to become an EU member state?

Why integrate?

A central question for any country wishing to join a regional organisation such as the EU is to consider the benefits and pitfalls of membership. Throughout the world there are various examples of regional IGOs, including the Association of South-East Asian

Nations (ASEAN), African Union (AU) and North American Free Trade Agreement (NAFTA). Although we looked in more detail at IGOs in Chapter 8, a general point that can be made is that countries that have become members of these organisations have done so out of a desire to deal with common issues, which can result in the formation of common identities. The issues that are dealt with at a regional level can vary tremendously, from trade to security concerns and the particular mix impacts on the members in different ways. One of the most common aspects of regional integration relates to economic issues, particularly the lowering and removal of customs duties between the member states to permit trade to move freely.

A focus on economic issues was the initial concern in the history of European integration. After the horrors of the Second World War many European nations realised that their economic and political problems could be tackled only by working together. This was a point which had been emphasised by the United States providing economic aid through the 1947 Marshall Plan, which led to the establishment in 1948 of the Organisation of European Economic Cooperation (OEEC) to supervise the Marshall aid programme that distributed some US$12.5 billion to Europe between 1948 and 1951. The OEEC was basically an IGO that assisted in processing payments between the relevant European countries, which would be superseded in September 1961 by the Organisation for Economic Cooperation and Development (OECD). The key point about the OEEC was that the individual European governments retained control. This was a situation that pleased some countries, such as Britain, which had a fear of losing control of their own national sovereignty through the establishment of an organisation at a level above the state – otherwise known as **supranationalism** (Box 11.1). But other European countries argued that the OEEC lacked the necessary supranational structures to bring long-term changes to the economic and political situation in Western Europe.

The key economic and military industries in the post-war period were coal and steel, and at the time it was argued that for European nations to recover their fortunes they would have to be bound up in a form of supranational co-operation which would entail governments giving up a degree of sovereign control. This resulted in a plan being

Box 11.1 Supranationalism

This refers to a method of decision-making in international organisations whereby representatives of member states and independent officials exercise power in addition to the role played by member state governments. The institutions of the EU have autonomy from national governments, EU law has primacy over national law, while decisions can be taken by a majority vote. Supranationalism has an impact on national sovereignty because it imposes certain limitations on member states. Supranationalism can be contrasted with intergovernmentalism, which is an approach that attaches greater emphasis to the role of member states in the decision-making process.

devised by Jean Monnet (who in 1946 had been appointed head of the French Planning Commission to oversee France's economic recovery) and Robert Schuman (French Foreign Minister from 1948–53) to place French and German coal and steel production under a supranational authority. It was their hope that in time integration in one area of the economy would **spill over** into other areas and this resulted in the creation of a European Coal and Steel Community (ECSC) which became the founding organisation of what we know today as the EU.

The ECSC, which began operating in August 1952, had six members: France; Germany; Italy; Luxembourg; Belgium; and the Netherlands. Britain chose not to join the ECSC on the basis of two concerns. First, an unwillingness to give up sovereign control of decisions on coal and steel matters. Secondly, an economic argument that Britain would not benefit from membership as its coal and steel production in the post-1945 period was more than two-thirds of the combined total of the other European members of the OEEC.

The ECSC sought to promote economic expansion, growth of employment and rising living standards among the member states through the creation of a common market for coal and steel. To facilitate this objective, four institutions were created: a High Authority; **Council of Ministers**; **Court of Justice**; and Common Assembly. The very creation of these institutions proved to be extremely significant as it took European integration down a different path than that of, say, regional integration in Asia through ASEAN. This is because the ECSC was not content with just providing a means of helping trade move between countries. Rather, the ECSC was an organisation that was concerned with regulating coal and steel production, and in so doing required institutions to be created that could make decisions on these matters (High Authority) and would represent the interests of the governments of the member states (Council of Ministers). At the same time, the ECSC had to take into consideration the views of the public in the member states (Common Assembly) and also be able to resolve conflicting interests (Court of Justice). Today these four institutions form the bedrock of the EU as we know it, although the High Authority has become the European Commission and the Common Assembly is now known as the European Parliament.

Because priority was attached to making a success of the ECSC, significant influence was given to the High Authority which acted as an executive institution independent of the member states and having responsibility for the coal and steel production of the member states. By contrast, the founders of the ECSC gave little influence to the Common Assembly as they were less concerned about the importance of democratic representation. The net effect of this decision was that the years which have followed have seen various efforts to reel back the influence of the European Commission and grant more power to the European Parliament.

From the foregoing information it should be evident that the founders of the ECSC established an organisation that set a mode of governance that was significantly different from other regional organisations. This was because the ECSC had at its heart the ability to make and take decisions that would impact on the member states as well as the legal capacity to resolve differences between the member states through the Court of Justice. In a nutshell, the participating member countries gave up independent sovereign control on coal and steel production out of a common belief that they could improve their economic and political conditions only by working together. Other countries, notably Britain, were not convinced by this argument and chose to stay outside the ECSC, and this tension between being prepared to relinquish independent sovereign control and to accept shared decision-making would be the key issue that would shape European integration in the years that followed.

Building a Community

In 1952 European integration was specifically focused on two sectors of the economy (coal and steel) and involved six participating member states. By 2009 European integration affected so many areas of national life that academics refer to the way in which domestic policies have become 'Europeanised'. From the origins of the ECSC there had emerged a whole range of institutions under a common umbrella that is now known as the EU. Moreover, the membership of the EU has grown to twenty-seven member states, with many of the members coming from behind the Iron Curtain that Winston Churchill pointed out had divided Europe after the Second World War (Chapter 2).

In examining the historical development of the EU, our first task is to find out why the original six members of the ECSC decided to expand beyond integration in the areas of coal and steel. European leaders were in part influenced by the Monnet spill over method of integration, whereby it was argued that integration in one sector would lead to demands to integrate in another.[1] In the post-war period a common concern to establish a strong defence in the face of the communist threat led policy-makers to hatch a plan to create a European Defence Community (EDC). Defence is, of course, a significantly different aspect of government policy to coal and steel. This is because whereas it might seem sensible to have shared decision-making on matters relating to coal and steel production, the possibility of having shared decision-making on defence matters was a considerably different issue. As we saw in Chapters 6 and 7, governments generally regard the protection of their own territory as one of their most important tasks, and in an emerging Cold War environment it was not surprising that some countries had concerns about giving up sovereign control of defence issues. This was certainly the view in France, where the National Assembly rejected the EDC Treaty on 30 August 1954 because of concerns about relinquishing national sovereignty over defence matters to a supranational organisation.

The collapse of the EDC provided an early lesson that while

member states acknowledged the benefit of European integration in certain policy areas where they could recognise the benefits of shared decision-making, some were less keen to integrate policies that they felt should be left to national decisions. In the years that followed this balance between European integration and preserving national autonomy would prove to be a delicate equilibrium to achieve.

Although the failure of the EDC Treaty was a notable setback to Monnet's approach to European integration, in March 1957 the six members of the ECSC agreed to the Treaty of Rome, creating a European Atomic Energy Community (Euratom) and European Economic Community (EEC). The key supranational element of the EEC and the main administrative hub was the European Commission. The interests of the member states were reflected in the Council of Ministers which had the primary task of legislating on the basis of the proposals arising from the Commission. Of the remaining institutions, the Parliamentary Assembly's influence was of a limited nature, while the Court of Justice played a more significant role by interpreting EEC decisions (see Box 11.2).

In its early years, a considerable proportion of the EEC's energies went on establishing a common customs union that would

Box 11.2 The main EU institutions

The Commission – The Executive Secretariat with rights of policy initiation, implementation and monitoring.

The Council of Ministers – a mainly intergovernmental body with final power over the decisions taken. The Council system has now been extended by the European Council which meets twice a year at the level of Heads of State.

The Parliament – initially an advisory and consultative body but now growing in power, directly elected since 1979.

The European Court of Justice – court of last resort for the enforcement and interpretation of EU legislation; its rulings supersede those of national courts.

permit free trade between the member states. In practical terms this involved getting rid of the tariff barriers which countries put in place to protect their own industries. So by getting rid of these the idea was to foster a culture of cross-border competition and consequently allow for the free movement of goods and people. This objective was achieved slightly ahead of schedule by 1968 and much of the credit for this lay with the European Commission.

One of the most important and influential policies that was included in the Treaty of Rome was the creation of a Common Agricultural Policy (CAP). Although the policy sought to alleviate the food shortages that existed in Europe after the Second World War, it also represented a classic compromise between the differing interests of the member states. This was because the French government had argued that in return for creating a common market – and thereby dismantling the trade barriers which protected its economy – the Community should establish an agricultural policy that would protect its farmers. While this objective was important to France, it was also the case that other member states were supportive of a policy which represented the interests of a significant proportion of the labour force and made a notable contribution to national wealth. For instance, in 1955 the respective figures were: France 25.9 per cent of the labour force and 12.3 per cent of GDP, Italy 39.5 per cent and 21.6 per cent, Germany 18.9 per cent and 8.5 per cent, Luxembourg 25 per cent and 9 per cent, the Netherlands 13.7 per cent and 12 per cent and Belgium 9.3 per cent and 8.1 per cent.[2]

The aim of improving agricultural production and guaranteeing farm income necessitated huge sums of money being spent on the CAP, with these accounting for approximately half of all Community expenditure right up until the 1990s. This inevitably resulted in the CAP being subject to criticism.

The very fact that the early years of the Community were dominated by efforts to establish common policies such as a customs union and CAP meant that the Commission exercised a strong influence over the direction of the Community. This did not last long. A significant dispute erupted in 1965 over the funding of the CAP. The Commission President, Walter Hallstein, proposed a package of measures that sought to combine a financial settlement for the CAP with a strengthening in the influence of the Parliament and the Commission. Member states were also concerned by the Treaty of Rome's provision to move from unanimity to majority voting in certain areas of the work of the Council of Ministers from 1966 onwards. The French President, Charles de Gaulle, refused to accept these proposals and the French government recalled its officials back to Paris. As France held the Presidency of the Council of Ministers, the period became known as the empty chair crisis. The crisis was resolved in January 1966 by what became known as the Luxembourg compromise. This provided member states with the ability to veto policies that they considered to be at odds with their national interests. In practical terms, it signalled a decline in the influence of the Commission and ascendancy in the power of the member states.

France's influence on the Community's affairs in the 1960s reflected its position as the major power among the member states, with Germany being reluctant to exercise influence in the wake of the Second World War. Such was the significance of French influence that it was twice able to veto Britain's application to join the Community in 1963 and 1967. In truth, Britain's decision to seek membership had been influenced by a decline in its own global influence (such as the Commonwealth replacing the Empire) and a weakening in its economic position vis-à-vis the Community members. For instance, having argued that non-participation in the Community was based on a fear of losing sovereign control of policy-making to a supranational body, policy-makers in Britain were soon to find out that the implication of this was that Britain could not enjoy the economic benefits of being part of a common market.

The replacement of De Gaulle as President of France by Georges Pompidou removed an obstacle to British membership of the Community, and in June 1970 enlargement negotiations started with the four applicant states of Britain, Denmark, Ireland and Norway. On 1 January 1973 Britain, Denmark and Ireland joined the Community. Norway, however, did not join because domestic concerns over the impact of Community membership on the agricultural industry resulted in the terms of membership being rejected in a popular **referendum**. The three new member states added sixty million people to the Community, which in 1973 had a combined population of 250 million. This was an amount broadly equivalent to the population of the United States at the time. Enlargement also increased the Community's economic and political influence, with it now accounting for approximately one-fifth of world trade. But contrary to expectations, the process of enlargement did not result in the Community making significant progress towards integration throughout the 1970s, as instability in the international economy meant that member states were not interested in deepening European integration.

As the Community entered the 1980s it was hoped that there would be an opportunity for renewed progress. The outlook appeared promising. The first direct elections to the **European Parliament** took place in 1979, while the same year also witnessed the creation of the European Monetary System (EMS) which offered a means of co-ordinating the economies of the member states. Two years later in 1981 the Community's membership increased to ten member states with the accession of Greece, and this enlargement to the south would soon be followed by Portugal and Spain in 1986.

Transformation

By the early 1980s there was a strong awareness that the economic competitiveness of the Community was lagging behind the United States and Japan. Within the Community there was a real concern that member states had become more concerned about protecting their own domestic markets through the use of non-tariff barriers, such as national product standards, rather than championing true European competition.[3]

A combination of the pressures of an ever more globalised marketplace (Chapter 9) and the need to develop a single approach across the member states resulted in a decision being taken to establish a single market by 1992. This commitment formed part of the Single European Act (SEA) agreement. As we show in Box 11.3, the SEA widened the scope of the Community's activities (such as the environment, social and technological policy) and made changes to the institutional and decision-making framework. Central to this was a strengthening of the European Parliament's powers through a new co-operation procedure (which ensured that it would be fully involved in the legislative process) and the introduction of **qualified**

Box 11.3 Key provisions of the Single European Act

- Established the objective of creating a single market by 31 December 1992 that would in turn be the biggest market in the world.
- Introduced QMV in the Council of Ministers for matters relating to the single market.
- Provided the institutions of the Community with influence over many policy areas, such as the environment, regional policy and research and development.
- Augmented the legislative powers of the European Parliament via the co-operation procedure.
- Gave legal status to European Council meetings of heads of state and government.
- Created a Court of First Instance.
- Incorporated European Political Cooperation (EPC) into the treaty and, therefore, enabled member states to progress toward a stronger foreign policy.
- Stressed the objective of Economic and Monetary Union (EMU) in a Preamble to the treaty.

majority voting (QMV) in the Council of Ministers. The latter led to a lessening of individual member state influence because they could no longer veto policies.

The ink was hardly dry on the SEA before questions were raised about expanding the Community's activities into other policy areas. This particularly applied to creating a single currency. It was a viewpoint that was influenced by the fact that, although the single market had made it possible for the free movement of people, services, goods and capital across the member states, the presence of distinct national currencies was regarded as a hurdle to the goal of free trade. 'For the single market's potential to be realised', Ben Rosamond has written, 'pure economic logic would contend that EMU is a necessity to maximise economic efficiency.'[4]

To look at this issue in more detail member states decided to hold an intergovernmental conference (IGC) negotiation that would formally set out the parameters for the creation of a single currency. The economic focus of the IGC negotiations was quickly widened to include political issues as the unforeseen collapse of communism in Eastern Europe in 1989 dramatically resulted in the dismantling of the Berlin wall on 11 November 1989 and the disintegration of Soviet-controlled governments in Central and Eastern Europe in 1990. These developments changed the map of Europe overnight and threw up a number of political concerns to which the Community needed to respond.

The product of the IGC negotiations on political union and economic and monetary union was the Treaty on European Union. Because the negotiations concluded at the Maastricht European Council of December 1991, the Treaty is commonly referred to as the 'Maastricht Treaty'. The Treaty made a number of significant changes to the Community, including the decision to set a firm timetable for the creation of a single currency by 1 January 1999. For member states to participate they would have to meet certain economic criteria to ensure that their economies were fit enough to join. For some less-developed member states, particularly Greece, Ireland, Portugal and Spain, the economic constraints that participation in the single currency required meant that they would require economic assistance from the Community in the form of a cohesion fund. Despite these challenges, the prospect of a single currency was welcomed by many governments who had lacked domestic economic stability. Britain did not share this view. Having argued against the need for a single currency, it achieved a compromise solution in the Maastricht Treaty that allowed it to opt-out from this commitment.[5]

The Maastricht Treaty was also significant for creating a new structure to the Community which would now resemble a Greek three-pillar temple, while the Community would be renamed the European Union.[6] The decision to create a pillar structure was taken because of a desire to separate the core common policies of the Community that involved supranational co-operation from new areas of intergovernmental co-operation on Common Foreign and Security Policy (CFSP) and Justice and Home Affairs (JHA). Of the three pillars, pillar 1 would include the common policies where the European Commission, European Parliament and European Court of Justice would be able to exercise their full influence. Co-operation on CFSP was set within pillar 2 and JHA in pillar 3, and in both of these areas decisions would be taken solely by the member states.

As far as the institutions were concerned, the Maastricht Treaty enhanced the power of the European Parliament which was now given the authority to approve (or not) the European Commission. A new co-decision procedure also meant that the Parliament would have the right to block or amend legislation through a series of discussions with the Council of Ministers and, therefore, ensured that the Parliament could 'no longer be accused of lacking teeth'.[7] The practicality of this change meant that the legislative process would no longer just represent a situation whereby the Commission proposed policies and the Council of Ministers took a decision after consulting the Parliament. Instead, the Council of Ministers would now have to co-decide with the Parliament on those policies that fell under the co-decision procedure. These various changes did not take effect at the European level until 1 November 1993. This delay between agreement on the treaty in December 1991 and implementation in November 1993 was because of the need for the member states to ratify the new treaty at the domestic level.

Enlargement and institutional reform

The acceleration in the process of European integration in the late 1980s and early 1990s resulted in many non-EU countries concluding that they were disadvantaged through being outside of the EU. The collapse of communism in Central and Eastern Europe also brought forward a number of countries who sought to join the Community.

The first group to seek EU membership comprised Austria, Finland, Norway and Sweden. These four countries did not raise significant issues for the design and operation of the EU as they were wealthy nations that did not place an extra burden on the EU's finances. However, while all four countries signed treaties of accession that would in turn require ratification at the national level, a referendum in Norway in November 1994 produced a no vote against membership which meant that only Austria, Finland and Sweden joined the EU on 1 January 1995.

The 'Nordic' enlargement meant that the EU now comprised

fifteen member states. The expansion in member states raised questions about the extent to which the existing institutional design of the EU was fit for purpose. This question over the nature and role of the EU institutions focused the minds of EU policy-makers because of the prospect of further enlargement to the countries of Central and Eastern Europe. Such an assessment was necessary because the 1995 enlargement did not produce a redesign of the institutions.

A further cause for concern was the way in which the EU budget was dominated by agricultural policy to the extent that it represented approximately 50 per cent of the budget in the early 1990s. Reform of the CAP was necessary because many of the prospective member states had large agricultural sectors and it was not financially possible to continue with a model of operation which subsidised farmers on the basis of production and guaranteed prices. As Friis has commented, 'if all farmers were to receive the level of agricultural subsidies received by existing member states, the EU budget would skyrocket'.[8] These concerns led to a decision to de-couple the linkage for agricultural support to farmers from production.

Questions over the nature of the institutional design of the EU resulted in member states taking the decision to hold another IGC that would examine the methods by which decisions were taken. There was also a desire among some member states to examine the effectiveness of the CFSP. Such a view was influenced by the inability of the EU to deal in an appropriate manner with the break up of the former Yugoslavia in the early 1990s, where member states were basically unable and unwilling to come to a consensus to stop 'ethnic cleansing' taking place.

The IGC which looked at these issues commenced work in March 1996 (less than three years since the Maastricht Treaty became law), with the work concluding at the Amsterdam European Council of June 1997. The product of these negotiations was the Treaty of Amsterdam which failed to address the significant institutional issues that dominated the EU.[9] Of the changes that the Treaty introduced, some of the most notable included the decision to create an area of freedom, security and justice which was further testament of the need by member states to respond in a co-ordinated way to the threat posed by organised crime. Another area of change included the decision to create a post of High Representative for the CFSP. The idea here was relatively simple: the existing member states needed to strengthen the co-ordination of the EU's newly formed foreign policy.

As the Treaty of Amsterdam skipped the big questions of institutional reform, the prospect of enlarging the EU (both in terms of number of countries and overall population) meant that there was a need to reform the EU institutional structure. This was a task that was partially dealt with in the Treaty of Nice that member states agreed to in December 2000 and which entered into force on 1 February 2003 after a period of national ratification. The Treaty of Nice helped to prepare the EU for further enlargement by making some changes to the institutional design of the EU, although, as with the Treaty of Amsterdam, the final outcome was not as significant as had been initially hoped for.[10] Thus, while the treaty set a limit of one Commissioner per member state (meaning that Britain, France, Italy, Germany and Spain gave up their right to have two Commissioners) and redistributed the number of MEPs, the Treaty did not make a wholesale change to the EU's institutional design; the large member states were reluctant to give up their power and influence within the EU.

In amongst the debates on the institutional design of the EU, the single currency successfully started operation on 1 January 2002. The new currency is called the euro, and twelve (out of a possible fifteen) member states were deemed to have met the economic convergence criteria that had been set for participation. For a number of reasons, Britain, Denmark and Sweden did not seek to join the single currency.

The countries which sought to join the EU in the twenty-first century therefore faced a more integrated EU than Austria, Finland and Sweden had when they joined in 1995. The issue of enlargement was not just more complex because there had been an expansion in the number of policies that were integrated at the EU level. It was rather because the economic levels of development in many of the former Soviet-dominated Central and Eastern European countries were considerably lower than the EU average. This economic discrepancy between existing and new member states had previously been evident with the Mediterranean enlargement of Greece (1981) and Portugal and Spain (1986). Yet, the prospect of such a significant enlargement meant that in 1993 the Community established a set of criteria that would have to be fulfilled if the countries of Central and Eastern Europe were to be able to join the EU.

Known as the Copenhagen Criteria, the EU emphasised the need for prospective applicant states to have stable political institutions that guaranteed human rights, to have a functioning market economy and for the governments to be able to adhere to the economic, political and monetary obligations of membership. Such criteria were a means for the EU to influence domestic economic and political reform within the applicant countries. In 2004 ten countries were deemed to have met the necessary requirements to join the EU: Cyprus, Czech Republic, Estonia, Hungary, Latvia, Lithuania, Malta, Poland, Slovakia and Slovenia.

As is highlighted in Box 11.4, this was the biggest enlargement in the EU's history and increased the EU population by more than 100 million people. The EU now comprised twenty-five member states. But whereas previous enlargements to Greece, Portugal and Spain had resulted in the EU providing significant financial assistance to offset the economic implications of membership, the new member states did not receive the same level of economic support with the implication being that they had to make changes to their economies from within. This state of affairs obviously resulted in the new member states complaining that one set of rules was being applied to existing member states and another to new member states. Yet, in leaving the process of reform to the new member states, it is nevertheless evident that the Commission's ability to influence the process

---

Box 11.4 Enlarging the EU

- 1973 Ireland, Denmark and the United Kingdom.
- 1981 Greece.
- 1986 Portugal and Spain.
- 1995 Austria, Finland and Sweden.
- 2004 Cyprus, Czech Republic, Estonia, Hungary, Latvia, Lithuania, Malta, Poland, Slovakia and Slovenia.
- 2007 Bulgaria and Romania.

of reform has tended to lessen once a country has joined the EU. It is a lot easier to apply pressure to an applicant state to make reforms because of the threat of vetoing their application.

The 2004 enlargement brought further to the fore the need for the EU to seriously reform its institutional and decision-making structures. To fully examine these issues member states agreed to establish a Convention on the Future of Europe. The Convention, which was chaired by the former French President, Valéry Giscard d'Estaing, met between March 2002 and June 2003 and discussed a number of proposals that reflected a desire to improve the quality of leadership offered by the EU, streamline its institutional structures and ensure that its range of policies reflect the challenges faced by the EU. Such points were set out in a series of recommendations that were presented in the form of a draft Constitutional Treaty in June 2003, which in turn served as the basis for IGC negotiations that commenced a few months later in October and concluded at the Brussels summit of 18 June 2004.

The final outcome of the IGC negotiations was agreement at the Brussels European Council of June 2004 on a new Constitutional Treaty consolidating all the previous treaties into one single document to provide the EU with a simpler and more accessible set of rules. This included extending QMV to new policy areas that had previously been primarily governed by intergovernmental methods of decision-making. The Treaty also proposed a new post of EU President to be elected by the heads of government for a term of two and half years. Agreement was reached on the creation of a new EU Minister for Foreign Affairs who would combine the existing positions of the Council's High Representative for foreign policy and the European Commissioner for external relations.

Despite the fact that many agreed that these changes were necessary to improve the EU's mode of operation, there was serious concern among the EU electorate that the Constitutional Treaty represented a significant erosion of national sovereignty. These concerns led to a ratification crisis for the treaty in 2005, when it was rejected in referendum votes in France (with a 'no' vote of 54.5 per cent) and the Netherlands (with a 'no' vote of 61.6 per cent). This resulted in the Constitutional Treaty grinding to a halt to provide a period of reflection, with member states agreeing at the June 2007

European Council to further examine developments with a view to the adoption of a new 'Reform Treaty'. By that stage the EU had undergone another enlargement with the accession of Bulgaria and Romania on 1 January 2007. This new Treaty was signed by the leaders of the EU's twenty-seven member states at the December 2007 Lisbon European Council and has become known as the 'Lisbon Treaty'. As with other treaties, it will be subject to a process of national ratification with the hope that it will come into force in 2009.

Critics of the Lisbon Treaty argue that it is basically the Constitutional Treaty in all but name as it contains many of the changes that the Constitutional Treaty attempted to introduce. This includes the creation of the post of EU President, combining of the jobs of the EU High Representative for foreign policy and the European Commissioner for external relations, redistributing QMV voting weights among the member states, slimming down the European Commission so that there are fewer commissioners than member states, removal of national vetoes in a number of policy areas and expansion of the influence of the European Commission, European Parliament and Court of Justice.

Yet, whereas the Constitutional Treaty sought to replace all the previous EU treaties so as to create a new simplified treaty, the Lisbon Treaty seeks merely to amend the previous treaties. Member state governments therefore argue that the dropping of all reference to an EU constitution – and the symbols that go with it (such as an EU flag and anthem) – mean that the Lisbon Treaty is less likely to create domestic problems.

Explaining integration

A key dividing line in the history of the EU has been between intergovernmental and supranational models of integration. Intergovernmental interpretations emphasise the fact that key decisions continue to be taken by member states. Supporters of the supranational viewpoint stress that the key dynamic of integration is determined by EU organisations and not as a result of the decisions taken by member states. Supranational models of EU integration therefore emphasise the policy outcomes of such EU institutions as the European Commission and the European Court of Justice. The European Commission (which acts as the central bureaucracy and executive body) has responsibility for upholding EU laws, monitoring patterns of implementing legislation, preserving the integrity of the single market, managing the annual budget of the EU and administering policies such as the CAP.

Not every EU government or every individual within a member state has welcomed the possibility of binding decisions being made beyond the realm of individual nation-state sovereignty. This has led to the emergence of the phenomenon of Euroscepticism in all EU countries, but it is particularly apparent in Britain and Denmark (Box 11.5). Eurosceptics stress that these viewpoints are first of all the product of EU membership having eroded the capacity of member states to administer policies at the national level. This inability to exercise independent authority is commonly viewed as a loss of sovereignty. At the same time, Eurosceptics also stress that the centralising of decision-making away from the nation-state creates a sense of remoteness that has been reflected in a general decline in voter turn-out at European Parliamentary elections, with the average level of voting falling for the fifth time running at the 2004 elections.

Those who subscribe to the Eurosceptic position draw on the argument that prior to joining the EU, member states were able to make their own decisions. Yet, it is important to point out that nation-states do not operate in a vacuum and that the globalisation of world politics has led to a level of interconnectedness between states which means that the fortunes of all states are increasingly interlinked between each other. This is particularly apparent with regard to financial matters, whereby it is virtually impossible to talk of national sovereignty with regard to economic issues. Consequently, EU membership has to be set within the context of a general trend toward increased levels of economic interdependence that affect all countries.

A more balanced view of European integration would be to say that while the activities of all member states have been constrained by EU membership, with governments being bound by a whole plethora of rules and regulations, it is also true that European integration has offered many opportunities to governments (Box 11.6). The establishment of a single market required member states to accept

Box 11.5 Britain and European integration

Britain is regularly mentioned as being one of the most Eurosceptic of all EU member states. When the first initiatives were taken towards European integration after the Second World War, successive British governments took the decision to support but not to be directly involved in the developments that led to the creation of the ECSC and subsequently the EEC. This decision was shaped by a belief that membership would conflict with Britain's position as a global trading power and its links to Empire (subsequently the Commonwealth). Britain, therefore, took the decision to defend its national interests and to protect is national sovereignty. Yet, only four years after the EEC started operating in 1958, Britain applied for membership in 1961. This change had been influenced by a concern that Britain's trading interests were being hampered by being outside the integrated market of the EEC. Concerns about national sovereignty were put into a wider context about the impact on the British economy. In the end, Britain did not actually become a member until 1973, by which time the economic need for it to have access to the markets of such countries as France and Germany was a paramount factor in determining membership.

Since 1973 Britain has regularly been portrayed as an 'awkward partner' as successive governments have sought to defend Britain's national interests. This became particularly apparent in the mid-1980s when the decision to establish a European single market brought with it a view among other European member states that the integration process should spread into areas of policy that had hitherto been dealt with principally at the national level. In time this meant that policy areas from the environment to social policy became subject to EU rules and regulations and lessened the room for member state governments to take independent decisions. Critics have inevitably stressed that British sovereignty has been eroded. Yet many would argue that there is little alternative. It could also be pointed out that the collective influence of the EU is crucial when negotiating in a global context with countries such as China, Russia and the United States and, therefore, Britain's membership of the EU enhances its position in world politics rather than actually diminishing its ability to take decisions.

Box 11.6 European integration and the challenge to national sovereignty

Hardly a day passes without some discussion regarding sovereignty within the context of European integration, and particularly with regard to whether a transfer of powers away from the member states to the EU institutions has occurred and, therefore, a concurrent reduction in the sovereignty of the member states. To this end, it is clear that because the EU institutions have the ability to take decisions that are binding on member states then there has been a transfer of sovereignty in those areas where the EU has responsibility. This is because in the context of a state, sovereignty refers to the ability of the institutions of the state to take decisions and implement laws. Within the context of European integration, the most common argument put forward by Eurosceptics is that there has been a loss of national sovereignty. While at first glance this may appear to be true, it is nevertheless the case that the member states have joined the EU voluntarily and, moreover, have played a leading role in shaping the powers of the EU institutions and determining the policies that are to be dealt with at the EU level.

new EU rules and standards to ensure fair competition across all EU member states. The European Commission was given increased powers to monitor the progress of member states in implementing these changes, while the Court of Justice had the power to implement fines where compliance did not take place. Such measures reduced national sovereignty. Yet, at the same time, the single market offered important benefits to the citizens of Europe, including the opportunity for cross-border trade, the free movement of people, as well as important practical points such as the recognition of educational qualifications from different EU countries.

The single market also acted as a catalyst for promoting further advances in European integration, including the promotion of a social dimension and the eventual creation of a single currency. The single currency is also representative of the EU's growing external influence, with the Euro increasingly being used as a reserve currency in the international economy.

The EU of today has become an important participant in international political and economic affairs. It is the largest contributor to the

UN budget and is the world's largest provider of development assistance. It is an economic powerhouse, playing a key role in international trading negotiations and is the single largest trading bloc in the world. The EU accounts for in excess of 20 per cent of all global imports and exports. These figures are all the more staggering since the twenty-seven member states of the EU account for approximately 7 per cent of the world's population. Yet despite these obvious strengths, the EU's ability to influence world affairs is often limited to specific policy areas. The EU might be an 'economic superpower', but in no way does this confer on it equal status with the United States.

It is a state of affairs which highlights the complexity of the EU. On the one hand, the EU enjoys a great deal of policy responsibility, is the most integrated of all international organisations and is widely regarded as a remarkable example of co-operation among states. On the other hand, its ability to achieve coherence in its policy objectives is often limited by the fact that it comprises twenty-seven sovereign nation-states. This has in turn focused attention on whether it is possible to categorise the EU in the same way as other IGOs, or whether it is indeed possible to continue to refer to the EU as an IGO at all.

The fact that the EU has many special characteristics that distinguish it from other IGOs has given rise to a number of debates over the extent to which it is possible to speak of the EU as an 'actor' in world politics in a manner similar to nation-states. This is because the EU addresses both internal issues, such as resolving conflicts between its members, and external issues, such as negotiating on behalf of the member states on matters of trade policy within the multilateral forum of the WTO negotiations or in the context of bilateral discussions, as with the United States (see Box 11.7). Yet, it is none the less apparent that despite the strengths of the EU, as on matters of trade policy, it is not a state and has not resulted in the withering away of the importance of its member states; they continue to exercise political power within the EU by taking the key decisions within the Council of Ministers.

Institutional balance of power

A significant amount of the debate that has taken place within the EU has accordingly focused on determining which policies should be

---

Box 11.7 EU trade policy

Although the twenty-seven member states of the EU represent just 7 per cent of the world's population, they nevertheless account for in excess of 20 per cent of all global imports and exports, making the EU the largest trading bloc in the world. The combined economic strength of the member states means that the EU is able to play an important role in matters relating to trade. To ensure that the EU acts collectively on these issues, member states have entrusted the European Commission with the responsibility for dealing with trade policy, such as handling negotiations in WTO discussions. This pooling of sovereignty on trade policy ensures that member states are able to maximise their influence in the international arena where the EU has traditionally been a strong advocate of free trade.

---

subject to decision-taking at a EU level and which should be retained solely for the preserve of the member states. At the same time, there has also been a significant amount of discussion as to which policies to be discussed at an EU level should be decided on a basis of QMV.

Within the EU the key decision-making body is the Council of Ministers which comprises member state representatives. While it is the responsibility of the European Commission to propose new EU laws and policies, the formal authority for acceptance rests with the Council of Ministers. Acceptance takes place after the Council has debated the policy with the European Parliament. The European Parliament's powers have increased in recent years and its influence now extends to being a co-legislator with the Council of Ministers over a majority of issues through the co-decision procedure. The European Parliament also possesses a number of supervisory powers over the appointment of the Commission and has influence over the non-compulsory expenditure of the EU budget.

We can see that although the EU is characterised as a supranational organisation, it comprises a number of institutions that reflect supranational as well as intergovernmental structures. Chief among the supranational institutions is the European Commission, which includes Commissioners (nominated by national governments) who are assisted by an administrative staff divided into directorate generals covering a range of EU policies. This structure is similar to that found in the government departments of member states. Other supranational institutions include the Court of Justice and European Parliament, while there are in addition a number of more specialised institutions such as the European Central Bank (which sets interest rate levels for those countries using the Euro – the so-called 'Euro zone') and Court of Auditors (which audits the accounts of the EU institutions).

Set against these institutions, the Council of Ministers acts as the main beacon of intergovernmentalism in the EU through its role as the key decision-making body. However, while decisions are taken by member states, the main method of agreement is QMV (where the votes of a member state are weighted partly to account for differences in the size of its population) which permits the possibility of a proposal being accepted if it receives the necessary number of votes and similarly being rejected if a sufficiently large number of states vote against it (commonly referred to as the blocking minority).

Summary

From the foregoing discussion, it is apparent that the EU comprises a mix of intergovernmental and supranational procedures, and this outcome is very much a product of the negotiating preferences of member states. In the post-war period many member states were willing to engage in new forms of co-operation and to create supranational structures to administer common policies because they considered that individual governments were not able to deal adequately with the challenges faced by Western Europe. In examining the factors that motivated states to engage in such a process of integration, Alan Milward has emphasised the point that the creation of the ECSC represented a desire to satisfy French national interests by ensuring the continued economic recovery of France.[11] This focus on the national interest has led Milward to argue that European integration took place only when it was demanded by nation-states and that supranational institutions were established for specific purposes and not as a means of eclipsing the nation-state.[12]

In contrast to this viewpoint, others have argued that the process of European integration will ultimately result in the creation of a new supranational state and thereby the demise of the nation-state.[13] This view is somewhat harder to sustain, not least because the national interest was a key factor propelling the strategies of nation-states. Indeed, as Milward has argued, rather than promoting the cause of federalism, European integration provided an opportunity to 'rescue the nation state'.[14] Germany was keen to participate in the ECSC because it provided a means of rehabilitation (as did Italy), while the smaller nations of Belgium, Luxembourg and the Netherlands realised that economically they could not afford to distance themselves from the markets of France and Germany.

Moves towards the taking of decisions at a European level and the transfer of power away from member states have been partly the result of the pragmatic decisions of member states. And even in those areas of decision-making that member states explicitly established on an intergovernmental basis, the practical experience of operating such policies has often resulted in the need to move away from intergovernmental procedures.

The examples that have been outlined in this chapter may lead some observers to consider that the present-day structure of the EU is the result of a series of bargains negotiated by member states. Certainly, it is the case that the various IGC negotiations that have become commonplace in the EU's calendar have been subject to agreement by member states. But at the same time, the institutions of the EU have provided a significant amount of the momentum behind European integration. This has been true particularly in the case of the European Commission and the European Court of Justice. To this end, the conflict between supranationalism and the ability of national governments to exercise their own decision-making remains a key feature of the process of European integration.

· ·

✅ What you should have learnt from reading this chapter

- The EU has developed primarily from the initial impetus to European integration that took place after the Second World War, with the ECSC providing the first significant development of supranational co-operation. Jean Monnet is regarded as the founding father of the EU.

- The key institutions in the EU are the Council of Ministers, European Council, European Commission, European Parliament and the Court of Justice. The increase in the powers of many of these institutions has been viewed as essential to aid the co-ordination of policy at the EU level.

- Over the years there have been several stages of EU enlargement, the most recent of which has included countries from Central and Eastern Europe. The fact that former Soviet-controlled countries have joined the EU highlights the broader changes that have taken place in world politics reflected in the spread of democracy, the demise of communism and the emergence of the United States as the only remaining superpower.

- More and more policies that were initially the preserve of decision-making at the national level are now being taken at the EU level.

- While many scholars argue that benefits come from having joint policies, as in the case of the environment, other commentators emphasise that this has led to an unacceptable transfer of sovereignty away from the member state.

- The process of European integration has been shaped by many factors that have included the member states, the EU institutions and external pressures such as the world economy. Many of the significant changes have come about because of the agreement of the member states. This particularly applies to the IGC negotiations.

- Although there are many ways to analyse the process of European integration, the principal dividing line is between intergovernmental and supranational viewpoints.

❓ Likely examination questions

Why did European integration initially start with the iron and coal industries?

How important is the European Commission in the EU?

Why have the European Parliament's powers been increased?

Why is it necessary to have a Court of Justice in the EU?

What factors influenced the relaunch of European integration in the 1980s?

In what ways has the recent enlargement of the EU from fifteen to twenty-seven member states changed the EU?

Why are EU member states represented solely by the European Trade Commission in external trade discussions such as those conducted through the World Trade Organisation?

Account for the fact that not every EU member state participates in the European single currency?

'European by name, Atlanticist by heart.' Is this an accurate reflection of British foreign policy?

Why did it take until 1973 for Britain to become a member of the European Community?

 ## Helpful websites

EU

European Union at: www.europa.eu.int

National governments

UK Foreign and Commonwealth Office at: www.fco.gov.uk

European governments at: http://europa.eu.int/abc/governments/index_en.html

UK Cabinet Papers on European co-operation at: www.nationalarchives.gov.uk/cabinetpapers/themes/european-co-operation.htm

Research institutes

The University Association for Contemporary European Studies at: www.uaces.org

The European Community Studies Association at: www.ecsanet.org

Centre for European Policy Studies at: www.ceps.be/index.php

The Federal Trust at: www.fedtrust.co.uk

Institute of European Affairs at: www/iiea.ie

 ## Suggestions for further reading

Textbooks

A. Blair, *The European Union since 1945* (Longman, 2005).

A. Blair, *Companion to the European Union* (Routledge, 2006).

M. Cini (ed.), *European Union Politics* (Oxford University Press, 2007).

D. Dinan (ed.), *Origins and Evolution of the European Union* (Oxford University Press, 2006).

S. George and I. Bache, *Politics in the European Union*, 2nd edn (Oxford University Press, 2007).

Thought-provoking studies

R. H. Ginsberg, *Demystifying the European Union: The Enduring Logic of Regional Integration* (Rowman and Littlefield, 2007).

C. Hay and A. Menon (eds), *European Politics* (Oxford University Press, 2007).

S. Hix, *What's Wrong with the European Union and How to Fix it* (Polity, 2008).

J. McCormick, *The European Superpower* (Palgrave, 2006).

J. McCormick, *Understanding the European Union*, 4th edn (Palgrave, 2008).

Conclusion

Contents

Overview

This book has aimed to provide an introduction to a broad range of subjects that are of relevance to international politics. This has included a focus on the role of nation-states and non-state actors and the way in which they operate in a regional and global context. We have also sought to understand these issues through a theoretical approach. The study of international politics is concerned with both specific issues and more general patterns of activity. In this sense, while our study of nation-states means that we are aware that each state has its own historical trajectory, its own peculiar circumstances and dynamics, our analysis of the broader international system means that we need to note similarities and general conclusions at the same time. In this chapter we review our analysis by identifying four defining features of international politics from the middle of the twentieth century to the present day.

Key issues to be covered in this chapter

- The impact of globalisation on contemporary world politics
- The rise of the nation-state as the predominant form of political community in the international system since 1945
- The continuing and changing importance of nuclear weapons in the post-Cold War order
- The spread of democracy and the prospects for world peace

Globalisation of international politics

The first defining feature of modern international politics has been the impact of globalisation. Although some commentators argue that globalisation can be traced prior to the nineteenth century, global issues of a common nature are primarily a phenomenon associated with the later years of the twentieth century and more particularly from the 1990s onwards. While it is possible to view globalisation as a recent development, there are nevertheless significant differences of opinion as to the impact of globalisation. Some scholars view globalisation as a positive development, while others view it in more negative terms. Despite these differences of opinion, it is evident that one of the most notable impacts of globalisation has been the dramatic acceleration in the speed with which issues affect individuals throughout the world, resulting in what Anthony Giddens has termed a 'runaway world'.[1] This, in conjunction with the withering of traditional definitions of society, centred on notions such as borders, time and distances, has led to an interconnected world where it is not always possible to distinguish the distinct influences that shape the world in which we live.

The concept of globalisation is itself based in Western beliefs and values and this has resulted in questions being raised about the extent to which a global culture is emerging based on these values. Globalisation in this sense represents the way in which the world is becomingly increasingly interdependent and shaped by ever more standard aspects of life. While it is certainly true that Western models of capitalism have spread throughout the world, it is also evident that there have been challenges to these developments. One response to the erosion of traditional cultures has been the rise of Islam. At the same time, the view that globalisation is being driven by corporate rather than social interests has resulted in campaigns by NGOs such as Greenpeace, Amnesty International and Oxfam.

In looking in more detail at what globalisation actually means, it is possible to identify three key concepts which demonstrate the nature of global change. The first of these is the way in which various networks now stretch across the world. Matters relating to culture, economics and politics are not just confined within one state or a particular region, but can impact on events on the other side of the world. This stretching of social relations links to our second key concept which is the extent to which distant cultural, social and economic practices increasingly penetrate localised activity. On the one hand this has resulted in a greater diversity of practices, but, on the other hand, has also resulted in certain practices becoming dominant and thereby lessening diversity. For instance, American movies have greater penetration throughout the world than Russian movies, while companies such as Microsoft and Apple dominate the global computer industry. Our third key concept refers to the way in which globalisation is supported by a range of institutions that assist with the governance of global issues. Examples here include the IMF and WTO which aim to regulate global finance and trade. To a large extent these institutions respond to the flow of global markets, in which the key decisions are taken in a small number of global financial centres, namely London, New York and Tokyo. The decisions that are taken in these centres of power not only affect the rise and fall of the stock markets in their own countries but also have a dramatic impact on the global economy as a whole.

It should be evident from the above comments that one of the most profound developments of globalisation has been the way in which the identity of the nation-state has been questioned. In basic terms, the concept of a state having control over all affairs within its borders no longer holds true. EU member states have reference to a superior authority as European law has precedence over domestic law. The economic pressures of globalisation mean that the contemporary state is not able to control its own economic fortunes as evidenced by economic crises. At the same time individuals within nation-states often have loyalty to communities that go beyond national boundaries that are driven by transnational concerns like the environment and shared beliefs such as religion. Thus, bonds are shared with those who have similar beliefs in other countries.

Yet, despite all these developments, it is nevertheless evident that the nation-state has not withered away as it continues to play a crucial role in the organisation of international politics. The very environment that favours an MNC establishing a base in a particular state is influenced by the prevalent conditions set by that government, including tax rates. Thus, while companies such as Microsoft exercise a great deal of influence throughout the world, they still operate within parameters established by states and institutions set up by states.

One of the most noticeable aspects of globalisation has been the emergence of global concerns, of which the rise of green politics has been of particular note. Since the 1970s there has been an increasing anxiety about the way in which the growth of the global economy is influenced by a limited number of key resources, particularly oil and gas. The reality of this situation hit home in 1973 when the Organisation of Petroleum Exporting Countries raised the price of oil fourfold, which had a dramatic and immediate effect in slowing economic growth in many of the world's countries and raised awareness of the importance of natural resources. Since then, energy politics has been joined by other modes of resource and producer politics that have included 'water politics'.

The rise of green politics has been stimulated by particular events, such as the disaster at the Chernobyl nuclear power plant in 1986 which highlighted the way in which the fall-out from an explosion in a nuclear reactor impacted on countries thousands of miles away. A further factor contributing to the rise of green politics has been the growth of environmental NGOs such as Greenpeace and Friends of the Earth, while the emergence of a global media has meant that environmental disasters on the other side of the world have become localised issues to everyone.

These issues have further brought to the fore an increasingly common view that such problems can be tackled only through co-operation at the global level. This has been particularly evident through the need to respond to the challenge of global warming, which has both domestic and international political dimensions. For those countries that are the main contributors to global warming through greenhouse gas emissions, such as the United States, the challenge to reduce these emissions will inevitably require costly adaptations to plant and machinery and could impede economic growth. Yet, at the same time, there are many countries in the world which have contributed little to the problems of global warming, such as Bangladesh, but which are nevertheless directly experiencing its consequences through rising sea levels and an increase in extreme weather conditions such as cyclones. Also, as the main polluters are the rich North, while the countries at present being most affected are in the poor South, global warming adds a further dimension to the **North–South division** in international politics.

The universalisation of the nation-state

The second defining feature of modern international politics has been the universalisation of the nation-state. Today practically 100 per cent of world's population lives within one nation-state or another, although many are without full citizenship and are mere residents. This is a remarkable and unprecedented development when one considers that as late as 1945 large populations lived under alternative forms of political organisation. For instance, India and most of Africa and southeast Asia were still under the colonial control of the European powers. Further back in history, we have examples of city-states co-existing with large empires and emerging nation-states. But in the period since 1945 the world has witnessed an end to colonies and mandated territories and the global spread of sovereign statehood.

In 1945, the world held just over fifty sovereign nation-states, albeit with some ambiguities (for example, while still a part of the British Empire, India was a founding signatory of the UN Charter, as it had been of the League of Nations). Today the international system comprises approximately 200 states. UN membership has expanded from fifty-one nation-states in 1945 to 192 at the last count in 2009 (Montenegro was the last to join in 2006). This increase in membership has been so great that the UN facilities in New York are hopelessly overstretched as the building was intended for only sixty to seventy national delegations. The end-product of this development is that nearly every individual on the planet now resides in one nation-state or another.

That is not to say that everyone is content to live where they do. There are groups of individuals who live in one state but who would prefer to reside somewhere else, for example, the Kurds who live in Turkey and Iran. A common feature of such groups is their belief that they should not be governed as part of the countries in which they live. A further point to note is that not all nation-states are similar. While the majority are democratic, many continue to be governed by unelected rulers. At the same time, some states continue to bear a resemblance to previous modes of political organisation. Notable examples include the PRC, which resembles an ancient empire, and Singapore and Lichtenstein, which in terms of geographical size are more like the city-states of ancient Greece and Renaissance Italy.

Despite these differences, it is nevertheless the case that the concept of the nation-state applies to all, and in terms of international law almost all are sovereign states (Taiwan is the most notable exception). But the globalisation of this one particular form of political organisation has not been all plain sailing or harmonious. When Woodrow Wilson advanced the idea of national **self-determination** in the Fourteen Points as proposed as the basis for the settlement after the First World War, he had hoped that this would result in the peaceful creation of new states and the dissolution of empires. Yet, the very drive to establish nation-states has at the same time generated new forms of discord, of which demands for secession have been particularly noticeable.

Demands for secession exist usually when a distinct ethnic group within one state seeks autonomy, thereby threatening to fracture the state into smaller territorial units. This has been a source of civil war and occasional interstate conflict in the period since 1945. In Nigeria in the mid-1960s the Ibo tribe sought an independent Biafra, resulting in a three-year civil war waged by the Nigerian state in its ultimately successful bid to hold the federal state together. More recently in 1993 Eritrea seceded from Ethiopia (Box 12.1). Where the nation is not homogeneous, there exists a potential for fragmentation. Africa is the most afflicted region as a consequence of rapid decolonisation. Its multi-tribal states often appear ripe for tribal conflict over who controls state institutions, with the ensuing risk of fragmentation as tribal identities outweigh feelings of unifying nationalism. But other regions are similarly predisposed, such as the Sikhs in India.

It used to be thought that these forms of conflict were peculiar to the states of the Third World which lacked cohesive national identities due to the affects of colonisation and rapid decolonisation. In the jargon of political scientists they are 'weak states', where local and tribal identities are frequently more powerful than national identity. However, since the end of the Cold War we have witnessed the appearance of such phenomena in Europe. For European

Box 12.1 Timeline of Eritrea

1890	Eritrea becomes an Italian colony.
1941	British forces occupy Eritrea.
1949	The United Kingdom administers Eritrea as a UN trust territory.
1952	UN decision to make Eritrea a federal part of Ethiopia.
1958	Formation of Eritrean Liberation Front.
1962	Ethiopia annexed Eritrea and turned it into a province: start of war of independence.
1974	Ethiopian Emperor Haile Selassie overthrown in a military coup.
1977–8	Cuban forces, aided by Soviet advisers, assist Ethiopian troops to reverse the advances made by Eritrean guerrillas.
1991	Eritrean People's Liberation Front capture the Eritrean capital, Asmara, and establish a provisional government; UN set a date for a referendum on Eritrean independence.
1993	Eritreans vote almost unanimously in support of independence.

examples of secession in the 1990s we have the decomposition of the former Soviet Union into fifteen states; Yugoslavia fractured violently into Slovenia, Croatia, Bosnia-Herzegovina, Macedonia, Serbia, Montenegro and Kosovo; and in 1993 the so-called Velvet Divorce saw the division of Czechoslovakia into the Czech and Slovak Republics. By 2008 Europe had twenty-one more sovereign states than it did in 1990.

Such pressures are also detectable in the more established nation-states of Europe. As examples we have devolution in the United Kingdom, the demands by Bretons for independence from France and ETA's terrorist activity on behalf of the Basques in Spain. It can, therefore, be seen that fragmentation in the form of secessionism does not just afflict the Third World, rather, similar movements also exist in the more developed world.

To conclude this section we can say that despite many movements that have sought to construct political formations other than the nation-state, such as pan-Arabism and pan-Africanism, the notion of an independent nation-state possesses a powerful logic. Thus, those groups that have attempted to break away from established states have envisioned the creation of their own sovereign states. This includes the demands of the Palestinians and Kurds, and the new nation-states created by the Bengalis (Bangladesh), the Slovaks and the Slovenians. The key point here is that ethnic groups which consider themselves oppressed demand their own states.

We can see, therefore, that the nation-state has basically become the sole legitimate form for the political organisation of community. One potential exception to this is in Western Europe, where some scholars argue that the creation of the EU reflects an effort to forge some form of post-national or transnational community. But even though the EU has some state-like qualities, such as diplomatic representation, it is fundamentally an organisation that is governed by its member states. More importantly, at a grass-roots level people in Europe tend not to identify with the EU and in this sense it can be concluded that even transnational economic attempts to forge unity appear ineffective at undermining the pull of the nation-state on the political imagination.

The enduring importance of nuclear weapons

A third defining feature of international politics since the Second World War has been the advent, adolescence and maturity of the nuclear age. Since the use of nuclear weapons on Hiroshima and Nagasaki, a Damocles' sword, in the form of a global nuclear conflagration, has been hanging over the head of humankind. Humans now possess the ability to destroy life on the planet, extinguishing human existence alongside that of many other species. In this way our era is unique: weapons exist that pose an existential threat to the human race.

Yet, it does need to be pointed out that the threat of MAD also brought safety and stability during the Cold War. It may seem strange, but during the Cold War many enlightened American officials recognised the importance of the Soviet Union gaining more nuclear warheads, since only through approximating nuclear parity with the United States would the Soviets feel more secure. This would alleviate their fear that a first strike by the United States would wipe out their capacity to respond in kind and hence a second-strike capability on both sides contributed to Cold War stability. The outcome of this state of affairs was that the Cold War did not escalate into a hot war. Instead, this era was characterised by proxy wars in many Third World countries and the development of crisis management mechanisms to prevent conflicts from escalating. The most notable example of this was the installation of the White House–Kremlin hot line after the Cuban missile crisis of 1962.

John Lewis Gaddis has since deemed the Cold War to be 'the long peace' for this very reason.[2] The possibility of world destruction forced the superpowers to be responsible. Likewise, according to John Mearsheimer, the presence of only two major powers and the reality of nuclear weapons were crucial in stopping the Cold War turning hot.[3] This means that some scholars, notably Kenneth Waltz, have been able to argue that 'more is better'.[4] Nuclear weapons, he has suggested, should be spread throughout the world in the interests of peace.

Nuclear weapons were certainly a defining motif of the Cold War, with the mushroom cloud image of a nuclear explosion being a dominant feature of books and television programmes which have dealt with the subject. However, nuclear weapons are also of continuing importance in the post-Cold War era. For example, Boris Yeltsin, powerless to stop NATO's bombardment of Serbia in 1999, threatened to station nuclear weapons in Belarus. It was the only card he could play. In terms of population and national income, Russia is comparable to Brazil; but the possession of nuclear weapons – along with the residues of its past greatness and the cachet of a permanent seat on the UN Security Council – gives Russia the continuing status of a world power.

But Russia is not the only nuclear power. Nuclear weapons remain important as status symbols. There is an element of prestige, an elevating aspect, which accompanies possession of 'the bomb' because there is the impression that it pushes states up the league table of world powers. For example, France insisted in conducting nuclear tests in French Polynesia in 1996 despite the offer of data by the United States that would have obviated any need for such damage to the environment. But President Chirac was concerned once again to demonstrate French independence from American control.

There are in fact five recognised and legitimate nuclear powers: the PRC, France, the United Kingdom, Russia and the United States. Under the terms of the Non-Proliferation Treaty (NPT) of 1968, they are the only powers in the world that can legally hold nuclear arsenals. They also happen to be the five permanent members (P5) of the UN Security Council. Is this accidental? To some extent, yes: the United States was the only nuclear power when the UN was created in 1945. In another sense, no: the P5 were the victors in the Second World War; other states with the level of economic development necessary for nuclear status were defeated in the war. Germany made a pact with the occupying powers after the Second World War never to develop its own nuclear or chemical weapons in return for regaining its sovereign independence, while Japan is also unlikely to pursue the nuclear option because it had a first-hand experience of the impact of nuclear weapons.

However, at present there are also three illegitimate nuclear powers (Box 12.2). Israel, surrounded by hostile states, developed nuclear weapons for its own protection in the Middle East. As it has not tested a nuclear device and has generally pursued a policy of neither confirming nor denying that it has such weapons – the 'bomb in the basement' policy[5] – analysts disagree over exactly when it developed them, but there seems to be a consensus that this threshold was crossed in the late 1960s or early 1970s. India and Pakistan's demonstrations of nuclear capability in a series of test in May 1998 developed out of their regional security concerns. India's fear of

Box 12.2 Timeline of emergence of the nuclear powers	
1945	United States
1949	Soviet Union
1952	United Kingdom
1960	France
1964	PRC
Late 1960s/early 1970s	Israel
1974	India
1998	Pakistan
2006	North Korea

China led to its successful test of a nuclear device in 1974. However, in the South Asian case there is another element also; for India at least, it is about status and prestige. India's development of nuclear weapons has seen the return of Nehru's rhetoric of non-alignment and anti-racism, but not in such a peaceful fashion. The BJP government that ordered the tests in 1998 claimed that the non-proliferation regime operates to deny one-fifth of the world's population the right to nuclear weapons and is, therefore, racist. Despite the crippling economic costs that both states have suffered, their leaders wager that this is a price worth paying for regional security and a world voice.

India and Pakistan also find hypocrisy in Western fears that Asian powers will be more likely to use nuclear weapons as if they are in some way less rational. However, proliferation in south Asia is worrying due to the lack of a second-strike capability on either side. With less fear of devastating retaliation, getting in a first strike against your opponent with the intention of destroying its nuclear silos may appear a rational option.

As if this wasn't worrying enough, we must add to these new nuclear dangers the threat of procurement by so-called rogue states. North Korea conducted what appeared to be a partially successful test explosion in October 2006 and is therefore on the threshold of becoming a nuclear power. Iran also appears to have a nuclear weapons development programme and, like North Korea, is in the advanced stages of producing medium- and long-range missile delivery systems. On a more positive note, in 2003 Libya buckled under the pressure of trade sanctions and agreed to demolish its nuclear weapons programme under UN inspection, as South Africa did after signing the NPT in 1991. But as the spread of nuclear weapons heightens the risk of accidents and miscalculations, and given post-Cold War instability, the world may indeed be a more dangerous place since the end of superpower tensions.

The 'end of history'

The fourth and by far the most optimistic recent development in international politics since 1945 has been the spread of democracy worldwide. Just as the nation-state is now the dominant model of political community across the planet, so can democracy increasingly lay claim to being the only legitimate form of government. Even dictatorships and authoritarian regimes claim to be democracies, as did the German Democratic Republic and most communist states during the Cold War.

Francis Fukuyama famously described this development as 'the end of history'.[6] In his account History has come to an end. By History (as opposed to mere history) Fukuyama refers not to the ongoing chronological stream of events (which, of course, has not come to an end), but to the era of conflict between ideological systems. In the twentieth century this conflict was fought out by three main ideological systems: fascism; communism; and liberal democracy. These battles were not fought purely on the plane of ideas, as the two world wars and the Cold War demonstrated. But the Second World War brought the defeat of fascism (although not the right-wing authoritarianism which persisted in Spain, Portugal and Latin America until the 1970s and 1980s), just as the end of Cold War saw the defeat of communism (with the largely insignificant exceptions of North Korea and Cuba).

Therefore, according to Fukuyama, the struggle between rival political ideologies is over. In a global, free-market economy, dictatorship has become a dysfunctional and outdated method of government due to the advent of information technology and mass tourism. In this sense, liberal democracy is the only tried, tested and viable form of government. To make this claim we do not have to insist that liberal democracy is perfect. A minimal defence would point to the fact that constitutional democracies have a mechanism for peacefully replacing one administration with another. Democracy in such a reading is little more that a mechanism for rotating the offices of government every so often; but given the problems that states with authoritarian regimes have in this area, it is a major achievement.

Samuel Huntington, among others, has identified three waves of democratisation that have swept the globe. The first wave took place in the nineteenth and early twentieth centuries, the second after 1945 and the third wave began in the mid-1970s.[7] But it is possible to break the 'third wave' itself down into three tranches in the spread of democracy. The first of these took place in Mediterranean Europe in the 1970s with the democratisation that took place in Greece and Portugal in 1974 and Spain in 1975. The second tranche took place in Latin America in the 1980s when Peru (1980), Argentina (following its defeat in the Falklands War in 1982), Uruguay (1983), Brazil (1984) and Paraguay and Chile (both 1990) embarked on the transition to democracy. The third tranche of democratisation took place in Eastern and Central Europe in 1989–90 when Gorbachev's reforms allowed freedom to return to Czechoslovakia, Poland, Hungary, Latvia, Lithuania, Estonia, Bulgaria and Romania. But the spread of democracy was not limited to these three areas. In 1986, Marcos was deposed by popular demonstrations in the Philippines. In 1990 the South African regime released Nelson Mandela as a first step towards replacing apartheid with a multi-racial democracy. Also in Africa in 1990, Benin became the first black African state to experience a change of government by peaceful, democratic means.

This globalisation of democracy is important not just for the spreading of freedom across the world, but also because of what has been described as the only law-like relationship in IR: the fact that no two democracies have ever been at war with each other – the so-called democratic peace thesis.

If it is true that democracies do not fight each other, and if every state in the international system becomes democratic, then we would approach the inter-war Idealists' dream: an end to war. This optimistic interpretation of the globalisation of democracy is based on two presumptions about relations between democratic states that makes such relations markedly different from interstate relations involving at least one non-democratic state.[8]

The first presumption concerns democratic institutions. Dictators can generally act as they choose because of the absence of domestic constraints. This means the actions of impetuous dictators can lead directly to war. But in democracies, power tends to be dispersed across a number of institutions. Hence, democratically-elected leaders tend to be more constrained, as they need to build up domestic support before embarking on a war. The existence of democratic institutions on both sides in a conflict thus creates a cooling-off period for peaceful solutions to conflicts of interest to be found. The second presumption concerns the nature of democratic values and norms. By definition, democracy promotes the resolution of conflict through the peaceful accommodation of clashing interests. The ideology of liberal democracy does not condone the lawless use of force; instead, it values attempts to achieve consensus. Therefore, when two or more democratic states find that their national interests collide, they will pursue peaceful means of finding a settlement.

Critics of the democratic peace thesis argue that there have been few opportunities for democracies to fight each other. As a general rule, states (except for great powers and superpowers) tend to go to war with their neighbours. The fact that until relatively recently democracies made up only a tiny proportion of states in the international system means that the absence of war between democracies shouldn't surprise us. But since 1945 there have been increasing numbers of democracies in existence, many of them sharing borders, and still we have no example of democratic war. (Russia's invasion of Georgia in 2008 can be disregarded on the grounds that at least one of these states is not a properly functioning democracy.) Therefore, due to the mutual constraints outlined above, Fukuyama and Robert Cooper, among others, have suggested we should expect the democracies in the world to form a zone of peace.[9]

Summary: world at war, world at peace?

There is another side of the coin to the democratic peace: the tendency to demonise and launch wars against dictators, for example, the invasion of Iraq in 2003 to remove Saddam Hussein from power.[10] The danger is that democracies may embark on moral crusades to liberate oppressed populations that actually increase the level of violence in the international system. Statistically democracies are just as likely to go to war as any other form of state, if not more so; they just do not fight other democracies. If this trend continues, we can project the emergence of two worlds of world politics: one at war, where democracies wage their military compaigns against dictators and authoritarian regimes, mainly in the developing world; and one at peace, primarily in the northern hemisphere. This development in contemporary world politics is a recent manifestation of the more general tension between reasons for optimism and sources of pessimism in international politics that has been a central theme running through this book and through the study of IR as a discipline.

. . . .

✔ What you should have learnt from reading this chapter

- Globalisation is a significant force in shaping the economic, social and cultural aspects of international politics.

- The nation-state is the predominant means of organising political community in the world, despite global and regional challenges.

- The presence of multicultural and multinational societies puts pressure on loyalties to nation-states.

- Many of the most serious conflicts are the result of struggles for statehood.

- Despite being a defining feature of the Cold War, nuclear weapons are of continuing relevance in the post-Cold War order.

- The spread of democracy across the world holds the possibility of an end to war, although there are dangers of crusades for the promotion of democracy.

? Likely examination questions

What is globalisation?

Is globalisation a primarily economic phenomenon?

Has globalisation transformed the nature of international politics?

Why has the nation-state emerged as the predominant form of political community?

What is secessionism and how does it destabilise the international system?

Why have nuclear weapons remained important in the post-Cold War order?

Has the spread of nuclear weapons made the world a safer or more dangerous place?

Why has democracy become the most favoured form of political system?

Why historically have democracies not fought each other?

Is there a danger that attempts to promote perpetual peace will result in perpetual war?

Helpful websites

See the websites listed at the end of Chapters 9 and 10.

United Nations Growth in Membership at: www.un.org/members/growth.shtml

 Suggestions for further reading

R. Cooper, *The Breaking of Nations: Order and Chaos in the Twenty-First Century* (Atlantic Books, 2004).

F. Fukuyama, *The End of History and the Last Man* (Hamish Hamilton, 1993).

D. Held and A. McGrew, *Globalization/Anti-Globalization: Beyond the Great Divide*, 2nd edn (Polity, 2007).

B. Russett, *Grasping the Democratic Peace: Principles for a Post-Cold War World* (Princeton University Press, 1993).

S. Sagan and K. Waltz, *The Spread of Nuclear Weapons: A Debate Revisited* (WW Norton and Company, 2003).

J. A. Scholte, *Globalization: A Critical Introduction*, 2nd edn (Palgrave Macmillan, 2005).

Glossary of key terms

Al-Qaeda is an international terrorist organisation founded by Osama bin Laden that has been attributed as the source of the 11 September 2001 (otherwise known as 9/11) terrorist attacks on the United States. The American-led war in Afghanistan of 2001 was a direct response to these attacks as the US government sought to topple the Afghan Taliban government that was acknowledged as having provided a safe haven for al-Qaeda. This attempt to eliminate the threat of al-Qaeda became known as the 'war on terror'.

Anarchy means the absence of government. Anarchy is often used in the context of the theory of Realism.

Appeasement is a term that is principally associated with the policies pursued by Britain and France towards Germany in the period between the First and Second World Wars. The readiness of Britain and France to accept Germany's expansionist policies at that time has meant that the term has become synonymous with giving in to the wishes of opponents.

Arms race takes place when a competition occurs between states to amass and/or to develop weapons. During the Cold War there was an arms race between the United States and the Soviet Union. It is also possible to have an arms race at a regional level, such as the competition between India and Pakistan to obtain nuclear weapons.

Balance of power refers to a situation whereby the relationship between any state(s) is such that no one should have greater power than the other.

Bipolar is a situation when two states are in competition for dominance over the other. During the Cold War the competition between the United States and the Soviet Union was regarded as that of a bipolar relationship.

Bretton Woods is synonymous with the negotiations that took place in the United States between 1944 and 1946 that sought to develop a structure for the international system after the end of the Second World War. This resulted in the establishment of the IMF, GATT, and the International Bank for Reconstruction and Development (IBRD), otherwise known as the World Bank. These organisations are collectively known as the Bretton Woods system that sought to promote economic stability centred on a process of trade liberalisation.

Brezhnev Doctrine takes its name from the former Soviet leader, Leonid Brezhnev. The doctrine basically said that the Soviet Union had the right to intervene to stop the overthrow of communism in the Soviet bloc of states in Central and Eastern Europe. The Doctrine ended when Gorbachev permitted these countries to make their own choices in 1989–91 and this resulted in the emergence of the so-called Sinatra Doctrine.

Capitalism is an economic system which stresses the private ownership of production and property with the exchange of goods taking place in a free market. It is a system that was subject to significant critique in the writings of Karl Marx and Friedrich Engels, whereby they argued that the tendency for capitalist systems to concentrate wealth and power in a small proportion of the population meant that the society could never be regarded as democratic.

City-states is a term that refers to cities that essentially performed the tasks of small countries. City-states were common in ancient Greece (such as Athens and Sparta) and in northern Italy (such as Florence and Venice). Today there continue to be a small number of city-states, notably Singapore, Luxembourg and Monaco.

Civil society is a broad and much used term which refers to the way in which individuals come together around shared interests and values that, in turn, result in certain structures being established to represent what is in essence a form of collective action. When civil society is mentioned it is often related to such organisations as NGOs, trades unions, social movements, faith-based associations and charities.

Civil war refers to wars that take place between factions within the same country.

Clash of civilisations is a term coined by Samuel P. Huntington which stressed that in the post-Cold War world culture will be the main source of conflict.

Climate change refers to the way in which the climate has changed as a result of human activity. Climate change is routinely used in the context of the way in which there has occurred a warming in the earth's atmosphere that is over and above what would be expected in historic terms.

Cold War is a phrase that emerged in the late 1940s to highlight the tension that developed in the wake of the Second World War between the United States and the Soviet Union and which came to an end with the collapse of the Berlin Wall in 1989. The term Cold War is used to demonstrate the fact that the United States and the Soviet Union did not engage in direct open conflict with each other.

Collective security is when states come to an agreement that their own security is bound up with the security of each other and also decide to take collective responsibility in response to any act of aggression.

Colonialism is when a power has control of another country.

Common market is a term that is often used to describe the original European Community with there being an emphasis on the removal of customs duties between the member states.

Communism is a political ideology based on the writings of Friedrich Engels and Karl Marx which stresses a common ownership of property and an absence of classes, with the state owning the means of production. It is a system of government that has been applied in the Soviet Union and the PRC.

Conference on Security and Cooperation in Europe (CSCE) was established in 1975 as a result of the signing of the Helsinki Final Act and was a key development during the period of détente. The CSCE represented a formal attempt to reconcile the different interests of the American-led NATO and the Soviet-led Warsaw Pact by providing a platform where Warsaw Pact and NATO countries could meet. In 1990 it was renamed the Organisation for Security and Cooperation in Europe (OSCE) and it commenced a process of expansion in membership and also the establishment of permanent institutions as well as operational capabilities. In 2008 the OSCE had fifty-six members and as such is the largest regional organisation in the world, with its work focused on aspects relating to human, political and military aspects of security.

Constructivism is a theory which is concerned with analysing the way in which the structure of world politics is constructed through the interaction of states. This basically means that whereas Realist theory argues that anarchy is a result of an inherent structural condition of world politics, Constructivists stress that there exists an opportunity to change the nature of the international system and state interaction.

Containment was the mainstay of American policy toward the Soviet Union throughout the Cold War. The policy was advanced in 1947 by the US diplomat, George Kennan, and had three aims. First, restoring the balance of power whereby the United States supported states that were threatened by the Soviet Union. Secondly, reducing the Soviet capability to project power by co-operating with communist regimes, such as Tito in Yugoslavia. Thirdly, to modify the Soviet concept of international politics through the negotiation of outstanding differences.

Council of Ministers is regarded as the most important EU institution. It comprises representatives from member states, with its work being divided between different policy areas ranging from finance to foreign affairs.

Court of Justice is the final arbiter of all legal issues in the EU, including the resolution of disputes between EU member states as well as between firms and individuals within the EU. The court has sometimes been criticised because its decisions have often favoured deeper European integration.

Customs union is when two or more countries establish a free trade policy among themselves by lifting duties and creating a common external tariff.

Decolonisation is a process that has principally taken place since the end of the Second World War, whereby colonial powers have granted independence to their former colonies. As the colonial powers were often faced with pressures for independence the transfers of power were not always planned.

Democracy is a political system where everyone has the right and ability to influence the decisions taken by government.

Dependency is a term that is applied to the historic and contemporary situation whereby the industrialised countries of the North have often established a set of relationships with less developed countries in the South, whereby the latter are in effect dependent and at the same time disadvantaged by these relations.

Détente was a period of relaxation in the tension between the Soviet Union and the United States as a result of foreign and defence policy decisions. It is most commonly associated with the 1970s as a result of the deliberate efforts by Western European governments and the United States to improve relations with the PRC and the Soviet Union. By the end of the 1970s the policy of Soviet intervention (for example, in Angola and Afghanistan) and the refusal of Eastern bloc states to observe human rights provisions led to a deterioration in relations with the West. When US President Ronald Reagan took office in 1981 the period of détente essentially came to an end.

Deterrence is a process by which a country seeks to persuade an opponent not to enter into conflict through having sufficient armed forces to stop an attack and in some instances also lead to a counter-attack. Deterrence was a regularly used term during the Cold War, when the capacity for the superpowers to inflict total damage on each other led to the term mutually assured deterrence (MAD) which actually created a climate of stability.

Developing countries have a low standard of living and often have significant debts which hamper their economic development. These countries are principally located in Africa, South America and parts of Asia. This is a term that is often used alongside the terms 'Third World', the 'South', and 'less developed countries'.

Devolution takes place when powers are transferred from national or central government to a lower level of state, regional or local government. This has taken place in the United Kingdom with the devolution of powers to Northern Ireland, Scotland and Wales.

Diplomacy refers to the conduct of relations between nation-states that take place through negotiations.

Domino theory originated in the 1950s when the United States believed that if the spread of communism was not stopped in Vietnam then it would spread to other countries in the manner of dominoes falling. Thus, when one country turned communist then another would do so and so on. Yet, the United States wrongly regarded the conflict in Vietnam as part of a broader spread of Communism and did not realise that it was a civil conflict that was less rooted in ideological divides. When the United States eventually pulled out of Vietnam a domino effect did not occur in southeast Asia.

East–West refers to the ideological division that took place after the Second World War between the Eastern and Western hemispheres, whereby the East was for the most part rooted in a communist system of government and the West rooted in a democratic system of government.

Eastern bloc was used to refer to the Soviet Union and its allies and satellite states in Central and Eastern Europe during the Cold War.

Ethnic group is a group of people that are regarded as being distinct from other groups as a result of cultural affiliation. In this sense, ethnicity is different from race, nationality and citizenship.

European Commission is the executive body of the EU and guardian of the treaties. Although it is often regarded as just the EU civil service, its role is far more important because it has the task of initiating EU legislation, implementing policies that have been agreed on, and it also plays an important role in negotiating on behalf of the EU on trade matters and with respect to relations with third countries. It can also refer matters to the Court of Justice when agreed policies have not been implemented by member states.

European Council comprises the heads of state or government of the member states and the President of the European Commission, and provides political direction to the EU.

European Parliament is the only directly-elected EU institution and comprises members of the European Parliament (MEPs) who are directly elected for a five-year term of office from each member state, with the number of national MEPs being in proportion to population. The European Parliament's most important area of influence is its power to amend and adopt legislation via the co-decision procedure, while its approval is also necessary for appointments to the European Commission.

Failed states occur when a functioning central government does not exist. As a result there is typically an absence of public services in failed states and consequently there is a great deal of corruption and crime. Because of the severe economic and political conditions in failed states it is often the case that there are significant movements in population as people seek to gain security in other states.

Fascism is an ideological approach that advances an extreme nationalism which is most commonly associated with the system of government that took hold in Italy and Germany in the 1920s and 1930s. It is a system that emphasises the importance of the nation, with power being centralised and often headed by a dictator and consequently resulting in the suppression of opposition parties.

Fossil fuels, notably coal, oil and natural gas, have been created over a very long period of time as a result of the decomposition of plants and animals. They are the main sources of power for many countries and the burning of these fuels is linked to an increase in global warming.

Glasnost was a process of 'openness' that was used by Mikhail Gorbachev to promote change in the Soviet Union from the mid-1980s onwards. This meant allowing the opportunity to debate formerly closed issues in Soviet society, such as the role of women, as well as issues relating to the environment (a point that was particularly relevant after the Chernobyl nuclear disaster of 1986). Glasnost spread to encompass other issues, including freedom of speech and publication and led to the toleration of criticism of Soviet history and the role of its leaders, including Lenin and Stalin. In conjunction with perestroika, glasnost was significant in promoting reform throughout Central and Eastern Europe, which in the end brought about the downfall of the Soviet Union.

Global warming is taking place as a result of the release of greenhouse gases.

Globalisation refers to the increasing interconnectedness and interdependence of the world's population.

Great Depression took place in the wake of the 1929 Wall Street crash. The crash triggered an economic crisis that plunged industrialised countries into an economic slump that resulted in mass unemployment.

Great Powers is a term that came to the fore at the time of the Vienna Congress of 1814–15 that brought the Napoleonic War to an end. The Great Powers at that time were considered to be Austria, France, Prussia, Britain and Russia. The twentieth century witnessed the rise of the United States and the Soviet Union as superpowers. The term is also used as part of a method of ranking states in the international system, whereby states can be referred to as great powers, medium powers and small powers.

Gross Domestic Product (GDP) is the total value of the goods and services produced in a country over period of one year. It excludes foreign exchange earnings.

Hallstein Doctrine was the claim made by the Federal Republic of Germany (FDR) (West Germany) that it was the sole representative of Germany because, in contrast to the government in the German Democratic Republic (GDR) (East Germany), the FDR's government had been democratically elected. Named after its author, Walter Hallstein, the Doctrine was set out in the 'Government Declaration' of Konrad Adenauer on 23 September 1955. The Doctrine was succeeded by the policy of Ostpolitik (relations with the East) which came to prominence after the election of Willy Brandt as Chancellor in 1969.

Hegemony refers to a situation when a particular country or leader is able to dominate an area. This usually referred to the influence exercised by superpowers during the Cold War.

Hot war is an international military conflict of a global or regional nature.

Human rights are internationally recognised to refer to the fact that all human beings are entitled to have the same moral and legal status. This includes the right to life, food, housing, health care, employment, education, liberty, privacy, as well as equality before the law and freedom of movement and freedom of religion.

Human security is a term which refers to the need to protect human life in the face of growing threats, such as drug and people trafficking, that are often influenced by the activities of organised crime groups.

Idealism is the belief that it is possible for co-operation to take place in international relations to put an end to war.

Idealist refers to the term that came to prominence after the First World War with the establishment of the League of Nations. The Idealist approach stresses the importance of promoting international co-operation between countries.

Imperial overstretch takes place when a country attempts to achieve dominance in a hegemonic manner over other countries which can result in it over committing its resources and can, in fact, be harmful to the very survival of the country.

Imperialism is the practice whereby states have sought to dominate other states through direct rule which in turn has often resulted in the establishment of an empire.

Interdependence refers to the situations whereby as more and more states become economically developed they develop increasingly close relations with other states, which in turn creates a level of connectedness which means that developments in one state often have an impact on others.

Interest group is a non-governmental group of individuals who share similar views and who seek to exert influence on national governments. In some instance interest groups also seek to exert influence on other organisations such as the UN and the EU.

Intergovernmental organisations (IGOs) are formed by nation states to promote their own interests through a collective organisation. Although IGOs exist to serve the interests of the member states, this can in certain instances, such as the EU, result in an IGO having powers that also constrain the choices that are available to member states.

International law are the rules that govern the relationships between states.

International system is a means of referring to the various interactions that take place among a variety of actors at the international level. This includes the activity of states, IGOs and MNCs. In this sense, the international system is at one end of a tier of levels of analysis which includes the state system as well as those activities that take place below the level of the state.

Iron curtain is a term that was used during the Cold War to refer to the East–West division of Europe. In March 1946 Winston Churchill made a speech in Fulton, Missouri which became famous for his concern that an 'iron curtain' had descended across Europe. In using this term, Churchill was highlighting the way in which the countries in Eastern Europe were being dominated by Soviet control.

Irredentism is a term which relates to the demands of ethnic groups to ensure that their fellow nationals are all located in one state. This situation often occurs when state boundaries have been established that divide ethnic groups.

Kyoto Protocol is an international agreement that has established binding targets for the reduction of greenhouse gas emissions. It falls under the United Nations Framework Convention on Climate Change.

Less developed countries (LDCs) is an expression that is used to refer to those countries that are principally situated in Africa, Asia and Latin America and which have a standard of living that is significantly less than that of industrialised countries. LDCs are primarily involved in the production of primary products, such as agriculture and raw materials, such as iron ore.

Liberalism stresses that nation-states are but one actor in world politics and notes the potential for states to enter into co-operation with each other.

Marshall Plan took place after the Second World War. In June 1947 the US Secretary of State, George Marshall, proposed a plan that would aid the rebuilding of European economies in the wake of the Second World War. The plan offered financial aid as well as other forms of assistance to the war-ravaged countries of Western Europe. The Marshall Plan played an important role in helping to foster the economic and political recovery of Europe, and was of considerable importance in promoting the concept of European integration as well as liberalising intra-European trade.

Marxism is a theory based on the philosophy of Karl Marx which emphasises that the nature of world politics has been structured to serve capitalist economies and that the inequalities that exist between states are the result of these structures.

Microstate is a state that often has a small land area and a small population.

Mujahideen refers to Islamic guerrilla warriors, primarily those who in the 1980s fought against the Soviet invasion of Afghanistan.

Multinational corporations (MNCs) are economic enterprises that have bases of operation in two or more countries.

Munich Agreement A meeting which took place between Britain, France, Germany, and Italy in 1938, at which it was accepted that Germany would be allowed to annex the Sudetenland, a part of Czechoslovakia, because of an unwillingness among the other countries to confront Germany. This was known as a policy of appeasement.

Mutual Assured Destruction (MAD) emerged as a term during the Cold War to emphasise the capability of both superpowers to launch second-strike nuclear weapon attacks against each other, meaning that it was not possible for either country to win a nuclear war. The reality of this situation gave rise to the term mutual assured destruction. American efforts to develop a Strategic Defence Initiative (SDI) in the 1980s created the possibility that the United States would be able to shield itself under a strategic umbrella that would protect it from nuclear attack. In such a theoretical setting, the United States would have the opportunity to win a nuclear war and as a result would erase the 'mutual' from mutual assured destruction.

National interest refers to the notion that each state has a clearly defined set of aims, usually with state security at the top of the list. However, Liberals challenge the idea that complex states have identifiable and internally consistent national interests.

Nationalism is the belief that every nation (usually defined in terms of ethnicity, language, culture and shared sense of belonging) should have its own state.

Neocolonialism is the way in which the governments of former colonial powers, as well as capitalist businesses located in developed countries, have often exercised undue influence over colonies when they became independent countries. The leaders of these new countries often criticise the way in which their countries are being subjected to rules, regulations and procedures that they argue constitute a new form of colonialism.

Non-Aligned Movement (NAM) is an organisation encompassing a large number of Third World countries, which emerged during the Cold War as a result of a desire to be independent from superpower rivalry. Since its first meeting in 1955 at Bandung, the NAM has issued a number of statements ranging from matters relating to development and trade to nuclear proliferation.

Non-governmental organisations (NGOs) are organisations which seek to promote specific policies that are independent of government and corporate interests. Notable examples include Amnesty International, Greenpeace and the Red Cross.

Non-state actors are those actors in international politics which are aside from nation-states. This would include NGOs and IGOs.

Non-tariff barriers are barriers to trade which do not take the form of physical barriers. Instead, they refer to factors which hinder trade between countries, such as different rules on product specification and different technical standards. These distinctions often mean that national governments can protect their own domestic markets from foreign competition.

North is an expression that refers to the world's economically developed countries which for the most part are in the Northern Hemisphere.

North–South division is the division between the economically developed countries that are principally located in the North and the less developed countries that are mainly located in the South. There are a greater number of less developed countries in the world than developed ones and it is generally acknowledged that the gap between rich and poor countries has widened over time.

Nuclear proliferation occurs when states that do not have nuclear weapons seek to develop or obtain them.

Ostpolitik was the policy towards Eastern Europe that was adopted by the coalition government of Social Democrats and Liberal Free Democrats that came to power in West Germany in 1969. The policy, under the leadership of Chancellor Willy Brandt, was described as 'change through rapprochement'. It set out to replace confrontation with the Eastern Bloc that had been a central feature of the Hallstein Doctrine.

Peacekeeping refers to the actions undertaken by international organisations, such as the UN, to despatch peacekeeping forces to conflict regions so as to act as a barrier between opposing forces. UN peacekeeping forces tend to be of an international nature and there has on occasion been criticism of both the mandate of the peacekeeping force to stop conflicts taking place and at the same time the robustness of the forces deployed.

Perestroika means 'restructuring' and was used by Mikhail Gorbachev in the same breadth as glasnost to refer to the need for change in the Soviet Union. Although Gorbachev initially thought that economic reform through perestroika was necessary to help to main the Soviet system, it quickly became evident that such reforms unleashed pressure which in the end brought about its downfall.

Post-industrial is an expression that is used to refer to those economies that have fewer workers employed in manufacturing industry because of technological advancements. To this end, a greater share of the economic wealth of the country rests in the service sector (such as banking and insurance) as well as information technology products (such as computer software).

Pressure groups primarily seek to influence the policy and direction of government. The term is interchangeable with others such as interest groups and lobby groups. Pressure groups vary considerably in their size and operation. Some are very large with formal structures like the Confederation of British Industry (CBI) or the Trades Union Congress (TUC). Others can be very small, representing only a few individuals and having no full-time employees. An example of the latter could be a local residents association campaigning for more street lights or a play area for children. The key point is that pressure groups seek to influence policy wherever the relevant decisions are being made, be that at the level of local government, such as a council, national government or indeed at the supranational level such as the EU.

Protectionism occurs when a country adopts a policy of restricting the amount of imports from other countries through a combination of tariff barriers (such as raising import taxes) and non-tariff barriers (such as noting that the imported product does not meet the required technical specifications).

Proxy wars are conflicts that are basically fought by third parties rather than countries directly fighting each other. This was principally the case during the Cold War as typified by the Korean War and Vietnam War.

Qualified majority voting (QMV) is a method of decision-making in the Council of Ministers of the EU, whereby decisions are taken that reflect the view of the majority of the member states. Individual member states can be required to accept a policy that they do not like. Over time a gradual expansion in the number of policy areas that are covered by QMV has taken place. Votes are divided among the member states in proportion to the relative size of their population. At the time of writing the twenty-seven member states of the EU have a total of 345 votes. For a proposal to succeed under QMV it must achieve a minimum of 255 out of the 345 votes.

Quasi-states is a term that has been developed to apply principally to Third World countries where states have been created (and survived) despite the fact that many of them are unstable. One of the reasons for this instability is that the state structures have often been welded onto existing tribal and ethnic communities, with the result that individuals often have a greater allegiance to their tribes than they do to the nation-state.

Realism stresses the anarchic nature of international politics and that nation-states are the main actor. Because of the existence of anarchy, the primary interest of states is to protect their sovereignty and this means that they will not enter into co-operation with each other.

Referendum is when the electorate are asked to either approve or disapprove of a matter that has been raised by government.

Reparations are the payments made by defeated powers at the end of a war to compensate the victorious countries for the cost of the war and to limit the potential of the defeated country to wage a future war. Reparations were imposed on Germany at the end of the First World War and their negative impact on the German nation is viewed as being one of the factors which led to the outbreak of the Second World War.

Rogue states are countries that are considered to disobey the rules and practices that are followed by the majority of nation-states.

Sanctions are the methods (mainly bans on trade) that can be imposed at an individual country and/or international level against specific countries that are viewed as being in violation of certain rules and norms. In the past sanctions have been applied against South Africa at a time when it operated a policy of apartheid against the majority black population. Sanctions have also been applied against Zimbabwe in response to the policies pursued by President Robert Mugabwe.

Secessionism is the name given to demands from groups within a state to break away and form their own state.

Second Cold War took place after the period of détente which dominated most of the 1970s. There was a heightening in superpower tensions from 1979 to 1985, a period otherwise known as the Second Cold War. It was a period dominated by an acceleration of the arms race, demonstrated in the United States by the announcement of the SDI and the building up of a large navy and heavy financial investment in the air force. The significant US military expenditure is often acknowledged to be a factor in bringing about the end of the Cold War as a crumbling Soviet Union was unable to match the United States in terms of the resources invested.

Security dilemma takes place when a state increases its military strength to protect itself and in so doing leads to other neighbouring states increasing their own military strength because they feel less secure.

Self-determination is the idea that individuals and countries should have the right to determine their own future. It is a concept that has been used principally in the context of decolonisation.

Sinatra Doctrine was the policy of non-intervention that was adopted by the Soviet Union in 1989 at the time of the collapse of the Berlin Wall. Named after the famous American singer, it basically meant that the countries in Central and Eastern Europe would go 'their own way'. As such, the emergence of this doctrine highlighted the end of the Brezhnev Doctrine which had been one of intervention and limited sovereignty for this group of countries.

Sovereignty is a feature of international politics which stresses that all states are equal, and that states have the right to take responsibility for the decisions within their own borders. Eurosceptics argue that EU integration has undermined national sovereignty because of the transfer of decision-making from the member states to the EU, while at the same time the legal decisions of the Court of Justice override national law.

South is a label that is given to the group of countries that are less well developed, which are for the main part located in the Southern Hemisphere.

Spheres of influence are the way in which a country is able to dominate another area without actually having formal sovereign control over it. During the Cold War this term was used to highlight the way in which the Soviet Union principally exercised control over the states of Central and Eastern Europe, while it also had influence over other countries such as Angola and Cuba. The United States sphere of influence included Western Europe and Latin America.

Spill over is an idea of European integration whereby one area of policy integration would spill over and impact on other areas of policy that might otherwise have been conducted at the member state level. Thus, the single market spilled over into the single currency.

Subnational refers to those levels of government that take place below the level of the state, such as regional or local government.

Summits are important diplomatic meetings between heads of states.
Superpower is a term that has been used to refer to those countries
that have resources (such as wealth, industrial production, raw materials,
military force, nuclear weapons) that are far greater than other countries.
During the Cold War it was recognised that the only superpowers were
the United States and the Soviet Union. Since the end of the Cold War
and the collapse of the Soviet Union the United States has generally been
acknowledged as the sole superpower. It could be possible that in the
future China's growing economic, political and military influence could
create a situation whereby it could be regarded as having superpower
status.
Supranational is a situation when national governments share sovereignty
with each other and establish supranational institutions above the nation-
state to co-ordinate policies. This term is commonly used in the context of
the EU because of the capacity of decisions taken at an EU level to have
an impact on the member states.
Terrorism is an unregularised form of violence that has a tendency to
attack civilians.
Third World was initially used during the Cold War to refer to LDCs in
Asia, Africa and Latin America, with the idea being that the other two
worlds were the American-led Western bloc and the Soviet-led Eastern
bloc. Today the phrase continues to be used, although much reference is
also given to LDCs.
Truman Doctrine evolved out of the March 1947 speech given by US
President Harry Truman, which said that 'it must be the policy of the
United States to support free peoples who are resisting attempted
subjugation by armed minorities or by outside pressures'. The statement
was initially intended to support American aid to Greece and Turkey, but
soon became an example of the policy of 'containment' as it was used
as the basis for the establishment of NATO and the longer-term global
presence of the United States.
Unipolarity is the situation when a single state dominates the international
system.
War on terror is a general term which gained prominence in the wake of
the 11 September 2001 terrorist attacks on the United States when the
US government responded by announcing a war on terror. At the heart
of this view is a desire to defeat terrorist groups, such as al-Qaeda and
those states that harbour terrorists. In 2003 the United States stressed
that its enemy in general was terrorism. Yet, the war on terror has proved
to be extremely problematic for the United States, not least because of
the difficulty of fighting a war which basically suggests that the means of
victory is the advancement of democracy.
Warsaw Pact was established in 1955 as a result of bilateral military
co-operation treaties that were signed between the Soviet Union and

seven countries of Eastern Europe: Albania, Bulgaria, Czechoslovakia, German Democratic Republic, Hungary, Poland and Romania (Albania withdrew in 1951). This was basically the Soviet Union's response to NATO. Following the collapse of communism in Central and Eastern Europe in 1989 and the ending of the Cold War, the Warsaw Pact was dissolved on 1 April 1991.

West was a term used during the Cold War which became a popular means of referring to those countries that were aligned to the United States and as a result opposed to the Soviet-led group of countries in the East. The term has, however, also had a wider reference as a means of highlighting the industrialised democracies of the world and as such also includes such countries as Japan.

Western bloc is a term that refers to the American-led group of states that principally included the countries of Western Europe and Canada during the Cold War.

References

Chapter 1

1. United Nations Development Programme, *Human Development Report 2007/2008* (Palgrave Macmillan, 2007), at: http://hdr.undp.org/en/media/HDR_20072008_EN_Complete.pdf.
2. Stern Review, *Report on the Economics of Climate Change*, HM Treasury (2006), at: www.hm-treasury.gov.uk/stern_review_final_report.htm.
3. United Nations Environment Programme is available at: www.unep.org/geo.
4. Intergovernmental Panel on Climate Change is available at: www.ipcc.ch.
5. The work conducted by Greenpeace on the environment can be found at: www.greenpeace.org/international/campaigns/climate-change.
6. The International Geosphere-Biosphere Programme (IGBP) is available at: www.igbp.kva.se/page.php?pid=100.
7. The Earth Charter can be found at: www.earthcharter.org.
8. Intergovernmental Panel on Climate Change, at: www.ipcc.ch.
9. Tearfund, *Feeling the Heat*, 2006, at: www.tearfund.org/webdocs/Website/News/Feeling%20the%20Heat%20Tearfund%20report.pdf.
10. R. Ramesh, 'Paradise almost lost: Maldives seek to buy a new homeland', *The Guardian*, 10 November 2008, at: www.guardian.co.uk/environment/2008/nov/10/maldives-climate-change.
11. D. Marples, *The Collapse of the Soviet Union, 1985–1991* (Longman, 2004).
12. UN Security Council Resolution 1368 (2001) at: http://daccessdds.un.org/doc/UNDOC/GEN/N01/533/82/PDF/N0153382.pdf?OpenElement.
13. UN Security Council Resolution 1373 (2001) at: http://daccessdds.un.org/doc/UNDOC/GEN/N01/557/43/PDF/N0155743.pdf?OpenElement.
14. R. Blakely, 'David Miliband: Bush's War on Terror was misleading and mistaken', *The Times*, 16 January 2009.
15. *Index of Weak States in the Developing World*, Brookings Institution (2008) at: www.brookings.edu/reports/2008/02_weak_states_index.aspx.

16. J. S. Nye, *Soft Power: The Means to Success in World Politics* (Public Affairs, 2004).

17. M. Leonard, *Why Europe Will Run the 21st Century* (Fourth Estate, 2005).

18. Thucydides, *History of the Peloponnesian War*, trans. R. Crawley (Everyman, 1993).

19. N. Machiavelli, *The Prince*, trans. P. Bondanella (Oxford University Press, 2005).

20. E. H. Carr, *The Twenty Years' Crisis* (Palgrave, 2001).

21. H. J. Morgenthau, *Politics Among Nations: The Struggle for Power and Peace*, revised 5th edn (McGraw-Hill, 1985).

22. J. L. Richardson, 'Contending liberalisms: past and present', *European Journal of International Relations*, Vol. 3, No. 1, 1997, pp. 5–33.

23. A. Wendt, 'Anarchy is what states make of it: the Social construction of power politics', *International Organization*, Vol. 46, No. 2, 1992, pp. 391–425.

24. A. Hurrell and N. Woods, 'Globalization and inequality', *Millennium: Journal of International Studies*, Vol. 24, No. 3, Winter 1995, p. 447.

25. United Nations Human Development Report 2007/8, available at: http://hdr.undp.org/en/reports/global/hdr2007-2008.

26. UNICEF, 'The State of the World's Children 1999', available at: www.unicef.org/sowc99/index.html.

27. B. Buzan and O. Wæver, *Regions and Powers: The Structure of International Security* (Cambridge University Press, 2003).

Chapter 2

1. D. G. Wright, *Napoleon and Europe* (Longman, 1985).

2. I. Porter and I. Armour, *Imperial Germany 1890–1918* (Longman, 1991).

3. P. Kennedy, *The Rise and Fall of the Great Powers: Economic Change and Military Conflict from 1500 to 2000* (Fontana Press, 1988), p. 327.

4. Z. Steiner, *The Lights that Failed: European International History 1919–1933* (Oxford University Press, 2005), p. 4.

5. S. L. Carruthers, 'International history, 1900–1945', in J. Baylis and S. Smith (eds), *The Globalization of World Politics*, 3rd edn (Oxford University Press, 2006), p. 68

6. R. J. Overy, *The Inter-War Crisis 1919–1939*, 2nd edn (Longman, 2007).

7. E. H. Carr, *The Twenty Years' Crisis* (Palgrave, 2001).

8. F. McDonough, *Hitler and Rise of the Nazi Party* (Longman, 2003).

9. H. Kissinger, *Diplomacy* (Touchstone, 1995), p. 245.

10. D. G. Williamson, *The Third Reich*, 3rd edn (Longman, 2002).

11. *Cabinet Conclusion 1. The International System. 2 September 1939*, p. 11, available at: http://filestore.nationalarchives.gov.uk/pdfs/small/cab-23-100-cc-48-39-16.pdf.

12. R. J. Overy, *The Origins of the Second World War*, 2nd edn (Longman, 1998).

13 J. Keegan, *The First World War* (Random House, 1998), p. 9.

14. M. Nicholson, *International Relations: A Concise Introduction*, 2nd edn (Palgrave, 2002), p. 57.

15. Quoted in P. Kennedy, *The Rise and Fall of the Great Powers: Economic Change and Military Conflict from 1500 to 2000* (Fontana Press, 1988), p. 447.

16. D. Engel, *The Holocaust: The Third Reich and the Jews* (Longman, 2000).

17. Tim Kirk, *The Longman Companion to Nazi History* (Longman, 1995), p. 172.

18. The Bretton Woods Agreements at: http://avalon.law.yale.edu/20th_century/decad047.asp.

19. C. Archer, *International Organizations*, 3rd edn (Routledge, 2001), p. 21.

20. The Berlin (Potsdam) Conference at: http://avalon.law.yale.edu/20th_century/decade17.asp.

21. S. R. Williamson Jr. and S. L. Rearden, *The Origins of US Nuclear Strategy, 1945–1953* (St Martin's Press, 1993), p. 20.

Chapter 3

1. Available at: www.yale.edu/lawweb/avalon/trudoc.htm.

2. H. Kissinger, *The White House Years* (Weidenfeld and Nicolson, 1979), p. 115.

3. M. McCauley, *Russia, America and the Cold War1949–1991* (Longman, 1998), p. 18.

4. M. E. Chamberlain, *The Scramble for Africa*, 2nd edn (Longman, 1999).

5. UN Resolution 181 of 29 November 1947 is available at: www.truman-library.org/israel/unres181.htm.

6. G. Lundestad, *The United States and Western Europe since 1945* (Oxford University Press, 2003), p. 11.

7. US Department of State: at: www.state.gov/r/pa/ho/time/cwr/82209.htm.

8. J. W. Young, *Cold War Europe, 1945–89: A Political History* (Edward Arnold, 1991), p. 13.

9. R. J. McMahon, *The Cold War: A Very Short Introduction* (Oxford University Press, 2003), pp. 96–7.

10. N. J. White, *Decolonisation: The British Experience Since 1945* (Longman, 1999), p. 97.

11. Ibid.

12. M. Hall, *The Vietnam War* (Longman, 2000), p. 13.

13. R. Nixon, *RN: The Memoirs of Richard Nixon* (Sidgwick and Jackson, 1978), p. 343.

14. M. Alexander, *Managing the Cold War: a view from the front line* (RUSI, 2005), p. 30.

15. Z. Brzezinski, *Power and Principle: Memoirs of the National Security Advisor* (Farrar-Straus-Giroux, 1983), p. 517.

Chapter 4

1. C. Weinberger, *Fighting for Peace* (Michael Joseph, 1990), p. 234.

2. E. Morris, *Dutch: A Memoir of Ronald Reagan* (Random House, 1999), pp. 461, 473,

3. J. L. Gaddis, *The Cold War* (Allen Lane, 2005), p. 217.

4. N. Chomsky, 'The United States: from Greece to El Salvador', in N. Chomsky, J. Steele and J. Gittings (eds), *Superpowers in Collision* (Penguin, 1982), p. 35.

5. S. Talbott, *Deadly Gambits: The Reagan Administration and the Stalemate in Nuclear Arms Control* (Picador, 1984), p. 227.

6. C. Weinberger, *Fighting for Peace* (Michael Joseph, 1990), p. 240.

7. Ibid., p. 28.

8. R. Reagan, *An American Life* (Hutchinson, 1990), p. 217.

9. Morris, *Dutch*, pp. 434–5.

10. R. Reagan, 'Remarks at the Brandenburg Gate', 12 June 1987, available at: www.reaganlibrary.com/reagan/speeches/wall.asp.

11. Quoted in Morris, *Dutch*, p. 450.

12. R. Stubbing, 'The defense program: buildup or binge', *Foreign Affairs*, Vol. 63, 1984–5, p. 858.

13. Quoted in S. Halper and J. Clarke, *America Alone: The Neo-Conservatives and the Global Order* (Cambridge University Press, 2005), p. 162.

14. F. Fitzgerald, *Way Out There in the Blue: Reagan, Star Wars and the End of the Cold War* (Simon and Schuster, 2000).

15. Morris, *Dutch*, pp. 169–70, 470.

16. M. McCauley, *Russia, America and the Cold War, 1949–1991* (Longman, 1998), p. 62.

17. Reagan, *An American Life*, p. 217.

18. S. Talbott, *Deadly Gambits: the Reagan Administration and the Stalemate in Arms Control* (Picador, 1984), p. 193.

19. Quoted in Morris, *Dutch*, p. 517.

20. Gaddis, *The Cold War*, pp. 247–8.

21. Quoted in E. Kantowicz, *Coming Apart, Coming Together* (Wm B. Eerdmans, 1999), p. 391

22. J. L. Gaddis, *The United States and the End of the Cold War: Implications, Reconsiderations, Provocations* (Oxford University Press, 1992), p. 131.

23. M. Sandle, *Gorbachev: Man of the Twentieth Century?* (Hodder Arnold, 2008).

24. Quoted in J. Isaacs and T. Downing, *The Cold War: For 45 Years the World Held its Breath* (Bantam Press, 1998), p. 417.

25. P. Kennedy, *The Rise and Fall of the Great Powers: Economic Change and Military Conflict from 1500 to 2000* (Unwin Hyman, 1988).

Chapter 5

1. G. H. W. Bush, 'State of the Union Address', 28 January 1992, available at: http://frwebgate.access.gpo.gov/cgi-bin/getdoc.cgi?dbname=1992 _public_papers_vol1_text&docid=pap_text-79.

2. F. Fukuyama, 'The end of history?', *The National Interest*, Summer 1989, p. 4.

3. S. P. Huntington, 'The clash of civilizations?', *Foreign Affairs*, Summer 1993, p. 22.

4. R. Haas, *The Reluctant Sheriff: The US after the Cold War*, Council of Foreign Relations, 1997, p. 21.

5. I. Clark, *The Post-Cold War Order* (Oxford University Press, 1999), p. 36.

6. E. Hobsbawm, *Age of Extremes, 1914–1991* (Penguin, 1994), p. 559.

7. G. H. W. Bush, 'Inaugural Address', 20 January 1989, available at: www. nationalcenter.org/BushInaugural.html.

8. J. Dumbrell, *American Foreign Policy: Carter to Clinton* (Macmillan, 1997), p. 143.

9. The 1991 coalition comprised Afghanistan, Argentina, Australia, Bangladesh, Canada, Czechoslovakia, Denmark, Egypt, France, Germany, Greece, Hungary, Honduras, Italy, Kuwait, Morocco, the

Netherlands, Niger, Norway, Oman, Pakistan, Poland, Portugal, Qatar, Saudi Arabia, Senegal, South Korea, Spain, Syria, Turkey, the United Arab Emirates, the United Kingdom and the United States.

10. G. H. W. Bush, 'Address Before a Joint Session of Congress', 11 September 1990 at: http://millercenter.org/scripps/archive/speeches/detail/3425.

11. D. Hannay, *New World Disorder* (Taurus, 1998), p. 138.

12. Quoted in D. Halberstam, *War in a Time of Peace: Bush, Clinton and the Generals* (Scribner, 2001), p. 305.

13. D. Brinkley, 'Democratic enlargement: the Clinton Doctrine', *Foreign Policy*, No. 106, Spring 1997, p. 113.

14. Quoted in ibid., p. 116.

15. Quoted in P. Krugman, 'Competitiveness: a dangerous obsession', *Foreign Affairs*, Vol. 73, No. 2, March/April 1994, p. 29.

16. Brinkley, 'Democratic enlargement', p. 116.

17. Quoted in F. Bruni, *Ambling into History: The Unlikely Odyssey of George W. Bush* (HarperCollins, 2002), p. 6.

18. UN Security Council Resolution No. 1441, 'The situation between Iraq and Kuwait', adopted 8 November 2002 at: http://daccess-ods.un.org/TMP/8639503.html.

19. D. Coates and J. Krieger, *Blair's War* (Polity Press, 2004).

20. P. Rogers, *Why We're Losing the War on Terror* (Polity Press, 2008).

21. Comprehensive Report of the Special Advisor to the DCI on Iraq's WMD, 30 September 2004 at: www.cia.gov/library/reports/general-reports-1/iraq_wmd_2004/index.html.

22. See, for instance, C. Johnson, *The Sorrows of Empire: Militarism, Secrecy and the End of the Republic* (Owl Books, 2005); L. Gardner and M. B. Young (eds), *The New American Empire: A 21st Century Teach-in on US Foreign Policy* (The New Press, 2005); A. J. Bacevich, *American Empire: The Realities and Consequences of US Diplomacy* (Harvard University Press, 2004); D. Harvey, *The New Imperialism* (Oxford University Press, 2005).

23. G. Lundestad, *'Empire' by Integration: United States and European Integration, 1945–97* (Oxford University Press, 1998).

24. B. Woodward, 'CIA told to do "whatever necessary" to kill Bin Laden', *The Washington Post*, 21 October 2001.

25. Quoted in J. K. White, *Still Seeing Red: How the Cold War Shapes the New American Politics*, revised edition (Westview Press, 1998), p. 256.

26. Quoted in ibid., p. 274.

27. Quoted in Bruni, *Ambling into History*, p. 44.
28. H. Seely (ed.), *Pieces of Intelligence: The Existential Poetry of Donald H. Rumsfeld* (Free Press, 2003), p. 2.
29. Quoted in White, *Still Seeing Red*, p. 203.
30. J. S. Nye, *Power in the Global Information Age: From Realism to Globalization* (Routledge, 2004), p. 98.

Chapter 6

1. K. Popper, *Conjectures and Refutations: The Growth of Knowledge*, 4th edn (Routledge and Kegan Paul, 1972), p. 46.
2. R. Rorty, *Contingency, Irony, and Solidarity* (Cambridge University Press, 1989), p. 5.
3. J. S. Nye, 'Hard power, soft power, and "the war on terrorism"', in D. Held and M. Koenig-Archibugi (eds), *American Power in the Twenty-First Century* (Polity Press, 2004), pp. 114–33.
4. K. N. Waltz, *Theory of International Politics* (McGraw-Hill, 1979).
5. H. Bull, 'International theory: the Case for a classical approach', *World Politics*, Vol. 18, No. 3, 1966, pp. 361–77.
6. Thucydides, *History of the Peloponnesian War*, trans. R. Crawley (Everyman, 1993).
7. T. Hobbes, *Leviathan* (Cambridge University Press, 1991).
8. N. Machiavelli, *The Prince*, trans. P. Bondanella (Oxford University Press, 2005).
9. E. H. Carr, *The Twenty Years' Crisis* (Palgrave, 2001).
10. Ibid.
11. K. N. Waltz, *Man, the State and War: A Theoretical Analysis* (Columbia University Press, 1959), p. 232.
12. A. Wolfers, *Discord and Collaboration: Essays on International Politics* (Johns Hopkins University Press, 1962), p. 19.
13. Waltz, *Theory of International Politics*, pp. 103, 107.
14. K. Booth and N. J. Wheeler, *The Security Dilemma: Fear, Cooperation and Trust in World Politics* (Palgrave, 2008), pp. 45–7; R. Jervis, 'The spiral of international insecurity', in R. Little and M. Smith (eds), *Perspectives on World Politics*, 3rd edn (Routledge, 2006).
15. Waltz, *Theory of International Politics*, p. 110.
16. M. Wight, 'Why is there no international theory', in H. Butterfield and M. Wight (eds), *Diplomatic Investigations* (George Allen and Unwin, 1966), p. 21.

17. H. J. Morgenthau, *Vietnam and the United States* (Public Affairs Press, 1965).

18. J. Mearsheimer and S. Walt, 'An unnecessary war', *Foreign Policy*, No. 134, Jan./Feb. 2003, pp. 50–9.

19. R. O. Keohane and J. S. Nye, *Power and Interdependence: World Politics in Transition*, 3rd edn (Longman, 2001).

20. Authors who use these terms include J. W. Burton, *World Society* (Cambridge University Press, 1972); Keohane and Nye, *Power and Interdependence*; R. O. Keohane, *International Institutions and State Power* (Westview Press, 1989); J. N. Rosenau, *Turbulence in World Politics* (Harvester Wheatsheaf, 1990).

21. Burton, *World Society*.

22. J. Nye, *Soft Power: The Means to Success in World Politics* (Public Affairs, 2005).

23. I. Kant, *Perpetual Peace*, 'Perpetual peace: a philosophical sketch', in *Political Writings*, H. Reiss (ed.) (Cambridge University Press, 1991); M. W. Doyle, 'Liberalism and world politics', *American Political Science Review*, Vol. 80, No. 4, 1986, pp. 1151–63.

24. I. Wallerstein, *World-Systems Analysis: An Introduction* (Duke University Press, 2004).

25. J. Rosenberg, *The Empire of Civil Society: A Critique of the Realist Theory of International Relations* (Verso, 1994).

26. I. Wallerstein, 'The rise and future demise of the world capitalist system', in Little and Smith (eds), *Perspectives on World Politics*, p. 250.

27. R. Cox, 'Social forces, states and world orders: beyond international relations theory', *Millennium Journal of International Studies*, Vol. 10, No. 2, 1981, pp. 125–55.

28. A. Linklater, *The Transformation of Political Community: Ethical Foundations of the Post-Westphalian Era* (Polity, 1998).

29. A. Wendt, 'Anarchy is what states make of it: the social construction of power politics', *International Organization*, Vol. 46, No. 2, 1992, pp. 391–425.

Chapter 7

1. T. Hobbes, *Leviathan*, R. Tuck (ed.) (Cambridge University Press, 1991).

2. J. Black, *European International Relations, 1648–1815* (Palgrave, 2002), p. 74.

3. S. Krasner, *Sovereignty: Organized Hypocrisy* (Princeton University Press, 1999).

4. W. Doyle, *The French Revolution: A Very Short Introduction* (Oxford University Press, 2001), p. 81.

5. Quoted in T. Skocpol, *States and Social Revolutions* (Cambridge University Press, 1979), p. 174.

6. J. Bentham, *Introduction to the Principles of Morals and Legislation* (Oxford University Press, 1970).

7. M. Kaldor, 'Nationalism and globalization', *Nations and Nationalism*, Vol. 10, Nos. 1–2, 2004.

8. R. Jackson, *Quasi-States: Sovereignty, International Relations and the Third World* (Cambridge University Press, 1990).

9. M. Leonard (ed.), *Re-Ordering the World: The Long-Term Implications of September 11th*, The Foreign Policy Centre, 2002, p. xi, at: http://fpc.org.uk/fsblob/36.pdf.

10. *National Security Strategy of the United States*, 2002, at: www.whitehouse.gov/nsc.

11. *European Security Strategy: A Secure Europe in a Better World*, 2003, at: http://ue.eu.int/uedocs/cmsUpload/78367.pdf.

12. *Index of Weak States in the Developing World*, Brookings Institution, 2008, at: www.brookings.edu/reports/2008/02_weak_states_index.aspx.

13. Center for the Continuing Study of the Californian Economy, *Numbers in the News September 2008 – Where Does California Rank – 2007 Update*, at: www.ccsce.com/pdf/Numbers-sep08-CA-Rank.pdf.

14. S. Strange, 'The Westfailure system', *Review of International Studies*, Vol. 25, 1999, pp. 345–54.

15. L. Weiss, *The Myth of the Powerless State: Governing the Economy in a Global Era* (Polity, 1998); L. Weiss (ed.), *States in the Global Economy: Bringing Domestic Institutions Back In* (Cambridge University Press, 2003).

16. W. F. Hanrieder, 'Dissolving international politics: reflections on the nation-state', *American Political Science Review*, Vol. 72, No. 4, 1978.

Chapter 8

1. J. Kurbalija, 'The World Summit on Information Society and the Development of Internet Diplomacy', in A. F. Cooper, B. Hocking and W. Maley (eds), *Global Governance and Diplomacy: Worlds Apart?* (Palgrave Macmillan, 2008).

2. UN World Summit on the Information Society, at: www.itu.int/wsis/tunis/newsroom/index.html.

3. For further information see UN Economic and Social Council website, at: www.un.org/ecosoc.

4. A. F. Cooper, *Celebrity Diplomacy* (Paradigm, 2008).

5. C. Hitchens, *The Missionary Position: Mother Teresa in Theory and Practice* (Verso, 1995).

6. www.unmillenniumproject.org/goals/index.htm.

7. C. Archer, *International Organizations*, 3rd edn (Routledge, 2001), p. 42.

8. D. Held and A. McGrew, *Globalization/Anti-Globalization: Beyond the Great Divide*, 2nd edn (Polity, 2007), p. 105.

9. J. S. Nye, *The Paradox of American Power* (Oxford University Press, 2002), p. 45.

10. M. E. Keck and K. Sikkink, *Activists Beyond Borders: Advocacy Networks in International Politics* (Cornell University Press, 1998).

11. 'The non-governmental order', *The Economist*, 9 December 1999.

Chapter 9

1. R. Biel, *The New Imperialism: Crisis and Contradictions in North–South Relations* (Zed, 2000).

2. M. Waters, *Globalization* (Routledge, 1995), p. 3.

3. A. Giddens, *Runaway World: The BBC Reith Lectures*, 1999, Lecture 1. Available at: http://news.bbc.co.uk/hi/english/static/events/reith_99/week1/week1.htm.

4. D. Nayyar, 'Globalization and development strategies', *UNCTAD X, High-Level Table on Trade and Development: Directions for the Twenty-first century*, Bangkok, 12 February 2000, p. 2, at: www.unctad-10.org/pdfs/ux_tdxrt1d4.en.pdf.

5. Information adapted from *Facts and Figures from World Development Indicators 2008*, http://siteresources.worldbank.org/DATASTATISTICS/Resources/reg_wdi.pdf.

6. P. Gowan, *The Global Gamble: Washington's Faustian Bid for World Dominance* (Verso, 1999).

7. 'More of less equal?', *The Economist*, 13 March 2004, pp. 69–71.

8. K. Ohmae, *The Borderless World: Power and Strategy in the Interlinked Economy* (Harper Business, 1999).

9. R. J. Barnett and J. Cavanagh, *Global Dreams: Imperial Corporations and the New World Order* (Simon & Schuster, 1994).

10. J. F. Helliwell, *Globalization: Myths, Facts and Consequences* (Howe Institute, 2000).

11. D. Held and A. McGrew (eds), *Global Transformations Reader* (Polity, 2000), p. 250.

12. J. A. Scholte, *Globalization: a critical introduction*, 2nd edn (Palgrave, 2005), pp. 19–20.

13. J. Bentham, *Introduction to the Principles of Morals and Legislation* (Oxford University Press, 1970).

14. P. Hirst and G. Thompson, *Globalization in Question: The International Economy and the Possibilities of Governance*, 2nd edn (Polity, 1999).

15. R. Ramesh, 'Paradise almost lost: Maldives seek to buy a new homeland', *The Guardian*, 10 November 2008, at: www.guardian.co.uk/environment/2008/nov/10/maldives-climate-change.

16. Joseph M. Grieco and G. John Ikenberry, *State Power and World Markets* (W.W. Norton, 2003), p. 207.

17. F. Abrams, 'Half of all high street clothes are made by cheap labour', *The Independent*, 27 September 1999, at: www.independent.co.uk/news/half-all-high-street-clothes-are-made-by-cheap-labour-1122578.html.

18. Report ILO Forum on Decent Work for a Fair Globalization, Lisbon, 31 October–2 November 2007, ILO, 2008, at: www.ilo.org/wcmsp5/groups/public/—dgreports/—integration/documents/meetingdocument/wcms_093827.pdf.

19. K. Ohmae, *The End of the Nation-State* (Free Press, 1995).

20. Ohmae, *The Borderless World*.

21. Ohmae, *The End of the Nation-State*, p. 7.

22. Ohmae, *The Borderless World*, p. 18.

23. Ohmae, *The Borderless World*.

24. R. O. Keohane and J. S. Nye, *Power and Interdependence: World Politics in Transition*, 3rd edn (Longman, 2001).

25. IMF Members' Quotas and Voting Power, at: www.imf.org/external/np/sec/memdir/members.htm#b.

26. IMF Staff, *Reform of IMF Quotas and Voice: Responding to Changes in the Global Economy*, March 2008, at: www.imf.org/External/NP/EXR/ib/2007/041307.pdf.

Chapter 10

1. D. Hannay, *New World Disorder* (Taurus, London, 2008), p. 15.
2. www.un.org/Depts/dpko/list/list.pdf.
3. Hannay, *New World Disorder*, p. 138.
4. Ibid., pp. 171–2.
5. Mary Kaldor, *Human Security: Reflections on Globalization and Interventions* (Polity, 2006), pp. 16–72.
6. B. Buzan, *People, States and Fear: An Agenda for International Security Studies in the Post-Cold War Order*, 2nd edn (Longman, 1991), chapter 5; B. Buzan and O. Waever, *Regions and Powers: The Structure of International Security* (Cambridge University Press, 2003).
7. Commission on Global Governance, *Our Global Neighbourhood* (Oxford University Press, 1995).
8. Sarah Boseley, 'Aids "bigger threat than terrorism"', *The Guardian*, 14 December 2001.
9. J. H. Herz, *International Politics in the Atomic Age* (Columbia University Press, 1959).
10. H. Bull, *The Anarchical Society: A Study of Order in World Politics* (Macmillan, 1977).
11. H. Bull, *Justice in International Relations: The Hagey Lectures* (University of Waterloo, 1984).

Chapter 11

1. F. Duchêne, 'Jean Monnet – pragmatic visionary', in M. Bond, J. Smith and W. Wallace (eds), *Eminent Europeans* (The Greycoat Press, 1996), p. 55.
2. S. Hix, *The Political System of the European Union* (Palgrave, 1999), p. 225.
3. D. Cameron, 'The 1992 initiative: causes and consequences', in A. M. Sbragia (ed.), *Euro-Politics: Institutions and Policymaking in the 'New' European Community* (Brookings, 1992), pp .43–4.
4. B. Rosamond, *Theories of European Integration* (Macmillan, 2000), p. 100.
5. A. Blair, *Dealing with Europe: Britain and the negotiation of the Maastricht Treaty* (Ashgate, 1999).
6. E. Denza, *The Intergovernmental Pillars of the European Union* (Oxford University Press, 2002).
7. R. Corbett, 'Representing the people', in A. Duff, J. Pinder and R. Pryce (eds), *Maastricht and Beyond* (Routledge, 1994), p. 210.

8. L. Friis, 'EU enlargement . . . and then there were 28', in E. Bomberg and A. Stubb (eds), *The European Union: How Does it Work?* (Oxford University Press, 2003), pp. 189–91.

9. K. Neunreither and A. Weiner (eds), *European Integration After Amsterdam* (Oxford University Press, 2000).

10. D. Galloway, *The Treaty of Nice* (Sheffield Academic Press, 2001).

11. A. W. Milward, *The Reconstruction of Western Europe, 1945–51* (Routledge, 1984).

12. A. W. Milward, *The European Rescue of the Nation State* (Routledge, 1994).

13. E. B. Haas, *The Uniting of Europe: Political, Social and Economic Forces, 1950–57*, 2nd edn (Stevens, 1968); W. A. Lipgens, *History of European Integration, Vol. 1, 1945–47* (Clarendon Press, 1982).

14. A. W. Milward, *The European Rescue of the Nation State*.

Chapter 12

1. A. Giddens, *Runaway World: The BBC Reith Lectures*, London, BBC Radio 4, 1999.

2. J. L. Gaddis, *The Long Peace: Inquiries into the History of the Cold War* (Oxford University Press, 1989).

3. J. Mearsheimer, 'Why we will soon miss the Cold War', *The Atlantic*, August 1990, pp. 35–50.

4. K. Waltz, 'The spread of nuclear weapons: more may be better', *Adelphi Papers*, No. 171, International Institute for Strategic Studies, 1981.

5. A. Shlaim, *The Iron Wall: Israel and the Arab World* (Allen Lane, 2000), p. 298.

6. F. Fukuyama, *The End of History and the Last Man* (Hamish Hamilton, 1992).

7. S. Huntington, *The Third Wave: Democratization in the Late Twentieth Century* (University of Oklahoma Press, 1993).

8. B. Russett, *Grasping the Democratic Peace: Principles for a Post-Cold War World* (Princeton University Press, 1993).

9. Fukuyama, *The End of History*, p. 276; R. Cooper, *The Breaking of Nations: Order and Chaos in the Twenty-First Century* (Atlantic Books, 2004).

10. A. Geis, L. Brock and H. Müller (eds), *Democratic Wars: Looking at the Dark Side of Democratic Peace* (Palgrave Macmillan, 2006).

Index

Bold indicates that the term is defined